Mometrix TEST PREPARATION

I0866838

TExES

Pedagogy and Professional Responsibilities for Trade and Industrial Education 6-12 (370)

Secrets Study Guide

Dear Future Exam Success Story

First of all, **THANK YOU** for purchasing Mometrix study materials!

Second, congratulations! You are one of the few determined test-takers who are committed to doing whatever it takes to excel on your exam. **You have come to the right place.** We developed these study materials with one goal in mind: to deliver you the information you need in a format that's concise and easy to use.

In addition to optimizing your guide for the content of the test, we've outlined our recommended steps for breaking down the preparation process into small, attainable goals so you can make sure you stay on track.

We've also analyzed the entire test-taking process, identifying the most common pitfalls and showing how you can overcome them and be ready for any curveball the test throws you.

Standardized testing is one of the biggest obstacles on your road to success, which only increases the importance of doing well in the high-pressure, high-stakes environment of test day. Your results on this test could have a significant impact on your future, and this guide provides the information and practical advice to help you achieve your full potential on test day.

Your success is our success

We would love to hear from you! If you would like to share the story of your exam success or if you have any questions or comments in regard to our products, please contact us at **800-673-8175** or **support@mometrix.com**.

Thanks again for your business and we wish you continued success!

Sincerely,
The Mometrix Test Preparation Team

TABLE OF CONTENTS

Introduction

Thank you for purchasing this resource! You have made the choice to prepare yourself for a test that could have a huge impact on your future, and this guide is designed to help you be fully ready for test day. Obviously, it's important to have a solid understanding of the test material, but you also need to be prepared for the unique environment and stressors of the test, so that you can perform to the best of your abilities.

For this purpose, the first section that appears in this guide is the **Secret Keys**. We've devoted countless hours to meticulously researching what works and what doesn't, and we've boiled down our findings to the five most impactful steps you can take to improve your performance on the test. We start at the beginning with study planning and move through the preparation process, all the way to the testing strategies that will help you get the most out of what you know when you're finally sitting in front of the test.

We recommend that you start preparing for your test as far in advance as possible. However, if you've bought this guide as a last-minute study resource and only have a few days before your test, we recommend that you skip over the first two Secret Keys since they address a long-term study plan.

If you struggle with **test anxiety**, we strongly encourage you to check out our recommendations for how you can overcome it. Test anxiety is a formidable foe, but it can be beaten, and we want to make sure you have the tools you need to defeat it.

Secret Key #1 – Plan Big, Study Small

There's a lot riding on your performance. If you want to ace this test, you're going to need to keep your skills sharp and the material fresh in your mind. You need a plan that lets you review everything you need to know while still fitting in your schedule. We'll break this strategy down into three categories.

Information Organization

Start with the information you already have: the official test outline. From this, you can make a complete list of all the concepts you need to cover before the test. Organize these concepts into groups that can be studied together, and create a list of any related vocabulary you need to learn so you can brush up on any difficult terms. You'll want to keep this vocabulary list handy once you actually start studying since you may need to add to it along the way.

Time Management

Once you have your set of study concepts, decide how to spread them out over the time you have left before the test. Break your study plan into small, clear goals so you have a manageable task for each day and know exactly what you're doing. Then just focus on one small step at a time. When you manage your time this way, you don't need to spend hours at a time studying. Studying a small block of content for a short period each day helps you retain information better and avoid stressing over how much you have left to do. You can relax knowing that you have a plan to cover everything in time. In order for this strategy to be effective though, you have to start studying early and stick to your schedule. Avoid the exhaustion and futility that comes from last-minute cramming!

Study Environment

The environment you study in has a big impact on your learning. Studying in a coffee shop, while probably more enjoyable, is not likely to be as fruitful as studying in a quiet room. It's important to keep distractions to a minimum. You're only planning to study for a short block of time, so make the most of it. Don't pause to check your phone or get up to find a snack. It's also important to **avoid multitasking**. Research has consistently shown that multitasking will make your studying dramatically less effective. Your study area should also be comfortable and well-lit so you don't have the distraction of straining your eyes or sitting on an uncomfortable chair.

The time of day you study is also important. You want to be rested and alert. Don't wait until just before bedtime. Study when you'll be most likely to comprehend and remember. Even better, if you know what time of day your test will be, set that time aside for study. That way your brain will be used to working on that subject at that specific time and you'll have a better chance of recalling information.

Finally, it can be helpful to team up with others who are studying for the same test. Your actual studying should be done in as isolated an environment as possible, but the work of organizing the information and setting up the study plan can be divided up. In between study sessions, you can discuss with your teammates the concepts that you're all studying and quiz each other on the details. Just be sure that your teammates are as serious about the test as you are. If you find that your study time is being replaced with social time, you might need to find a new team.

Secret Key #2 – Make Your Studying Count

You're devoting a lot of time and effort to preparing for this test, so you want to be absolutely certain it will pay off. This means doing more than just reading the content and hoping you can remember it on test day. It's important to make every minute of study count. There are two main areas you can focus on to make your studying count.

Retention

It doesn't matter how much time you study if you can't remember the material. You need to make sure you are retaining the concepts. To check your retention of the information you're learning, try recalling it at later times with minimal prompting. Try carrying around flashcards and glance at one or two from time to time or ask a friend who's also studying for the test to quiz you.

To enhance your retention, look for ways to put the information into practice so that you can apply it rather than simply recalling it. If you're using the information in practical ways, it will be much easier to remember. Similarly, it helps to solidify a concept in your mind if you're not only reading it to yourself but also explaining it to someone else. Ask a friend to let you teach them about a concept you're a little shaky on (or speak aloud to an imaginary audience if necessary). As you try to summarize, define, give examples, and answer your friend's questions, you'll understand the concepts better and they will stay with you longer. Finally, step back for a big picture view and ask yourself how each piece of information fits with the whole subject. When you link the different concepts together and see them working together as a whole, it's easier to remember the individual components.

Finally, practice showing your work on any multi-step problems, even if you're just studying. Writing out each step you take to solve a problem will help solidify the process in your mind, and you'll be more likely to remember it during the test.

Modality

Modality simply refers to the means or method by which you study. Choosing a study modality that fits your own individual learning style is crucial. No two people learn best in exactly the same way, so it's important to know your strengths and use them to your advantage.

For example, if you learn best by visualization, focus on visualizing a concept in your mind and draw an image or a diagram. Try color-coding your notes, illustrating them, or creating symbols that will trigger your mind to recall a learned concept. If you learn best by hearing or discussing information, find a study partner who learns the same way or read aloud to yourself. Think about how to put the information in your own words. Imagine that you are giving a lecture on the topic and record yourself so you can listen to it later.

For any learning style, flashcards can be helpful. Organize the information so you can take advantage of spare moments to review. Underline key words or phrases. Use different colors for different categories. Mnemonic devices (such as creating a short list in which every item starts with the same letter) can also help with retention. Find what works best for you and use it to store the information in your mind most effectively and easily.

Secret Key #3 – Practice the Right Way

Your success on test day depends not only on how many hours you put into preparing, but also on whether you prepared the right way. It's good to check along the way to see if your studying is paying off. One of the most effective ways to do this is by taking practice tests to evaluate your progress. Practice tests are useful because they show exactly where you need to improve. Every time you take a practice test, pay special attention to these three groups of questions:

- The questions you got wrong
- The questions you had to guess on, even if you guessed right
- The questions you found difficult or slow to work through

This will show you exactly what your weak areas are, and where you need to devote more study time. Ask yourself why each of these questions gave you trouble. Was it because you didn't understand the material? Was it because you didn't remember the vocabulary? Do you need more repetitions on this type of question to build speed and confidence? Dig into those questions and figure out how you can strengthen your weak areas as you go back to review the material.

Additionally, many practice tests have a section explaining the answer choices. It can be tempting to read the explanation and think that you now have a good understanding of the concept. However, an explanation likely only covers part of the question's broader context. Even if the explanation makes perfect sense, **go back and investigate** every concept related to the question until you're positive you have a thorough understanding.

As you go along, keep in mind that the practice test is just that: practice. Memorizing these questions and answers will not be very helpful on the actual test because it is unlikely to have any of the same exact questions. If you only know the right answers to the sample questions, you won't be prepared for the real thing. **Study the concepts** until you understand them fully, and then you'll be able to answer any question that shows up on the test.

It's important to wait on the practice tests until you're ready. If you take a test on your first day of study, you may be overwhelmed by the amount of material covered and how much you need to learn. Work up to it gradually.

On test day, you'll need to be prepared for answering questions, managing your time, and using the test-taking strategies you've learned. It's a lot to balance, like a mental marathon that will have a big impact on your future. Like training for a marathon, you'll need to start slowly and work your way up. When test day arrives, you'll be ready.

Start with the strategies you've read in the first two Secret Keys—plan your course and study in the way that works best for you. If you have time, consider using multiple study resources to get different approaches to the same concepts. It can be helpful to see difficult concepts from more than one angle. Then find a good source for practice tests. Many times, the test website will suggest potential study resources or provide sample tests.

Practice Test Strategy

If you're able to find at least three practice tests, we recommend this strategy:

Untimed and Open-Book Practice

Take the first test with no time constraints and with your notes and study guide handy. Take your time and focus on applying the strategies you've learned.

Timed and Open-Book Practice

Take the second practice test open-book as well, but set a timer and practice pacing yourself to finish in time.

Timed and Closed-Book Practice

Take any other practice tests as if it were test day. Set a timer and put away your study materials. Sit at a table or desk in a quiet room, imagine yourself at the testing center, and answer questions as quickly and accurately as possible.

Keep repeating timed and closed-book tests on a regular basis until you run out of practice tests or it's time for the actual test. Your mind will be ready for the schedule and stress of test day, and you'll be able to focus on recalling the material you've learned.

Secret Key #4 – Pace Yourself

Once you're fully prepared for the material on the test, your biggest challenge on test day will be managing your time. Just knowing that the clock is ticking can make you panic even if you have plenty of time left. Work on pacing yourself so you can build confidence against the time constraints of the exam. Pacing is a difficult skill to master, especially in a high-pressure environment, so **practice is vital**.

Set time expectations for your pace based on how much time is available. For example, if a section has 60 questions and the time limit is 30 minutes, you know you have to average 30 seconds or less per question in order to answer them all. Although 30 seconds is the hard limit, set 25 seconds per question as your goal, so you reserve extra time to spend on harder questions. When you budget extra time for the harder questions, you no longer have any reason to stress when those questions take longer to answer.

Don't let this time expectation distract you from working through the test at a calm, steady pace, but keep it in mind so you don't spend too much time on any one question. Recognize that taking extra time on one question you don't understand may keep you from answering two that you do understand later in the test. If your time limit for a question is up and you're still not sure of the answer, mark it and move on, and come back to it later if the time and the test format allow. If the testing format doesn't allow you to return to earlier questions, just make an educated guess; then put it out of your mind and move on.

On the easier questions, be careful not to rush. It may seem wise to hurry through them so you have more time for the challenging ones, but it's not worth missing one if you know the concept and just didn't take the time to read the question fully. Work efficiently but make sure you understand the question and have looked at all of the answer choices, since more than one may seem right at first.

Even if you're paying attention to the time, you may find yourself a little behind at some point. You should speed up to get back on track, but do so wisely. Don't panic; just take a few seconds less on each question until you're caught up. Don't guess without thinking, but do look through the answer choices and eliminate any you know are wrong. If you can get down to two choices, it is often worthwhile to guess from those. Once you've chosen an answer, move on and don't dwell on any that you skipped or had to hurry through. If a question was taking too long, chances are it was one of the harder ones, so you weren't as likely to get it right anyway.

On the other hand, if you find yourself getting ahead of schedule, it may be beneficial to slow down a little. The more quickly you work, the more likely you are to make a careless mistake that will affect your score. You've budgeted time for each question, so don't be afraid to spend that time. Practice an efficient but careful pace to get the most out of the time you have.

Secret Key #5 – Have a Plan for Guessing

When you're taking the test, you may find yourself stuck on a question. Some of the answer choices seem better than others, but you don't see the one answer choice that is obviously correct. What do you do?

The scenario described above is very common, yet most test takers have not effectively prepared for it. Developing and practicing a plan for guessing may be one of the single most effective uses of your time as you get ready for the exam.

In developing your plan for guessing, there are three questions to address:

- When should you start the guessing process?
- How should you narrow down the choices?
- Which answer should you choose?

When to Start the Guessing Process

Unless your plan for guessing is to select C every time (which, despite its merits, is not what we recommend), you need to leave yourself enough time to apply your answer elimination strategies. Since you have a limited amount of time for each question, that means that if you're going to give yourself the best shot at guessing correctly, you have to decide quickly whether or not you will guess.

Of course, the best-case scenario is that you don't have to guess at all, so first, see if you can answer the question based on your knowledge of the subject and basic reasoning skills. Focus on the key words in the question and try to jog your memory of related topics. Give yourself a chance to bring the knowledge to mind, but once you realize that you don't have (or you can't access) the knowledge you need to answer the question, it's time to start the guessing process.

It's almost always better to start the guessing process too early than too late. It only takes a few seconds to remember something and answer the question from knowledge. Carefully eliminating wrong answer choices takes longer. Plus, going through the process of eliminating answer choices can actually help jog your memory.

Summary: Start the guessing process as soon as you decide that you can't answer the question based on your knowledge.

How to Narrow Down the Choices

The next chapter in this book (**Test-Taking Strategies**) includes a wide range of strategies for how to approach questions and how to look for answer choices to eliminate. You will definitely want to read those carefully, practice them, and figure out which ones work best for you. Here though, we're going to address a mindset rather than a particular strategy.

Your odds of guessing an answer correctly depend on how many options you are choosing from.

Number of options left	5	4	3	2	1
Odds of guessing correctly	20%	25%	33%	50%	100%

You can see from this chart just how valuable it is to be able to eliminate incorrect answers and make an educated guess, but there are two things that many test takers do that cause them to miss out on the benefits of guessing:

- Accidentally eliminating the correct answer
- Selecting an answer based on an impression

We'll look at the first one here, and the second one in the next section.

To avoid accidentally eliminating the correct answer, we recommend a thought exercise called **the $5 challenge**. In this challenge, you only eliminate an answer choice from contention if you are willing to bet $5 on it being wrong. Why $5? Five dollars is a small but not insignificant amount of money. It's an amount you could afford to lose but wouldn't want to throw away. And while losing $5 once might not hurt too much, doing it twenty times will set you back $100. In the same way, each small decision you make—eliminating a choice here, guessing on a question there—won't by itself impact your score very much, but when you put them all together, they can make a big difference. By holding each answer choice elimination decision to a higher standard, you can reduce the risk of accidentally eliminating the correct answer.

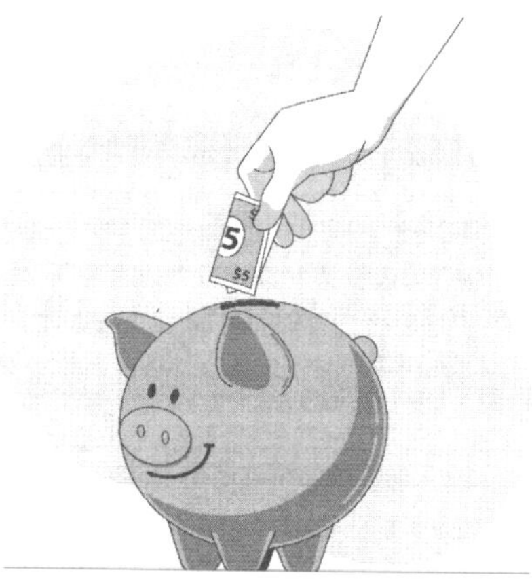

The $5 challenge can also be applied in a positive sense: If you are willing to bet $5 that an answer choice *is* correct, go ahead and mark it as correct.

Summary: Only eliminate an answer choice if you are willing to bet $5 that it is wrong.

Which Answer to Choose

You're taking the test. You've run into a hard question and decided you'll have to guess. You've eliminated all the answer choices you're willing to bet $5 on. Now you have to pick an answer. Why do we even need to talk about this? Why can't you just pick whichever one you feel like when the time comes?

The answer to these questions is that if you don't come into the test with a plan, you'll rely on your impression to select an answer choice, and if you do that, you risk falling into a trap. The test writers know that everyone who takes their test will be guessing on some of the questions, so they intentionally write wrong answer choices to seem plausible. You still have to pick an answer though, and if the wrong answer choices are designed to look right, how can you ever be sure that you're not falling for their trap? The best solution we've found to this dilemma is to take the decision out of your hands entirely. Here is the process we recommend:

Once you've eliminated any choices that you are confident (willing to bet $5) are wrong, select the first remaining choice as your answer.

Whether you choose to select the first remaining choice, the second, or the last, the important thing is that you use some preselected standard. Using this approach guarantees that you will not be enticed into selecting an answer choice that looks right, because you are not basing your decision on how the answer choices look.

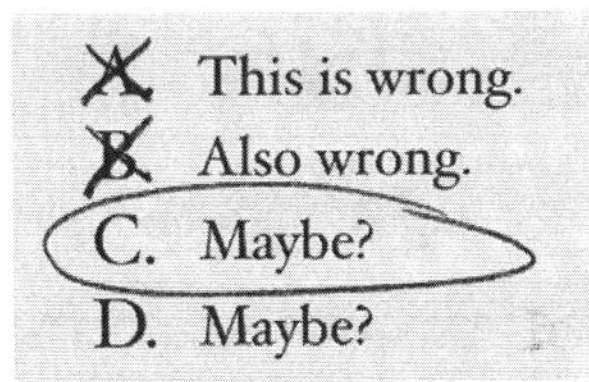

This is not meant to make you question your knowledge. Instead, it is to help you recognize the difference between your knowledge and your impressions. There's a huge difference between thinking an answer is right because of what you know, and thinking an answer is right because it looks or sounds like it should be right.

Summary: To ensure that your selection is appropriately random, make a predetermined selection from among all answer choices you have not eliminated.

Test-Taking Strategies

This section contains a list of test-taking strategies that you may find helpful as you work through the test. By taking what you know and applying logical thought, you can maximize your chances of answering any question correctly!

It is very important to realize that every question is different and every person is different: no single strategy will work on every question, and no single strategy will work for every person. That's why we've included all of them here, so you can try them out and determine which ones work best for different types of questions and which ones work best for you.

Question Strategies

☑ Read Carefully

Read the question and the answer choices carefully. Don't miss the question because you misread the terms. You have plenty of time to read each question thoroughly and make sure you understand what is being asked. Yet a happy medium must be attained, so don't waste too much time. You must read carefully and efficiently.

☑ Contextual Clues

Look for contextual clues. If the question includes a word you are not familiar with, look at the immediate context for some indication of what the word might mean. Contextual clues can often give you all the information you need to decipher the meaning of an unfamiliar word. Even if you can't determine the meaning, you may be able to narrow down the possibilities enough to make a solid guess at the answer to the question.

☑ Prefixes

If you're having trouble with a word in the question or answer choices, try dissecting it. Take advantage of every clue that the word might include. Prefixes can be a huge help. Usually, they allow you to determine a basic meaning. *Pre-* means before, *post-* means after, *pro-* is positive, *de-* is negative. From prefixes, you can get an idea of the general meaning of the word and try to put it into context.

☑ Hedge Words

Watch out for critical hedge words, such as *likely, may, can, often, almost, mostly, usually, generally, rarely,* and *sometimes.* Question writers insert these hedge phrases to cover every possibility. Often an answer choice will be wrong simply because it leaves no room for exception. Be on guard for answer choices that have definitive words such as *exactly* and *always.*

☑ Switchback Words

Stay alert for *switchbacks.* These are the words and phrases frequently used to alert you to shifts in thought. The most common switchback words are *but, although,* and *however.* Others include *nevertheless, on the other hand, even though, while, in spite of, despite,* and *regardless of.* Switchback words are important to catch because they can change the direction of the question or an answer choice.

☑ Face Value

When in doubt, use common sense. Accept the situation in the problem at face value. Don't read too much into it. These problems will not require you to make wild assumptions. If you have to go beyond creativity and warp time or space in order to have an answer choice fit the question, then you should move on and consider the other answer choices. These are normal problems rooted in reality. The applicable relationship or explanation may not be readily apparent, but it is there for you to figure out. Use your common sense to interpret anything that isn't clear.

Answer Choice Strategies

⊘ Answer Selection

The most thorough way to pick an answer choice is to identify and eliminate wrong answers until only one is left, then confirm it is the correct answer. Sometimes an answer choice may immediately seem right, but be careful. The test writers will usually put more than one reasonable answer choice on each question, so take a second to read all of them and make sure that the other choices are not equally obvious. As long as you have time left, it is better to read every answer choice than to pick the first one that looks right without checking the others.

⊘ Answer Choice Families

An answer choice family consists of two (in rare cases, three) answer choices that are very similar in construction and cannot all be true at the same time. If you see two answer choices that are direct opposites or parallels, one of them is usually the correct answer. For instance, if one answer choice says that quantity *x* increases and another either says that quantity *x* decreases (opposite) or says that quantity *y* increases (parallel), then those answer choices would fall into the same family. An answer choice that doesn't match the construction of the answer choice family is more likely to be incorrect. Most questions will not have answer choice families, but when they do appear, you should be prepared to recognize them.

⊘ Eliminate Answers

Eliminate answer choices as soon as you realize they are wrong, but make sure you consider all possibilities. If you are eliminating answer choices and realize that the last one you are left with is also wrong, don't panic. Start over and consider each choice again. There may be something you missed the first time that you will realize on the second pass.

⊘ Avoid Fact Traps

Don't be distracted by an answer choice that is factually true but doesn't answer the question. You are looking for the choice that answers the question. Stay focused on what the question is asking for so you don't accidentally pick an answer that is true but incorrect. Always go back to the question and make sure the answer choice you've selected actually answers the question and is not merely a true statement.

⊘ Extreme Statements

In general, you should avoid answers that put forth extreme actions as standard practice or proclaim controversial ideas as established fact. An answer choice that states the "process should be used in certain situations, if..." is much more likely to be correct than one that states the "process should be discontinued completely." The first is a calm rational statement and doesn't even make a definitive, uncompromising stance, using a hedge word *if* to provide wiggle room, whereas the second choice is far more extreme.

⊘ Benchmark

As you read through the answer choices and you come across one that seems to answer the question well, mentally select that answer choice. This is not your final answer, but it's the one that will help you evaluate the other answer choices. The one that you selected is your benchmark or standard for judging each of the other answer choices. Every other answer choice must be compared to your benchmark. That choice is correct until proven otherwise by another answer choice beating it. If you find a better answer, then that one becomes your new benchmark. Once you've decided that no other choice answers the question as well as your benchmark, you have your final answer.

☑ Predict the Answer

Before you even start looking at the answer choices, it is often best to try to predict the answer. When you come up with the answer on your own, it is easier to avoid distractions and traps because you will know exactly what to look for. The right answer choice is unlikely to be word-for-word what you came up with, but it should be a close match. Even if you are confident that you have the right answer, you should still take the time to read each option before moving on.

General Strategies

☑ Tough Questions

If you are stumped on a problem or it appears too hard or too difficult, don't waste time. Move on! Remember though, if you can quickly check for obviously incorrect answer choices, your chances of guessing correctly are greatly improved. Before you completely give up, at least try to knock out a couple of possible answers. Eliminate what you can and then guess at the remaining answer choices before moving on.

☑ Check Your Work

Since you will probably not know every term listed and the answer to every question, it is important that you get credit for the ones that you do know. Don't miss any questions through careless mistakes. If at all possible, try to take a second to look back over your answer selection and make sure you've selected the correct answer choice and haven't made a costly careless mistake (such as marking an answer choice that you didn't mean to mark). This quick double check should more than pay for itself in caught mistakes for the time it costs.

☑ Pace Yourself

It's easy to be overwhelmed when you're looking at a page full of questions; your mind is confused and full of random thoughts, and the clock is ticking down faster than you would like. Calm down and maintain the pace that you have set for yourself. Especially as you get down to the last few minutes of the test, don't let the small numbers on the clock make you panic. As long as you are on track by monitoring your pace, you are guaranteed to have time for each question.

☑ Don't Rush

It is very easy to make errors when you are in a hurry. Maintaining a fast pace in answering questions is pointless if it makes you miss questions that you would have gotten right otherwise. Test writers like to include distracting information and wrong answers that seem right. Taking a little extra time to avoid careless mistakes can make all the difference in your test score. Find a pace that allows you to be confident in the answers that you select.

☑ Keep Moving

Panicking will not help you pass the test, so do your best to stay calm and keep moving. Taking deep breaths and going through the answer elimination steps you practiced can help to break through a stress barrier and keep your pace.

Final Notes

The combination of a solid foundation of content knowledge and the confidence that comes from practicing your plan for applying that knowledge is the key to maximizing your performance on test day. As your foundation of content knowledge is built up and strengthened, you'll find that the strategies included in this chapter become more and more effective in helping you quickly sift through the distractions and traps of the test to isolate the correct answer.

Now that you're preparing to move forward into the test content chapters of this book, be sure to keep your goal in mind. As you read, think about how you will be able to apply this information on the test. If you've already seen sample questions for the test and you have an idea of the question format and style, try to come up with questions of your own that you can answer based on what you're reading. This will give you valuable practice applying your knowledge in the same ways you can expect to on test day.

Good luck and good studying!

Instructional Planning, Delivery, and Assessment

Student Motivation

Internal and External Motivation

Internal motivation is the desire to perform an activity for personal enjoyment, reward, and satisfaction. In the classroom, students with strong internal motivation engage in learning because they enjoy it and are interested in the topic of instruction. The overall learning atmosphere contributes to internal motivation. A positive, welcoming, and interesting environment excites students and promotes genuine curiosity for learning. In addition, attitudes and behaviors modeled by the teacher influence the classroom atmosphere and, ultimately, student motivation. When teachers are enthusiastic about learning, they positively affect students' internal motivation to participate in instruction. In employing multiple instructional strategies, the teacher effectively elicits internal motivation by providing an engaging environment that addresses students' needs and interests. **External motivation** is the desire to complete a task for a tangible reward, such as extra credit, prizes, or special privileges, or to avoid something unwanted, such as bad grades or punishment. Students' individual backgrounds heavily influence external motivation. Additionally, the value placed on education at home and parental expectations contribute to students' engagement as motivational factors. The frequency of external rewards ultimately determines the effectiveness of external motivation. While external motivation can promote a desired outcome, when used too frequently, it can diminish students' internal motivation for learning.

Instructional Strategies for Activating Students' Internal Motivation

When teachers employ multiple instructional strategies, create engaging environments that activate students' **internal motivation** for success in learning. Community building strategies establish an engaging, respectful, and welcoming environment that fosters positive attitudes toward learning, which activates students' internal motivation. Modeling is an effective technique for engaging students in learning. When teachers demonstrate enthusiasm toward education, they positively influence students' excitement and desire for learning. Incorporating growth-mindset strategies serves to develop students' self-esteem and self-concept, which empowers them and enhances their personal desire to actively engage in learning and achieve success. In addition, when the teacher is cognizant of students' needs, interests, backgrounds, and preferences, they can employ a variety of strategies to individualize instruction and enhance relevancy, thus establishing a clear purpose for learning that activates internal motivation. Providing multiple active and self-directed learning opportunities that promote inquiry and curiosity further motivates and engages students in learning. Such opportunities create a personalized learning experience that promotes autonomy and ownership over learning, thus encouraging active participation. When students have an internal drive to participate in their own learning, they are ultimately more engaged, productive, and successful throughout the learning process.

Instructional Strategies for Activating Students' External Motivation

External motivational strategies are effective for promoting engagement in achieving **short-term** desired outcomes or behaviors, particularly when internal motivation is already present. Implementing tangible rewards such as extra credit, class prizes, or special privileges when students accomplish a specific task enhances students' desire to engage and succeed in learning. In addition, incorporating competition amongst students by gamifying instruction or creating class contests is another strategy for providing external motivation that excites students for success in learning. By establishing clear academic and behavioral expectations, the teacher can effectively activate students' external motivation for academic success. When students understand classroom operations and what is expected of them, they are more willing to engage in learning. This includes establishing a clear classroom management plan with explicit procedures, expectations, and consequences as well as utilizing and maintaining an effective grading system. It is important to note that although external motivation techniques can be immediately successful in promoting engagement and learning, the teacher must be selective in implementing them because they may diminish students' internal motivation and the overall effectiveness of instruction when they are used too frequently.

SELF-MOTIVATION

SIGNIFICANCE IN THE LEARNING PROCESS AND INFLUENTIAL FACTORS

Student **self-motivation** is necessary for a productive learning experience. The student must be personally motivated to actively engage in learning. Students' internal drive for academic success affects their willingness to achieve learning goals, participate in instructional activities, and perform well on assignments. When students are self-motivated, they are more likely to put forth strong effort toward understanding and considering complex ideas on a deeper level to enhance comprehension and retainment. Students' **self-esteem** and **self-concept** influence their motivation toward learning, as students that feel poorly about themselves are less likely to actively engage in learning, whereas students with a high sense of self-worth feel confident and empowered to succeed. Students' self-concept is influenced by the interactions and methodology of the teacher, as the teacher's attitudes and behaviors can either empower and excite students for learning or hinder their self-confidence and, therefore, motivation to participate. In addition, **parental expectations** and the value placed on education at home can determine students' attitudes toward learning and whether they are self-motivated to achieve academically. **Peer relationships** are highly influential on students' self-motivation as well, as the regard a student's peers place on learning affects his or her own attitudes toward academic success.

STRATEGIES TO ENHANCE SELF-MOTIVATION

The teacher's role in enhancing students' **self-motivation** is integral to a productive and successful learning environment. An effective teacher implements a variety of teaching strategies throughout instruction to activate students' self-motivation by addressing their individual learning needs and providing variation in instruction to enhance engagement. By learning the unique needs, interests, and preferences of students, the teacher can locate and implement **authentic materials** that make learning relevant and enable students to make personal connections. This creates a clear purpose for students and promotes self-motivation. **Modeling** enthusiasm for learning and ensuring all interactions in the classroom are positive fosters positive attitudes toward learning and establishes a welcoming, engaging environment that enhances excitement and motivation for success. In addition, incorporating **growth-mindset** strategies, such as goal setting and teaching students to overcome obstacles, empowers students to become confident learners, thus developing students' self-esteem and self-motivation to engage in learning. Furthermore, when students feel they have control over their learning, they are more motivated, engaged, and successful in learning. By incorporating several opportunities for autonomy through student-choice and self-directed learning opportunities, the teacher effectively enhances self-motivation that promotes success in learning.

IMPACT OF ENCOURAGING STUDENTS' SELF-MOTIVATION

When students' **self-motivation** is encouraged in the academic setting, they develop vital life skills necessary for real-world situations that serve as a foundation for lifelong success. Self-motivated students are more inclined to take initiative in setting goals and taking active steps to achieve them for a sense of personal accomplishment and satisfaction rather than a tangible reward. In addition, when self-motivation is promoted, students develop the ability to commit to a goal, navigate obstacles, and reflect on their performance to seek areas for improvement, thus enabling them to be successful in a real-world, professional setting. When self-motivation is established early, students develop the desire to continuously pursue goals, challenge themselves, and learn through improvement, thus becoming lifelong learners with the necessary real-world skills for success.

Learning Goals and Objectives

Determining Instructional Goals and Objectives

Role of Assessment in Meeting Individual Student Learning Needs

Assessing students' prerequisite skills and knowledge is integral in gaining the understanding necessary to effectively determine instructional goals and objectives. This understanding provides the teacher with information about students' background knowledge, diverse experiences, and individual needs. With this information in mind, the teacher can establish goals and objectives based on state standards that are tailored to meet students' individual learning needs and ensure that learning targets are relevant, challenging, and attainable. In assessing background knowledge, teachers can develop high quality instruction that builds on students' prior experiences, thus fostering engagement in learning by allowing students to make personal connections in their learning. Additionally, assessing prerequisite skills and knowledge allows the teacher to identify gaps in learning, misunderstandings, or specific learning needs. This information allows the teacher to adjust and adapt instructional goals and objectives that align with students' abilities, learning styles, and knowledge, thus maximizing student learning potential by establishing student-centered instruction.

Assessment Strategies

Several assessment strategies can be utilized when determining the prerequisite knowledge and skills of students. Assessments may be either formal or informal and serve to provide valuable information to the teacher for effectively determining an instructional plan that is tailored to students' individual needs. Before introducing new content, teachers can administer a formal diagnostic test that contains the new material to assess prior knowledge and skill level. Teachers can then analyze the results to adjust goals and objectives as necessary. Additionally, knowledge and abilities can be evaluated by analyzing prior test scores or project portfolios to gauge student understanding of previously taught material. This allows the teacher to identify gaps in knowledge or make necessary clarifications to information. Some informal methods of assessment include conducting individual or whole-class formative assessments such as concept maps, polls, or observations to gain understanding of students' background knowledge on new material prior to teaching it. Teachers can also have students self-assess their prerequisite knowledge on new instruction through administering a test or questionnaire about content material. Often, when assessing prerequisite knowledge and skills, it is important that teachers keep assessments anonymous to ensure they receive accurate and unbiased data on student understanding and ability.

Role of Standards in Determining Instructional Goals and Objectives

State standards for achievement provide a guideline and reference point for specific benchmarks of student academic progress based on grade level. Additionally, they serve to ensure that teachers and students are held to the same expectations for teaching and learning, thus focusing instructional goals and objectives. Teachers must have a solid understanding of state standards, as they are responsible for referring to them as an outline for planning instruction, lessons, learning outcomes, and assessments and ensuring that students achieve these learning targets. State standards provide a structure for teachers to effectively plan and adjust instructional goals and objectives based on individual student learning needs and ensure that all students have the necessary support to reach these academic standards. State standards are also the reference point for establishing the pace of instruction, monitoring student progress, and determining if learning goals have been met before progressing through the curriculum.

Appropriate Learning Goals and Objectives

Setting appropriate learning goals and objectives is an integral component of quality, effective instruction that communicates high expectations, is developmentally appropriate, and is tailored to students' individual learning needs. Specific learning targets allow the teacher to effectively determine the path of instruction based on students' skills and abilities in a manner that is challenging and attainable while supporting students in achieving state academic standards. Through focusing the method of instruction on specific targets, teachers can better determine which lesson materials, activities, and assessments will best support students' learning needs to achieve success in learning. Additionally, appropriate learning goals and objectives are necessary for student academic success because they communicate clear expectations and the purpose of learning. When students understand why they are learning a given concept and what they are expected to achieve, they are encouraged to be engaged and focused in learning. Clear learning goals and objectives are also important for monitoring student progress, as they allow teachers to concretely measure student achievement and provide specific, meaningful feedback that allows for student growth.

Elements of Appropriate Learning Goals and Objectives

When determining learning outcomes, the teacher must consider the elements of appropriate learning goals and objectives. Effective **learning goals** communicate long-term learning targets, such as at the end of a unit or chapter, whereas **objectives** should dictate what students are expected to learn at the end of a daily lesson or activity. Proper learning goals and objectives are derived from state academic standards and simultaneously reflect individual student learning needs. They are age- and grade-level-appropriate, challenging, and aimed toward higher-order thinking while still attainable to students according to their developmental level and learning differences. Appropriate learning goals and objectives clearly and succinctly communicate measurable expectations and define a clear purpose for instruction to make learning relevant. Additionally, they consider students' current skills and abilities in order to set targets that build upon background knowledge and allow students to make personal connections in their learning.

Determining Effectiveness of Learning Goals and Objectives

Learning goals and objectives provide a necessary foundation for successful students. Proper learning targets clearly and succinctly communicate expectations, engagement, and achievement. The effectiveness of goals and objectives can be determined by their level of clarity, relevance, and significance of desired outcomes to students, thus allowing for focused instruction and learning. Goals and objectives are most successful when they are relevant to both curriculum material and students' individual experiences, as this fosters engagement through allowing students to forge personal connections and apply new concepts to their own experiences. Moreover, appropriate goals and objectives convey significance to overall learning. When students understand why what they are learning is important, they are more likely to be engaged and focused on instruction, and ultimately, achieve success in learning.

Framing Learning Goals and Objectives to Promote Student Understanding

The language of learning objectives and goals must be **age-appropriate, clear**, and **succinct** for students to comprehend them. Learning goals must represent broader learning outcomes, whereas learning objectives outline the steps for doing so. This includes utilizing verbs that align with the level of understanding that teachers intend for their students to achieve. For example, when introducing a concept, learning objectives may include verbs such as *identify, match*, or *define*. As students develop mastery, the language of objectives should incorporate **higher-order thinking** verbs, such as *analyze, interpret*, or *predict*. Learning objectives and goals should also be measurable in order to communicate to students exactly what they are expected to achieve by the end of the lesson or unit. For example, a learning objective written as, "students will be able to discuss the economic impact of World War II," provides students with a specific and tangible goal to work toward. Academic goals and objectives should include the **purpose** for learning, such as to prepare for an assessment or complete part of a project, and should be connected to state or district standards.

Review Video: Learning Objectives
Visit mometrix.com/academy and enter code: 528458

Determining If Learning Goals and Objectives Are Responsive to Student Needs

In order for instruction and learning to be successful, goals and objectives must be responsive to the developmental levels and individual needs of the students. Teachers must determine the responsiveness of learning targets by their age-appropriateness, consideration of students' skills and abilities, and reflection of their needs, interests, cultures, and backgrounds. Age-appropriate goals and objectives promote student achievement by providing realistic yet rigorous expectations based on developmental level that facilitate academic success. In order to design instruction and activities that are challenging but not overwhelming, expectations must match students' individual skill levels and abilities. Finding the right difficulty for students can ensure that students feel empowered in their learning. Responsive learning goals and objectives also consider students' individual needs and interests, thus allowing for instruction that is relevant and engaging. Additionally, learning targets should be sensitive to and incorporate elements of students' cultures and backgrounds. This fosters engagement and success in learning through allowing students to make personal connections between instruction and their own experiences.

Evaluating Appropriateness of Learning Goals and Objectives

When evaluating the appropriateness of learning goals and objectives, teachers should first consider their relevance and specificity to the academic standards from which they are deriving learning targets as well as how well they facilitate the design of effective instruction. Learning goals should express the desired outcomes of long-term learning, whereas objectives should measure daily achievement as students work toward the learning goal and the specified state standard. Teachers should evaluate whether the goals and objectives precisely communicate what the students are expected to achieve to effectively design instruction that supports students in achieving learning targets. Furthermore, they must ensure that learning targets are tailored to students' individual learning needs to design challenging and realistic instruction. Additionally, teachers should consider the purpose of the learning goals and objectives to determine whether they communicate clear intentions for learning to students. Teachers must then decide which activities, instructional strategies, materials, and resources are most effective for supporting the achievement of learning targets and how they will design assessments to determine student achievement.

Role of Campus and District Goals in Student Academic Readiness

Aligning instructional learning goals and objectives with campus and district goals is imperative for student academic readiness. These standards indicate benchmarks of achievement that students are expected to reach at a given grade level and act as a framework for the design of goals and objectives that help facilitate this achievement. This allows for the focusing of instruction and learning as well as providing a measurable framework for assessing student progress. Additionally, it ensures that all students are held to the same academic expectations and that all students are given the same opportunities for learning. Creating learning targets based upon campus and district goals ensures that students are successfully able to advance to the next grade level with the same academic preparedness relative to their peers.

Designing Goals and Objectives to Address Different Skills and Ability Levels

While learning targets must be aligned with state academic standards, they simultaneously must be tailored to address students' unique skills and abilities. By differentiating instructional goals and objectives, teachers ensure that the instructional strategies, activities, and materials that they implement are effectively varied to meet students' individual learning needs. Additionally, they ensure that instructional expectations challenge students based on their skill and ability while supporting all students in meeting academic benchmarks. The language of objectives and goals should be layered to include varying levels of rigor to accommodate students' differing abilities as they work toward achieving intended learning outcomes. Learning targets should include scaffolding in order to ensure students have necessary supports and allow opportunities for expansion or enrichment as necessary. They should include differentiation in skills students are expected to attain based on their background knowledge and ability as well as variances in approaches to completing tasks and demonstrating understanding. In differentiating objectives and goals, teachers ensure that all students are challenged and supported as they work to achieve grade-level academic standards.

Instructional Planning

Designing Lesson Plans and Units to Align with Instructional Goals

The effective sequencing of units and lesson plans is key to developing coherent, comprehensible instruction that aligns with instructional goals and fosters success in learning. Teachers must first determine the instructional goals that students will be expected to achieve based on state academic standards as a framework and students' individual needs, knowledge, and abilities. Teachers must then logically arrange specific units of instruction aimed toward achieving the determined instructional goals. Each unit should build upon knowledge from the prior unit. Within each unit, teachers must determine what students must achieve as they work toward instructional goals and determine objectives that facilitate success based on individual need and ability. Once objectives are defined, teachers must design lesson plans in a logical sequence that will facilitate students in reaching these objectives and increasingly build upon knowledge as students work toward achieving the learning goal. When planning lessons, teachers must decide which activities, procedures, and materials are necessary for successfully completing lesson objectives while ensuring that individual learning needs are met. The teacher must also decide what will be assessed at the end of each lesson and unit to determine student success in achieving instructional goals.

Review Video: Creating Effective Lesson Plans
Visit mometrix.com/academy and enter code: 100377

Creating Developmentally Appropriate Learning Experiences and Assessments

Multiple factors must be considered when designing developmentally appropriate learning experiences and assessments that effectively facilitate student growth and achievement. Teachers must consider the general cognitive, physical, social, and emotional developmental levels of students as well as individual differences in background, skill, knowledge, and learning needs. With this understanding, teachers must then evaluate whether learning experiences are simultaneously appropriate to students' developmental levels and individual needs. This includes ensuring that learning activities and teaching strategies are varied in approach, are tailored to students' interests, and that they incorporate student choice in learning. Learning experiences must build upon students' background knowledge and experiences and provide challenging yet attainable learning opportunities based on individual skills and abilities. Additionally, teachers must consider whether learning experiences promote student participation and engagement as well as cooperative learning to ensure development across domains. Just as with learning experiences, the developmental appropriateness of assessments must also be evaluated. The teacher must consider whether assessments allow for choice in how students demonstrate their learning so as to address individual learning needs. Furthermore, it is important that teachers consider the purpose of each assessment regarding the feedback they are seeking and how it can help determine further instruction.

Role of Learning Theory in Instructional Process and Student Learning

Multiple learning theories exist to explain how people acquire knowledge, abilities, and skills. Each theory proposes its own approach for best practices in teaching and learning, and their effectiveness varies depending on the context of learning and individual student needs. These theories serve as frameworks for the instructional process and facilitating student learning. Teachers must understand the principles of various learning philosophies as well as their students' unique learning needs to effectively design and implement instruction from the perspective of the most applicable theory. Upon identifying desired learning outcomes, teachers can draw on applicable learning theories to make informed decisions about designing instruction, activities, and assessments that are most effective based on their students' learning styles, skills, and abilities.

The following are examples of some common learning theories that can be used as a framework in the instructional process:

- **Constructivism (Jean Piaget):** This theory proposes that students learn by interacting with the learning environment and connecting new information to their background knowledge to build understanding. This active process allows students to personalize their learning and construct their own perceptions of the world through the lens of their previous experiences.
- **Humanism (Abraham Maslow, Carl Rogers):** This theory proposes that learning should take a person-centered approach, with a focus on the individual's innate capacity for personal growth and self-actualization. It operates axiomatically from the principle that all humans have a natural desire to learn; therefore, a failure to learn is due to the learning situation or environment rather than a person's inability to learn. Teachers should act as facilitators and strive to create a safe, accepting learning environment, celebrate students' differences, and praise academic and personal achievement.
- **Connectivism (George Siemens, Stephen Downes):** This theory proposes that learning occurs by making a series of connections across pieces of information, ideas, concepts, and perspectives. Connectivism is rooted in the notion that learning occurs externally, and technology facilitates connections by giving learners access to several outlets for acquiring and processing new information.
- **Experiential Learning (David Kolb):** This theory proposes that students learn and retain information best through physical exploration and interaction with the learning environment. In the classroom, teachers can facilitate this student-led approach by providing students with varying relevant experiences and opportunities for hands-on learning, such as projects or learning centers.
- **Multiple Intelligences (Howard Gardner):** Gardner's theory proposes there are several versions of intelligence, and as such, the process of learning differs among individuals. Some learners may have a stronger intelligence in one domain but have difficulty in another and, therefore, learn best when instruction is presented through the lens of their dominant intelligence. Intelligences are categorized as logical-mathematical, verbal-linguistic, visual-spatial, bodily-kinesthetic, interpersonal, intrapersonal, musical, and naturalistic.

Connecting New Information and Ideas to Prior Knowledge

When students connect new information to prior knowledge, learning becomes relevant and engaging. Effective instruction encourages students to connect learning to background knowledge and experiences, which increases retainment, deepens understanding, and enhances the effectiveness of the overall learning experience. Fostering personal connections to learning is achieved through incorporating an array of strategies and technologies into instruction. Activities including KWL charts, anticipatory guides, graphic organizers, and brainstorming encourage students to consider what they know before learning new concepts, thus allowing them to build upon their prior knowledge and ability to make connections that strengthen learning. Cooperative learning strategies promote sharing and building prior knowledge with other students, thus increasing students' connections to new information. Numerous technologies exist to enhance the learning experience by fostering connections between prior knowledge and new information. Teachers can incorporate a wide range of apps and games across subject areas that build upon prior knowledge by providing activities with increasing levels of difficulty. Online polls, surveys, and word association websites allow students to demonstrate prior understanding of a topic to begin making connections. Self-reflection and closure opportunities at the end of instruction further strengthen learning by encouraging students to connect new material to prior knowledge and experiences.

Making Learning Meaningful and Relevant

Effective instruction occurs when learning is meaningful and relevant. When the purpose of learning is clear, students are engaged, motivated, and retain new information. Instruction must be student-centered, foster personal connections, and be applicable to real-life situations to create meaningful and relevant instruction. Teachers achieve this through an array of methods and technologies that are tailored to students' learning needs. Through forging positive relationships with students, teachers learn their unique interests, preferences, and experiences. Activities such as interest inventories, surveys, and community building develop a positive rapport between teachers and students. This allows teachers to make learning meaningful by creating learner-centered instruction that facilitates personal connections and builds upon prior knowledge. Field trips and community outreach programs are effective in enhancing relevancy through demonstrating the real-world applications of instruction. Additionally, technologies including virtual field trips and tours, videos, and documentaries assist in increasing students' understanding the purpose of learning by illustrating the real-world applications of instruction. Self-assessments make learning meaningful and relevant through encouraging student ownership and responsibility over learning as students seek areas for improvement. Moreover, closure activities serve to demonstrate overall purpose for learning through encouraging students to connect learning to the lesson's objective and their prior knowledge.

Intradisciplinary and Interdisciplinary Instruction

Intradisciplinary and interdisciplinary instruction are both valuable strategies for teaching and learning. In **intradisciplinary** instruction, several elements of a single broad subject area are incorporated into the lesson. For example, in a science lesson, the teacher could incorporate elements of chemistry, biology, and physics into instruction. This method of instruction is beneficial in deepening students' understanding of the nuances of a particular subject area through demonstrating the various components that comprise the overarching discipline. **Interdisciplinary** instruction refers to the simultaneous integration of ideas, knowledge, and skills from several subject areas when approaching an idea, problem, or theme and applying principles of one subject area to another. For example, in an interdisciplinary unit on food, the teacher could incorporate elements of math by teaching students to measure ingredients, language arts by teaching them to read or write a recipe, science through examining chemical reactions of the cooking process, and social studies through having students explore the impact of food agriculture on economy and society. Interdisciplinary instruction is beneficial in deepening students' understanding across subject areas and developing real-world critical thinking skills by encouraging them to make connections between disciplines and teaching them to consider an idea or problem from multiple perspectives.

Examples of Intradisciplinary Instruction

- **Language arts:** A single language arts lesson can incorporate components of reading, writing, grammar, and listening skills. For example, a lesson on a particular poem can include a close reading of the poet's use of grammar, symbolism, imagery, and other literary techniques as well as an audio recording of the poet reading aloud. At the end of the unit, students can be assigned to use what they learned to compose their own original poems.
- **Social studies:** Social studies units can incorporate elements of history, anthropology, archaeology, sociology, psychology, or any other field that involves the study of humans, civilizations, cultures, and historical events. For example, a unit on the Aztec people may include an examination of their religious beliefs, customs, architecture, and agricultural practices.
- **Science:** Intradisciplinary units in science can include several branches within the field, such as chemistry, biology, physics, earth science, botany, or geology. For example, a unit on volcanoes may incorporate lessons on plate tectonics, the Earth's layers, chemicals released during a volcanic eruption, islands formed from cooled volcanic rock, as well as plants that grow best near volcanoes.
- **Mathematics:** An intradisciplinary math lesson may simultaneously include several branches within the field, such as arithmetic, algebra, or geometry. For example, in a geometry lesson on the Pythagorean theorem, students must utilize algebraic equations and arithmetic to determine the length of the sides of a right triangle.

Examples of Interdisciplinary Instruction

- **Language arts:** A unit based in language arts may also incorporate several other disciplines, such as social studies, art, or music. For example, a unit on William Shakespeare's *Romeo and Juliet* may include a reading of the play, an analysis of the use of literary techniques within it, and study of William Shakespeare's life and the society in which he lived, thereby incorporating social studies into the language arts lesson. Students can also act out the play to incorporate the arts and participate in a rhythmic study on iambic pentameter to incorporate music.

- **Social studies:** Units based in social studies can include lessons focused on multiple disciplines, including language arts, music, science, and math. For example, an interdisciplinary unit on Ancient Egypt may include a historical study of the culture, religion, architecture, and practices of the Ancient Egyptians while integrating other subject areas, such as a study of hieroglyphics to incorporate language arts and creating Egyptian masks to incorporate art. Students can also study the scientific advancements of the Ancient Egyptians and incorporate math to study how the ancient pyramids were constructed.
- **Science:** Scientific units can also incorporate elements of art, math, social studies, and language arts in order to become interdisciplinary. For example, a unit on Punnett squares focuses on biology and genetics but can also include several other subject areas. Math can be incorporated by integrating lessons on probability or students can be assigned to research their genetics, create a family tree, and write a report on their findings to incorporate language arts and social studies. Art can also be incorporated by having students create portraits of the potential outcomes from Punnett squares.
- **Mathematics:** Interdisciplinary units in mathematics can also include lessons focused on art, social studies, science, and music. For example, a geometry unit on measuring triangles may also incorporate songs to memorize equations, lessons on the pyramids of Ancient Egypt to incorporate social studies, as well as an art project in which students use only triangles to create an original piece.

Incorporating Cooperative Learning and Consideration from Multiple Viewpoints

In any classroom, teachers will encounter a wide range of diversities among students' backgrounds, cultures, interests, skills, and abilities. Thus, providing students with several opportunities for cooperative learning gives them access to others' perspectives and is highly valuable in teaching students to consider ideas from multiple viewpoints. As each student has different experiences and background knowledge, collaborative learning allows them to share their views on ideas with others. Additionally, in working together, students have the opportunity to work with others from different backgrounds that they may have otherwise never encountered and gain exposure to approaching ideas from multiple viewpoints. Cooperative learning opportunities allow students to understand and appreciate others' perspectives and teach them that there are multiple approaches to problem solving and ideas.

Learning Experiences That Develop Real-World Life Skills

The ultimate goal of education is to develop the whole child into a productive, contributing member of society; therefore, it is imperative to provide learning experiences that will develop life skills that are applicable and beneficial in the real world. In an increasingly fast-paced global society, students must be prepared to enter the professional and societal world as confident, independent, responsible, and adaptive individuals. They must have the leadership skills necessary to compete in the professional arena. Students must be able to work cooperatively with others, respect and value multiple perspectives, and be effective problem solvers and critical thinkers in order to be successful outside of the classroom. Teachers must also aim to help students develop the skills necessary to become lifelong learners to ensure continuous growth and development as they enter society; therefore, learning experiences that promote the development of real-world life skills in addition to academic skills are necessary in adequately preparing students for success.

Cross-Curricular Instruction for Exploring Content from Varied Perspectives

Cross-curricular instruction allows teachers to demonstrate that elements from one subject area can be applied to ideas or problems in another. Thus, this instructional strategy is highly valuable in developing students' abilities to explore content from varied perspectives. As this method incorporates several disciplines in approaching a topic, it deepens students' understanding that there are several perspectives that one can take when solving a problem and that elements of one subject area are relevant in another. In addition, cross-curricular instruction prepares students for the real world through developing critical thinking skills and allowing them to make connections between disciplines, thus allowing them to understand how to successfully approach ideas from varied perspectives.

Benefits of Multicultural Learning Experiences

Multicultural learning experiences demonstrate to students the array of diversities that exist both inside and outside of the classroom. Just as each culture has its own values, norms, and traditions, each has its own perspectives and approaches to ideas and problem solving. Incorporating multicultural experiences in the classroom exposes students to cultures and groups that they may have otherwise never encountered and teaches them to respect and value perspectives outside of their own. As students learn other cultures' beliefs, customs, and attitudes, they develop the understanding that each culture solves problems and considers ideas from multiple viewpoints and that each approach is valuable. As students learn other perspectives, they can apply this knowledge and build problem solving and critical thinking skills that will be beneficial in developing successful lifelong learning habits.

Incorporating Multiple Disciplines into a Thematic Unit

In **cross-curricular** (or **interdisciplinary**) instruction, multiple disciplines are incorporated into a thematic unit in order to deepen students' understanding through fostering connections and demonstrating multiple perspectives and methods of problem solving. Effective interdisciplinary instruction requires careful planning to ensure that all activities are relevant to the overall lesson theme and effectively support students in achieving desired learning outcomes. Teachers must first select a thematic unit based on state academic standards and then determine desired learning outcomes. Then, teachers must design lessons and activities for students to reach learning goals and objectives. When integrating multiple disciplines into a thematic unit, teachers must seek out materials, resources, and activities from various subject areas that are applicable to the main topic and reinforce lesson objectives. Teachers can then integrate these elements into lesson planning to create multifaceted instruction. Additionally, teachers can create activities that approach the overarching lesson theme from the perspective of different subject areas. The activities and materials should be coordinated and relate to one another in order to deepen students' understanding of the overall concept.

Effectively Allocating Time When Creating Lessons and Units

Effective time management is vital for successful teaching and learning. To ensure that all academic standards are covered within a school year, teachers must consider how to best allocate specific amounts of time for units and lessons that allow for review, enrichment, and reteaching. A unit plan for the school year is an effective strategy in allowing the teacher to visualize and plan the amount of content that must be covered. A unit plan can also be utilized on a smaller scale, as a framework for designing and allotting time for instructional goals, objectives, and lessons within each unit. By setting learning goals and daily objectives within individual units, teachers can determine the amount of time available for completing each unit. This ensures more effective lesson planning by allowing teachers to develop daily schedules with dedicated time for teaching and learning. When planning lessons, teachers must consider how much instructional time is necessary to cover each topic and the time students will need to complete lesson activities. Additionally, teachers must ensure that they allow time at the end of each lesson for reteaching if students have misconceptions, as extra time can be utilized for enrichment if reteaching is unnecessary.

Opportunities for Reflection

Opportunities for reflection within lesson plans enhance learning experiences through strengthening student understanding and influencing further instruction. When students are given the opportunity to reflect, they are able to connect their learning back to the original objective and better understand the overall purpose for learning, thus fostering engagement. Reflection deepens students' understanding by allowing them to connect new concepts to their own personal experiences, which ultimately helps in comprehension and retainment by making learning relevant. Reflecting on performance empowers students to become self-motivated lifelong learners by allowing them to analyze what they understood and did well. Reflection also encourages students to identify areas for improvement. Teachers can utilize students' reflections to influence and drive further instruction. Students' reflections allow teachers to identify areas in which students excelled and areas in which they need improvement. They can also aid teachers in tailoring future lesson plans to adapt to students' needs and interests.

Opportunities for Self-Assessment

Including self-assessments within lessons is a valuable formative assessment strategy that enriches student learning and provides insight to the teacher. Providing students with the opportunity to monitor their progress and assess their learning supports them in developing a wide range of skills that are beneficial both inside and outside of the classroom. Self-assessments create a sense of ownership and responsibility over learning, which foster self-motivation and engagement. They also serve to create a sense of independence and objectivity within students to effectively review their own work and identify areas of improvement, which is a vital skill needed to become a lifelong learner. When students evaluate their own performance, teachers are able to effectively assess student understanding, thus allowing them to identify areas of weakness or misconception for reteaching.

Opportunities for Closure Activities

Closure activities at the end of each lesson or topic are short activities that allow teachers to formatively assess student understanding of content covered within a lesson and identify areas of misconception for reteaching. Additionally, closure activities are valuable in measuring whether the intended lesson objective was achieved before moving to the next topic. For students, closures at the end of a lesson provide structure and organization to learning as well as emphasize the purpose for instruction by allowing them to connect what they learned back to the original objective. Moreover, in having students restate what they have learned in a closure activity, learning is strengthened by giving students the opportunity to internalize new information. In demonstrating their understanding, they can better make personal connections between their own learning, background knowledge, and experiences.

Instructional Techniques

Implementing Multiple Instructional Techniques to Maximize Student Learning

Incorporating multiple instructional techniques into the classroom maximizes student learning by enhancing intellectual involvement and overall engagement. When instructional material is presented through a variety of means, it facilitates an **active learning** environment in which students' interest is captured and they are motivated to participate in learning. Varying teaching strategies stimulates engagement and fosters achievement by encouraging students to actively participate in their own learning and implement critical thinking skills to consider information more deeply. Students' understanding is strengthened when content is presented in different ways through various instructional techniques by providing them with multiple frames of reference for making connections and internalizing new concepts. In addition, utilizing multiple instructional techniques allows the teacher to effectively **differentiate instruction** to access multiple learning styles and address individual student needs to ensure understanding and enhance the overall learning process.

Instructional Strategies to Differentiate Instruction

Implementing a variety of strategies for differentiation helps to ensure that instruction appeals to students' varying learning styles and needs. By incorporating **multiple modalities** into direct instruction, such as visual representations, written directions, video or audio clips, songs, graphs, or mnemonic devices, teachers can differentiate the presentation of new concepts and information. Using strategies to differentiate instructional activities is also beneficial in diversifying the learning experience. By providing opportunities for **independent, collaborative**, and **hands-on** learning, teachers can ensure that learning is accessible and engaging to all students. In addition, learning activities should allow for a degree of flexibility in order to appeal to students' varying needs and preferences. Activities such as task cards, educational technology resources, and learning stations provide this **flexibility** and allow for a student-directed experience in which students can choose to learn in the way that best suits their needs. Similarly, assigning open-ended projects as summative assessments allows for a degree of **student-choice**, thus differentiating the method in which students demonstrate their understanding.

Varying the Teacher and Student Roles in the Instructional Process

Varying the roles of the teacher and students as an instructional technique is beneficial in creating an engaging, dynamic classroom environment that maximizes learning. When different roles are implemented, instruction is diversified, thus stimulating student interest and engagement. In addition, certain teacher and student roles are most applicable and effective in specific learning situations. When teachers acknowledge this and understand when to adopt and assign particular roles, they can effectively deliver instruction in a way that deepens student understanding and fosters success in learning. In presenting new content, directions, or modeling new skills, for example, the roles of **lecturer** and student **observer** are effective. In hands-on learning situations, students can take on the role of **active participant** while the teacher acts as a **facilitator** to create a student-centered and engaging learning environment in which students are given ownership over their own learning. Such variation enhances intellectual involvement by promoting critical thinking and problem-solving skills through self-directed learning. Skillfully assigning different roles throughout the learning process also allows the teacher to effectively address students' individual learning needs and preferences to promote engagement and enhance the learning experience.

Fostering Intellectual Involvement and Engagement

Effective instruction includes a variety of strategies for fostering intellectual involvement and engagement to promote academic success. Presenting instruction using various approaches provides multiple avenues for learning new content, thus ensuring and strengthening student understanding to facilitate achievement. In addition, diversifying instructional strategies creates variety in the classroom that effectively stimulates students' interest and motivation to engage in learning. Strategies such as **cooperative learning**, **discussion**, and **self-directed opportunities** encourage active student participation that enhances intellectual involvement by allowing students to build on background knowledge, deepen understanding by exploring others' perspectives, and take ownership over their own learning. This ultimately increases student engagement and motivation for success in learning. Similarly, incorporating **inquiry**, **problem-solving**, and **project-based** strategies promotes curiosity in learning, creativity, and the development of critical thinking skills that stimulate intellectual participation and engagement to create a productive learning environment. Implementing **digital resources** and media throughout instruction is integral in enhancing academic success by making learning relevant, interesting, and differentiated to accommodate various learning needs. At the end of a lesson or activity, allowing students the opportunity to reflect is a valuable strategy in increasing intellectual involvement, retainment, and academic success by facilitating personal connections with learning to build understanding.

Actively Engaging Students by Incorporating Discussion into Instruction

Classroom discussion is a valuable instructional technique in engaging students throughout the learning process. When teachers skillfully pose higher-level questions in discussions, they establish an active learning environment in which students are encouraged and motivated to participate, thus enhancing overall engagement. Effective discussions prompt students to become **intellectually invested** in instruction by promoting the use of **critical** and **higher-order thinking** skills to consider information more deeply and devise creative solutions to problems. In addition, discussions stimulate engagement by providing students the opportunity to express their own thoughts and reasoning regarding a given topic to establish a sense of ownership over their learning. Furthermore, discussions foster a collaborative learning environment that actively engages students by prompting them to understand others' perspectives, consider alternative approaches, and build on one another's experiences to make deeper connections to learning.

Promoting Student Inquiry

The promotion of inquiry is a valuable instructional technique in enhancing student engagement and intellectual involvement. In an **inquiry-based** learning environment, students are encouraged to explore instructional material and devise their own conclusions or solutions to problems. This increases the effectiveness of the learning process by providing students with a sense of agency over their own learning. In addition, implementing this strategy fosters curiosity, self-motivation, and active participation, as it allows for hands-on, **student-led** learning that increases overall engagement. Incorporating inquiry into the classroom stimulates critical and higher-order thinking skills as students construct their own understanding by interacting with learning materials, analyzing their findings, and synthesizing their learning to create new conclusions, results, and responses. To effectively incorporate inquiry into the learning process, the teacher must provide several opportunities for self-directed learning, project-based learning, and student choice to stimulate curiosity. Questions must be open-ended, and students must be encouraged to hypothesize, predict, and experiment in their learning. The teacher must be flexible in instruction to allow space and opportunity for exploration and allow time for reflection and extended learning opportunities to facilitate further inquiry.

Incorporating Problem-Solving into Instruction

Providing opportunities for creative problem solving within instruction effectively creates an engaging and successful learning experience. Students become more **intellectually involved** when encouraged to actively participate in learning and utilize **critical thinking skills** to test hypotheses, analyze results, and devise creative solutions to problems. This hands-on, **student-directed** approach promotes success in learning by allowing students to interact with learning materials as they seek answers to complex ideas and problems in an engaging environment. Problem-solving enables students to make deeper connections to their learning to enhance understanding, as this strategy prompts them to employ and develop background knowledge. In addition, problem-solving activities allow for collaborative learning in which students can actively engage with peers to build on one another's knowledge and experience, thus enhancing successful learning.

Intellectual Involvement, Active Student Engagement, and Success in Learning

A productive learning environment is composed intellectually involved students that are actively engaged in successful learning. A strong correlation exists between **intellectual involvement**, **active student engagement**, and **success in learning**, and each component is necessary for effective instruction. Effective instruction consists of challenging students based on their abilities and teaching them to think deeply about new ideas and concepts. This ultimately encourages students' intellectual involvement, as it prompts them to utilize their critical thinking skills to build on their background knowledge, consider alternative perspectives, and synthesize their learning to devise creative solutions. When students are intellectually involved in instruction, they become more personally invested and engaged, as learning becomes relevant, interesting, and challenging. Engaged students are active participants in their learning, thus enhancing their overall productivity and academic success.

Effectively Structuring Lessons

When developing instruction, it is imperative that the teacher is knowledgeable on how to effectively structure lessons to maximize student engagement and success. Each lesson must include a clear **objective** and explicitly state the process for achieving it. To initiate engagement, effective lessons begin with an **opening**, or "warm-up," activity to introduce a new topic, diagnose student understanding, and activate prior knowledge. Instruction of new material must be delivered through a variety of teaching strategies that are consciously tailored to students' individual learning needs to enhance participation and ensure comprehension. Direct instruction should be followed by **active learning** activities with clear directions and procedures to allow students to practice new concepts and skills. Throughout a successful lesson, the teacher checks frequently for understanding and comprehension by conducting a variety of **formative assessments** and adjusts instruction as necessary. Including **closure** activities is essential to successful learning, as it gives students the opportunity to reflect, process information, make connections, and demonstrate comprehension. In structuring lessons effectively according to students' learning needs, the teacher establishes a focused and engaging learning environment that promotes academic success.

Example of a Daily Lesson Plan Structure

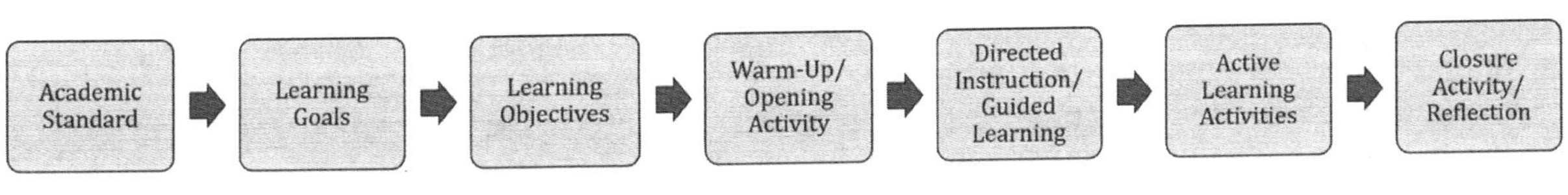

Flexible Instructional Groupings

Flexible instructional groupings provide the teacher and students with a versatile, engaging environment for successful learning. Skillfully grouping students allows for productive, cooperative learning opportunities in which individual strengths are enhanced and necessary support is provided, thus enhancing motivation and engagement. When working in groups, students' understanding of instruction is strengthened, as they are able to learn and build upon one another's background knowledge, perspectives, and abilities. Instructional groups can include students of the **same** or **varied abilities** depending on the learning objective and task to increase productivity and provide scaffolding as necessary for support. This strategy is effective in enabling the teacher to **differentiate** instruction and adjust groups as needed to accommodate varying learning styles, abilities, and interests to maximize engagement and success in learning.

Effective Pacing of Lessons and Importance of Flexibility to Students' Needs

Effective pacing is imperative to focused and engaging instruction. Teachers must be conscientious of the pace of their instruction and ensure that it is reflective of their students' learning needs and sustains their attention. Instruction that is delivered too quickly results in confusion and discouragement, whereas if instruction is too slow, students will lose interest and become disengaged. A well-paced lesson states clear learning goals and objectives while clearly outlining the means to achieve them to elicit student motivation. The teacher must consider the most **efficient** and **engaging** instructional strategies for presenting new material to establish a steady pace and maintain it by incorporating smooth **transitions** from one activity to the next. It is important that teachers are conscious of the rate of instruction throughout all stages of learning while maintaining **flexibility** in pacing in order to be responsive to their students. As individual students have different learning needs and processing times, they may require a faster or slower rate of instruction to understand new concepts and remain engaged in learning. Frequent checks for understanding and reflection activities are essential strategies in determining if the pace of instruction must be adjusted to accommodate students' needs.

Connecting Content to Students' Prior Knowledge and Experiences

Implementing effective instructional strategies for connecting content to students' prior knowledge and experiences enhances the relevancy of learning and fosters deeper connections that strengthen understanding. To achieve this, teachers must educate themselves on students' backgrounds, experiences, communities, and interests to determine what is important and interesting to them. With this knowledge in mind, teachers can successfully locate and implement **authentic materials** into instruction to enhance relevancy. Additionally, encouraging students to bring materials to class that reflect their backgrounds and including these materials in instruction makes learning relevant by allowing students to make **personal connections** to content. Instructional strategies such as brainstorming, KWL charts, prereading, and anticipation guides allow the teacher to determine what students know prior to learning a new concept, thus enabling them to connect content to students' background knowledge in a relevant way. Incorporating digital resources further enhances relevancy in learning. Teachers can locate videos or audio clips that relate to instruction and reflect students' background experiences and interests. Using digital resources to introduce a new concept is a valuable strategy in developing students' **schema** on a topic to build prior knowledge and make learning meaningful by fostering connections.

Making Learning Relevant and Meaningful

For learning to be relevant and meaningful, it is essential that teachers present content in a way that connects with students' **prior knowledge** and experiences. When students are able to apply new ideas and information to what they already know through effective instructional techniques, it facilitates strong **personal connections** that make learning relevant and meaningful. In addition, personal connections and **relevancy** are strengthened when teachers consciously incorporate materials to reflect students' individual backgrounds and experiences in instruction. Linking content to students' background experiences enables them to relate instruction to real-world situations, thus establishing a sense of purpose for learning by making it applicable to their lives. Intentionally connecting content with students' prior knowledge and experiences enhances the effectiveness of the instructional process and fosters positive attitudes toward learning.

Enhancing Student Engagement and Success in Learning

Engaging instruction employs a variety of instructional strategies and materials to create a relevant, meaningful, and successful learning experience. Effective content establishes a clear and applicable purpose for instruction that increases student participation in the learning process. Presenting relevant and meaningful content enhances understanding and engagement by enabling students to create real-world, **personal connections** to learning based upon their own backgrounds and experiences. In addition, when instruction is tailored to reflect students' unique interests and preferences, content becomes more appealing and students' willingness to learn is enhanced. When students can perceive content through their own frames of reference with instructional materials that reflect their unique differences, they are able to effectively internalize and relate information to their lives, thus increasing engagement. Engaged learning ultimately facilitates academic success in that when students are motivated to learn, they demonstrate positive attitudes toward learning and are more likely to actively participate.

Adapting Instruction to Individual Needs

Evaluating Activities and Materials to Meet Learning Needs

The careful selection of instructional activities and materials is integral to accommodating students' varying characteristics and needs. When evaluating the appropriateness of activities and materials, several considerations must be made. Teachers must consider whether activities and materials align with state and district **academic standards**. Teachers must also evaluate the quality and effectiveness of the activities and materials in supporting students' unique differences as they achieve learning goals and objectives. All materials and activities must be **developmentally appropriate** across domains yet adaptable to individual students' learning needs. In addition, they must be challenging yet feasible for student achievement relative to students' grade levels and abilities to promote engagement and the development of critical and **higher-order thinking** skills. Teachers must evaluate activities and materials for versatility to allow for student choice and differentiation in order to address varying characteristics and needs. Teachers must also ensure that activities and materials are accurate, **culturally sensitive**, and reflective of students' diversities to foster an inclusive learning environment that promotes engagement.

Instructional Resources and Technologies

The implementation of varied instructional resources and technologies is highly valuable in supporting student engagement and achievement. Effective use of resources and technologies requires teachers to evaluate their appropriateness in addressing students' individual characteristics and learning needs for academic success. Teachers must be attuned to students' unique differences in order to seek high quality technologies and resources that address their students' needs and support the achievement of learning goals and objectives. Technologies and resources must be **accurate**, **comprehensible**, easily **accessible** to students, and **relevant** to the curriculum and the development of particular skills. Teachers must also consider the grade-level and **developmental appropriateness** of technologies and resources as well as their adaptability to allow for differentiation. Effective technologies and resources are interactive, engaging, and multifaceted to allow for varying levels of complexity based on students' abilities. This allows teachers to provide appropriate challenges while diversifying instruction to appeal to varied characteristics and learning needs, thus fostering an engaging environment that supports success in learning for all students.

Adapting Activities and Materials to Meet Individual Characteristics and Needs

In effective instruction, activities and materials are adapted to accommodate students' individual characteristics and needs. Teachers must be attuned to students' unique differences and understand how to adjust activities and materials accordingly to facilitate academic success and growth. To achieve this, teachers must incorporate a **variety** of activities and materials that appeal to all styles of learners. Activities and materials should provide **student choice** for engagement in learning and demonstration of understanding. By differentiating instruction, teachers can effectively scaffold activities and materials to provide supports as necessary as well as include extensions or alternate activities for enrichment. **Chunking** instruction, allowing extra time as necessary, and accompanying activities and materials with aids such as graphic organizers, visual representations, and anticipation guides further differentiates learning to accommodate students' learning characteristics and needs. Conducting **formative assessments** provides teachers with valuable feedback regarding student understanding and engagement, thus allowing them to modify and adjust the complexity of activities and materials as necessary to adapt to varied characteristics and learning differences.

Instructional Resources and Technologies

When teachers understand students' individual characteristics and needs, they can adapt instructional resources and technologies accordingly to maximize learning. To do so effectively, the teacher must incorporate a diverse array of **multifaceted** resources and technologies that support and enhance learning through a variety of methods. This ensures that varying learning needs are met, as students of all learning styles are provided with several avenues for building and strengthening understanding. Additionally, the teacher can adapt resources and technologies to accommodate individual students by **varying the complexity** to provide challenges, support, and opportunities for enrichment based on ability level. Supplementing technologies and resources with **scaffolds**, such as extra time, visual representations, or opportunities for collaborative learning, further enables the teacher to adapt to individual learning needs. When effectively implemented and adapted to students' characteristics and needs, instructional technologies and resources serve as valuable tools for differentiating curriculum to enhance the learning experience.

Flexible and Responsive Instructional Practices

Evaluation of Instruction

Evaluating the appropriateness of instructional materials, activities, resources, and technologies is integral to establishing a successful learning environment. Doing so provides students with high-quality and inclusive instruction by ensuring **clarity**, **accuracy**, **relevancy**, and **reflection** of student diversities. By determining whether these components of instruction meet varying characteristics and learning needs, the teacher can deliver **student-centered** instruction that is challenging based on individual ability and promote development and academic success. This process also allows the teacher to effectively **differentiate** instruction to provide necessary personalized support for success in achieving learning targets as well as create engaging learning opportunities tailored to students' unique differences and interests. Effectively determining the appropriateness of activities, materials, resources, and technologies in meeting students' learning needs ultimately maximizes academic achievement and fosters positive attitudes toward learning that establish a foundation for future success.

Continuous Monitoring of Instructional Effectiveness

Successful instruction must be flexible and adaptable to meet students' dynamic learning needs. To achieve this, teachers must continuously monitor the effectiveness of their instruction to determine if their teaching strategies, activities, and communication are effective. Frequent evaluation of instructional effectiveness is necessary to ensure that students understand **foundational concepts** before moving on to more advanced concepts. **Adaptations** to instruction, communication, or assessment may be necessary to ensure students are able to comprehend and retain concepts before moving on to more advanced topics. **Remediation** of missed concepts is often much more challenging and less successful than checking for comprehension within context and providing more detailed instruction. This ultimately fosters long-term achievement, as the teacher can identify and address student needs as they arise and prevent compounding issues. Continuous monitoring enables the teacher to ensure that learning opportunities are engaging, relevant, and challenging based on students' ability levels, as it provides immediate feedback on the effectiveness of instruction, which allows the teacher to make necessary changes. This ultimately enhances instruction by establishing a student-centered learning environment that is tailored to individual needs, interests, and abilities.

Pre-Instructional, Peri-Instructional, and Post-Instructional Strategies

Instructional effectiveness must be monitored on a whole-class and individual level throughout all stages of teaching. Prior to instruction, administering **pre-tests** provides teachers with insight regarding whole-class and individual understanding. This enables teachers to select effective and appropriate instructional strategies that can be differentiated to meet individual needs. Pre-tests allow teachers to identify and clarify misunderstandings before instruction to ensure effectiveness. During instruction, **observation** of students' participation in instruction during independent and group activities enables the teacher to evaluate overall and individual understanding and engagement. Frequent checks for understanding and **formative assessments** throughout instruction provide feedback on whole-group and individual learning, as the teacher can assess understanding and participation to adapt teaching strategies or individualize instruction. Leading student discussions allows the teacher to identify areas of misunderstanding among the class or individuals who may need reteaching through a different approach. Closure and reflection activities after instruction are valuable in monitoring effectiveness, as they indicate both whole-class and individual comprehension and retainment of new concepts. Likewise, incorporating **summative assessments** and analyzing the results provides teachers with information regarding the overall effectiveness of their teaching process as well as students' individual strengths and weaknesses to consider for future instruction.

Applying Feedback to Make Necessary Changes to Instruction

Continuous monitoring of instruction indicates the instruction's effectiveness on a **whole-class** and **individual** level, as it provides the teacher with immediate insight into student understanding, progress, and areas for improvement. Monitoring instructional effectiveness enables the teacher to evaluate students' **pace** in achieving learning goals and adjust the rate of instruction as necessary. Additionally, it allows the teacher to identify whole-class and individual **misconceptions** that require correction to ensure students do not fall behind schedule in meeting academic benchmarks. If monitoring reveals misunderstanding among the whole class, the teacher must alter the overall instructional approach and teaching strategies to clarify and regain understanding. Individual misconceptions indicate the need to differentiate instruction, adjust groupings, and provide supports and remediation as necessary to ensure the student progresses at the same rate as the rest of the class. By identifying student strengths and weaknesses through consistent monitoring of instructional effectiveness, the teacher can effectively make instructional decisions that are attuned to whole-class and individual student needs to maximize learning.

Flexibility in Instruction

Situations Requiring Flexibility

The classroom environment is dynamic in nature. Teachers will inevitably encounter situations throughout instruction and assessment in which **flexibility** is integral to successful teaching and learning. As students have varying learning styles, needs, and interests, teachers may find that their instructional approaches are ineffective in maintaining engagement and may need to adjust strategies, activities, or assessments to better meet learning needs. Students may have difficulty grasping new material, which could result in a lack of engagement in instructional activities and, potentially, disruptive behavior. Teachers must consistently be attuned to students' levels of comprehension and allow flexibility in their lesson plans to modify strategies, activities, or pacing as necessary to facilitate engagement and understanding before advancing in instruction. Students may also progress more quickly than others through instructional activities or assessments. **Scaffolding** activities to include opportunities for extension and enrichment allow for flexibility within instruction and ensure that all students are adequately challenged and engaged in learning. Throughout instruction and assessments, teachers may find valuable, unexpected learning opportunities. By remaining open and flexible to these instances, teachers can enhance the learning process and strengthen student understanding by incorporating them into instruction.

Enhancing the Overall Learning Experience

Flexibility is an integral component of effective instruction, as it enables the teacher to adequately address and accommodate students' individual needs and interests for maximized success in learning. When teachers consider their lesson plans as **frameworks** while allowing for flexibility, they demonstrate an awareness of their students' individual differences and the potential for deviation from original instruction. This enables them to more effectively modify instructional and assessment strategies, activities, and approaches to create a **responsive, student-centered** environment that enhances the overall learning experience and promotes achievement. When instructional activities and assessments are adaptable to accommodate students' needs and interests, learning becomes more personalized and relevant, thus strengthening understanding and increasing motivation to engage in active learning. A flexible approach to instruction and assessment also provides students with the ability to explore content of interest on a deeper level and potentially encounter unanticipated learning opportunities that foster personal connections and enhance learning. In addition, this approach allows for **versatility** in assessment, as flexibility enables the teacher to modify assessments by providing necessary support to meet students' individual needs and supports students' choice in demonstrating learning.

Poor Student Comprehension

Throughout instruction and assessments, students may have difficulty **comprehending** new or difficult material despite being engaged in instruction. This may lead to confusion that can cause students to become discouraged and disengaged in learning as well as have continued and compounded difficulty in grasping increasingly complex concepts. Difficulties with comprehension hinders academic success, as students who struggle face challenges in building the foundation of understanding necessary for advancing through curriculum. To ensure student comprehension throughout all stages of learning, the teacher must be aware of students' individual learning styles and needs and be able to respond flexibly to obstacles they may encounter. **Formative assessments** during instruction enable the teacher to evaluate the level of student comprehension and identify areas of need for flexible **adjustment** or additional support. This includes modifying **pacing** and allowing additional time for student processing to ensure understanding. In addition, the original lesson plan may require **chunking** into smaller, more manageable parts to allow students to internalize new concepts before moving on. The teacher may also need to respond flexibly to students' needs during instruction by **differentiating** teaching strategies, activities, groupings, or assessments to ensure that material is accessible and comprehensible to all students for enhanced success.

Unanticipated Learning Opportunities

Unanticipated learning opportunities, when embraced by the teacher, are often highly valuable in establishing a classroom environment that promotes student engagement, motivation, and success. These instances often divert from the original lesson plan, but when utilized effectively, they serve to strengthen student understanding and foster **personal connections** for an enhanced learning experience. Facilitating such opportunities allows students to investigate topics that are interesting and relevant to them on a deeper level, thus increasing active engagement and promoting **self-directed** learning. This ultimately supports students in forming connections and recognizing the real-world applications of their learning, which increases the likelihood that they will internalize and **retain** new information. Responding flexibly to unanticipated learning opportunities includes acknowledging students' questions and comments as well as demonstrating an awareness of their individual differences and learning needs. This enables the teacher to maximize the effectiveness of these opportunities by facilitating student-led instruction that is attuned to their learning styles, interests, and preferences for enhanced engagement and achievement.

Conducting Ongoing Assessments and Making Adjustments

Conducting **ongoing assessments** throughout instruction provides teachers with continuous feedback regarding student comprehension, engagement, and performance. When practiced consistently, teachers are more attuned and responsive to students' individual learning needs. This enables them to effectively modify instructional strategies, activities, and assessments accordingly for a **student-centered** learning environment that provides the support necessary for enhanced engagement, comprehension, and achievement. It allows teachers to identify and address areas of **misconception** and student need to ensure understanding prior to progressing through the curriculum. Feedback from ongoing evaluation of student performance indicates areas of instruction in which adjustment is necessary to effectively support students in achieving learning goals. Teachers may need to adjust their pacing to ensure comprehension and engagement as well as differentiate instruction based on feedback regarding individual progress to ensure all students are adequately challenged and supported based on their ability levels. Student groupings may need to be adjusted to scaffold instruction and facilitate increased comprehension. When teachers effectively apply feedback from ongoing assessments of student engagement and performance, they can tailor instruction to accommodate their individual needs and interests to enhance success in learning.

Progressing Ahead of Schedule

Throughout instruction, teachers will encounter instances in which individual students or the whole class progresses **faster than anticipated**. When this arises, the teacher must be prepared to respond flexibly to ensure that all students are engaged, on task, and challenged based on their ability levels. Lesson plans should be **scaffolded** to include opportunities for enrichment and extended learning for students who finish before others. This includes incorporating materials such as increasingly complex texts, practice activities, and project opportunities. Teachers can also establish a designated area in the classroom in which individuals or small groups that finish early can participate in **extended learning** or **review** activities that reinforce learning objectives. Such activities allow students to explore instructional topics on a deeper level for strengthened understanding and ensure they are engaging productively in meaningful activities that are relevant to instruction. When the whole class progresses faster than expected, the teacher can respond flexibly by incorporating **total participation** activities to reinforce instructional material. Activities such as review games, class discussions, and digital resources for extra practice ensure that the class remains engaged in instruction when they finish a lesson early.

Communicating Effectively with Students

Clear and Accurate Communication

Significance

Successful teaching and learning is reliant on clear, accurate communication throughout all stages of the learning process. To create a positive and productive learning environment, it is vital that the teacher practice effective speaking, listening, reading, and writing skills to ensure focused instruction in which students understand expectations and desired learning outcomes. When communication is clear and accurate, learning becomes relevant and engaging, as students understand the purpose of instruction and are more successfully able to complete tasks and achieve learning targets. This ultimately enhances the overall learning experience in that it allows teachers to efficiently progress through the curriculum and challenge students with increasingly complex material as they master desired learning outcomes. Effective communication is multifaceted, it increases student comprehension, and it deepens their understanding of subject matter. When the teacher skillfully communicates instruction through a variety of methods, students of varying learning styles are better able to internalize new information according to their individual needs. By enhancing teaching and learning through clear and accurate communication, the teacher establishes positive attitudes toward learning among students that serve as a foundation for future academic success.

Appropriate Language for Varying Age Groups

Students' cognitive abilities develop as they mature, and the ability to focus, comprehend, and process information differs among age groups. For successful teaching and learning, the teacher must be aware of these variances to clearly and accurately communicate in an age-appropriate manner that facilitates student understanding. The use of age-appropriate language throughout the teaching and learning process is vital in supporting students' attention and ability to focus. Age-appropriate language also challenges students according to their developmental levels to ensure prolonged engagement in instruction. Furthermore, age-appropriate language is necessary in promoting student understanding through making information accessible and relevant. When designing and communicating instruction, the teacher must consider students' cognitive and linguistic abilities as well as their attention span relative to their age group to ensure a comprehensible, rigorous, and engaging learning environment. The teacher must also be sure to support verbal communication with eye contact, body language, and visuals appropriate to the specific age group to reinforce and deepen understanding.

Tailoring Communication to Students' Interests

Communicating instruction to reflect students' interests enhances the teaching and learning process by fostering an engaging, student-centered environment. Instruction that appeals to students by incorporating their interests strengthens comprehension and understanding through increasing relevancy by allowing for personal connections to learning. To accomplish this, the teacher must get to know individual students and work to build positive relationships to gain an understanding of their unique interests and preferences. With this understanding in mind, the teacher can provide learning experiences that reflect individual interests through examples, relevant activities, and encouraging active participation to allow students to express their own interests and connections when learning. In addition, the teacher must seek feedback from students and evaluate their reactions when delivering instruction to determine whether it is reflective of their interests and adjust accordingly. When instruction is communicated according to students' interests and preferences, the teacher creates an inclusive and personalized learning experience that fosters positive attitudes toward learning and enhances academic achievement.

Using Language Appropriate to Students' Backgrounds

Understanding students' backgrounds and adjusting language accordingly is imperative for ensuring clear, accurate, and respectful communication that promotes success in learning. When communicating in the classroom, using language appropriate to students' individual backgrounds is essential in ensuring culturally **relevant**, **sensitive**, and **responsive** instruction. When teachers understand what is important to students based on their background experiences, beliefs, and values, they can more effectively and accurately communicate instruction, as they can tailor their language in a manner that is responsive to students' needs and avoids misunderstanding. Such **culturally competent** communication promotes academic success by fostering an inclusive environment in which all students feel respected and are therefore motivated to learn. Moreover, using language that is appropriate to students' backgrounds enhances the teaching and learning process by making instruction engaging and relevant to students, as it enables personal connections to deepen understanding. When the language of instruction is easily accessible to students and reflective of their experiences, they can apply their learning to their own personal contexts. This ultimately fosters positive attitudes toward learning among students that promote academic success.

Instructional Strategies for Ensuring Clear and Accurate Communication

In effective instruction, the teacher frequently implements strategies to ensure and evaluate the clarity and accuracy of communication and adjusts accordingly to meet students' individual needs. In order to provide instruction that is easily accessible to students, the teacher must incorporate a variety of **verbal** and **nonverbal** communication techniques to strengthen understanding. Verbal information must be accompanied by nonverbal means of communication, such as proper eye contact, body language, gestures, visuals, and written information. Additionally, teachers can determine whether they are communicating clearly and accurately by asking students to repeat instructions and key information. Frequently monitoring student progress by conducting formative assessments throughout the learning process allows the teacher to determine student comprehension and adjust communication techniques as necessary to enhance clarity and accuracy. Moreover, allowing students opportunities to provide feedback on the learning process through discussions and reflection activities is an effective strategy in providing insight on the clarity and accuracy of communication. By implementing cooperative learning and small group activities, the teacher can further ensure clarity and accuracy of communication by allowing for more focused instruction that is tailored to students' individual learning needs.

Ensuring Student Understanding

Effectively Communicating Directions, Explanations, and Procedures

Successful learning requires the effective communication of directions, explanations, and procedures to ensure student understanding. When this information is clearly communicated, confusion and misconceptions are avoided, allowing for smoother and more focused instruction. Effective and skillful communication eliminates distractions from instruction, thus allowing students to engage in learning confidently and successfully because they clearly understand the objectives, expectations, and methods for completing tasks. In addition, allocating specific time to provide specific directions, explanations, and procedures enhances student understanding by establishing consistency, order, and effective classroom management that enables students to focus on learning. This creates a safe, predictable, and more engaging classroom environment that facilitates student understanding and success in learning.

Strategies for Adjusting Communication

In all stages of the teaching and learning process, teachers must be flexible in instruction and implement strategies for adjusting communication to ensure student understanding. Teachers may have to adapt communication by adjusting their tone, pace, vocabulary, or method of communicating to meet students' individual learning needs. Teachers must get to know their students to understand their unique needs as well as what is interesting and relevant to them to tailor their communication accordingly. By building positive relationships and learning students' communication styles, teachers can effectively deliver instruction that is easily understandable to students. Modeling good active listening skills, conducting formative assessments throughout instruction, and eliciting student feedback allows teachers to evaluate student understanding and adjust their communication style as necessary. In addition, incorporating technology into instruction is a valuable strategy for adapting communication to meet students' needs and ensure understanding. By accompanying instruction with digital resources, teachers can deliver information, directions, and explanations through a variety of methods to make communication accessible and comprehensible to students of varying learning styles.

Providing Examples When Communicating Directions, Explanations, and Procedures

When the teacher skillfully provides examples to support directions, explanations, and procedures, instruction is more effective because students' overall understanding is enhanced. In selecting appropriate, relevant examples, the teacher makes learning concrete and establishes a frame of reference for students to visualize the real-world application of the given information. Effective examples allow students to make personal connections to their learning by relating information to their own experiences, thus enhancing their understanding by making learning more engaging and meaningful. Additionally, as modeling is an influential instructional strategy, incorporating practical examples enhances student understanding by providing them with a model to reference, compare, and replicate. The use of effective examples in communicating directions, explanations, and procedures ultimately increases retainment of information, thus fostering success when students engage in learning.

Types of Examples

Accompanying directions, explanations, and procedures with a variety of examples is beneficial in strengthening students' connections and enhancing understanding. **Visual representations**, such as images, illustrations, diagrams, graphs, or charts, serve as valuable examples for student reference, as reminders, and as supplements to instruction. Modeling is a highly effective instructional strategy, and **demonstrating** to students how to perform directions, routines, and procedures ensures that students are clear regarding what is expected of them. When communicating criteria for assignments, showing examples of **past student work** provides students with clarity regarding how they will be graded and the characteristics of quality work. In addition, using real-life **scenarios** or **personal experiences** as examples is beneficial in making new information relevant, applicable, and easier for students to comprehend.

Simplifying Complex Ideas

To strengthen student understanding of educational content, complex ideas often must be simplified. Teachers must communicate carefully and implement teaching strategies to provide comprehensible instruction. The language of instruction must be clear, succinct, free of distractions, and age-appropriate to ensure that new content is easily accessible to students. Complex ideas should be **chunked** into smaller parts when teaching to allow for focused instruction that avoids misconceptions and builds a solid foundation of understanding. This also enhances student understanding by allowing the teacher the opportunity to formatively assess comprehension throughout the learning process and adjust instructional strategies as necessary to simplify difficult content. Accompanying instruction with visual aids, such as graphic organizers, anchor charts, or infographics, makes complex topics easier to internalize by emphasizing key information. Likewise, incorporating media and other digital resources enhances student understanding by diversifying the instructional approach to make learning more accessible and reinforcing complex ideas.

Effective Communication Tools

In a productive learning environment, the teacher implements a variety of communication tools to ensure that students have a clear understanding of directions, explanations, and procedures. **Visual aids** throughout the classroom in the form of posters, anchor charts, and class bulletin boards serve to reinforce and remind students of pertinent information and expectations. Effective **transitions** communicate to students the process for moving from one activity or subject to the next. Allowing students opportunities for **reflection** provides the teacher with feedback on the clarity of directions, explanations, and procedures and enables them to adjust communication as necessary to enhance understanding. In addition, several digital communication tools are available to increase communication and understanding, including interactive apps that enable teachers to formatively assess clarity and apps to remind students and families of important information to reinforce understanding. Establishing communication with families by creating a classroom newsletter or website and requiring students to keep a daily agenda book are examples of valuable tools for ensuring understanding, as these allow students to be reminded of events, assignments, and expectations at home.

Verbal and Nonverbal Means of Communication

Directions, explanations, and procedures often must be communicated throughout instruction to enhance student understanding. In communicating this information through a variety of **verbal** and **nonverbal** methods, the teacher ensures that students are aware of every part of the instructional process, thus allowing for a focused and productive learning experience. When introducing a new lesson or activity, using effective speaking and listening skills, repeating explanations as necessary, and varying tone, pacing, and inflection to verbally communicate pertinent information and processes effectively establishes understanding. Verbally conducting formative assessments during instruction further supports student understanding by providing the teacher with feedback to adjust communication as needed for clarity. In addition, verbal instructions can be strengthened to increase student understanding by incorporating media such as videos and audio clips. Nonverbal communication is highly effective in reminding students of and reinforcing directions, explanations, and procedures. Gestures, facial expressions, body language, eye contact, and proximity are valuable tools for highlighting key information and reminding students of expectations and instructional steps. In addition, visual reminders around the classroom in the form of posters, charts, and presentation slides act as nonverbal reminders of processes and expectations to enhance understanding and allow for focused engagement in instruction.

Significance of Effective Communication Skills in Meeting Specified Goals

Effective communication skills are essential to successfully meeting learning goals across various contexts. When the teacher skillfully communicates desired outcomes in the instructional process and the steps to achieve them, students are able to meet learning goals because they have a focused understanding and purpose for learning. When communication is clear and free of distractions, students' engagement in instruction is enhanced, thus making it easier for them to achieve learning targets. In addition, using a variety of techniques to effectively communicate material across subject areas enhances understanding by providing multiple avenues for students to internalize, apply, and ultimately retain new information. Furthermore, when teachers are conscientious of their communication, they become more attuned to students' individual learning needs and communication styles. This allows teachers to effectively instill necessary supports and adjust communication to meet students' needs when meeting specified learning goals.

Significance of Effective Interpersonal Skills in a Positive Learning Environment

Interpersonal relationships are a vital aspect of successful teaching and learning. When positive interpersonal skills are demonstrated and promoted, the teacher effectively establishes a supportive, inviting classroom environment in which students are empowered and motivated to learn. Strong interpersonal skills allow the teacher to build positive, respectful relationships with students, instilling in them a sense of confidence and engagement that fosters academic achievement. In understanding how to interact with students in a way that is relevant and meaningful to them, the teacher can enhance learning and achievement by tailoring instruction to students' unique interests and experiences. In addition, establishing a positive rapport with students enables the teacher to identify, address, and adapt instruction to students' individual learning needs, thus enhancing instruction to promote engagement and achievement.

Verbal and Nonverbal Communication

When developing and delivering instruction to meet specified goals across varying learning contexts, it is imperative that the teacher implement a variety of verbal and nonverbal communication techniques. **Verbal communication** methods, including repetition, providing explanations and examples, and changing the pace, tone, and inflection of speech are effective when introducing new, complex concepts and emphasizing key information to students. Incorporating videos and audio clips enhances verbal communication by providing an additional method for understanding when working to achieve learning goals. Incorporating clear **nonverbal communication** techniques is effective in reinforcing and reminding students of instructional targets and content. Body language, gestures, facial expressions, and eye contact highlight important information to support verbal communication and strengthen understanding when explaining new concepts or modeling new skills to students. Visual aids such as posters, anchor charts, presentation slides, and images are tools for nonverbally restating procedures and concepts. They can also be used to simplify complex ideas to enable students to successfully reach specified learning goals.

Electronic Communication

In an increasingly digital world, electronic communication has become integral in enhancing teaching and learning to efficiently meet specified goals across learning contexts. Digital resources improve clarity by providing teachers with multiple means of communicating learning targets, delivering instruction, and providing feedback. Electronic communication makes learning more accessible and comprehensible, as teachers can utilize it to deliver information and instruction in a variety of ways according to students' individual learning needs. Digital communication platforms, such as virtual classrooms and interactive apps, promote interaction and participation, which increase student engagement in the learning process. In addition, such platforms increase the efficiency of meeting specified learning goals by allowing for immediate communication and feedback between teachers and students throughout all stages of instruction. Such platforms also allow the teacher to provide instructional materials that students can easily reference to increase understanding. Electronic tools such as email, class websites, and communication apps establish open communication between teachers, students, and families. This is beneficial in meeting learning goals because it allows the teacher to easily provide pertinent information that can be reinforced at home.

Effective Feedback and Self-Assessment

Timely Feedback

Timely feedback improves the effectiveness of teaching and learning for enhanced student achievement. When the teacher consistently provides feedback on students' progress throughout all stages of instruction, it is more relevant, thus enabling students to effectively connect it to the context of their learning. Providing timely feedback also ensures that instructional content is at the forefront of students' minds, thus increasing the likelihood that students will effectively apply it for enhanced learning. Immediate feedback increases student motivation and allows for more focused instruction, as students are continuously aware of their strengths and areas for improvement. In addition, efficient feedback enables the teacher to quickly identify areas of misconception before advancing in instruction, thus ensuring student understanding before moving forward and avoiding the need for remediation. This allows the teacher to progress smoothly through instruction while ensuring comprehension to enhance student achievement.

Appropriate Language for Providing Feedback

The language of feedback influences its effectiveness in fostering student achievement. When providing students with feedback regarding their progress, teachers must be mindful of their approach to ensure that it is properly received. It is important that teachers consider students' **age** and **grade levels** to tailor language accordingly and present feedback in a relevant and meaningful way. When the language of feedback is comprehensible to students, they are more effectively able to apply it to the context of their learning. The teacher's language must be **respectful, positive**, and **encouraging** while constructively suggesting areas for improvement so as to support students' self-concept and positive attitudes toward learning. This includes framing feedback with remarks that identify and reinforce students' **strengths** while offering support and guidance to enhance development. Language must be **direct** and **specific** to ensure understanding and that necessary changes are made as students progress through instruction. The teacher must also be attuned to students' individual characteristics in order to address them with language that is responsive and considerate of their needs. When the appropriate language is applied in presenting feedback, it increases student motivation, engagement, and ability to make improvements that enhance their learning experience.

Effective Formats for Feedback

Successful instruction is reliant on continuous feedback through a variety of **formats** to ensure that the teacher's guidance is accurate, constructive, substantive, and specific. Varying formats for providing formative and summative feedback are applicable and effective in different stages of the learning process. **Formative feedback** is often informal and occurs throughout instruction to guide student learning. Some methods include oral feedback in the form of asking students open-ended questions and providing suggestions for improvement, written comments on assignments, and peer-to-peer feedback in which students can offer one another support to build understanding. **Summative feedback** is often formal and occurs at the end of a lesson or unit to evaluate students' progress in achieving learning goals. **Rubrics** are a versatile tool for providing summative feedback, as they vary in complexity and the criteria within them can be tailored to specific learning objectives. This format is valuable for communicating expectations and clearly demonstrating the characteristics of quality work. In utilizing rubrics to provide feedback, the teacher can outline specific areas for evaluation, assign point values, and explicitly specify areas of strength and skills that need improvement.

Substantive Feedback

When teachers provide **substantive feedback**, they ensure that students are given focused, useful, and relevant direction regarding their progress throughout the learning process. This feedback should provide students with **concrete information** regarding ways in which they can improve their performance in a given area. This ultimately strengthens students' connections between the teacher's substantive feedback and their work, thus enhancing understanding and success in learning. In addition, the nature of substantive feedback facilitates **personalized learning**, as it is tailored to address individual student progress and areas for improvement. This allows for student-centered instruction that enhances learning by addressing the needs of all students.

Constructive Feedback

Feedback on students' progress must always be **constructive** in nature to facilitate successful learning and development. Constructive feedback ensures students maintain a positive **self-concept** and attitude toward learning, which is integral to increasing self-motivation and engagement. When students are motivated and engaged, they are more likely to apply the teacher's suggestions to enhance their learning and understanding. When providing constructive feedback, it is important that the teacher consider the specific area in which the student needs improvement in order to provide effective guidance for enhancing comprehension and progress. In addition, teachers must consider their approach to providing feedback to ensure that all suggestions are productive, encouraging, and helpful to the student. This includes presenting feedback through **positive** and **supportive language** that is free of negative connotations or inferences. The teacher should accompany feedback with comments that highlight students' **strengths** while offering **suggestions** and **guidance** on specific areas in which they can improve. Constructive feedback must include clear explanations on ways in which students can improve their performance as well as establish how the teacher's suggestions will enhance their overall learning and growth.

Specific Feedback

Specific feedback provides students with clarity regarding how to effectively improve their progress as they work toward achieving learning targets. When the teacher consistently delivers specific feedback, students are clear on expectations, can identify areas for improvement within their performance, and make necessary changes. Students are more likely to effectively apply feedback that specifies areas for development as they progress toward learning goals. If feedback is too vague, students may either disregard it or make incorrect, uninformed changes that hinder understanding and progress. Providing detailed suggestions and guidance enhances student engagement and motivation, as it increases their focus on particular areas for improvement to allow for success in learning. In addition, highlighting students' strengths through specific feedback encourages them to apply their abilities to other areas of instruction, thus enhancing student productivity and success in achieving learning targets.

Promoting Use of Feedback

The ability to use feedback allows students to enhance their own learning. To develop this skill among students, the teacher must emphasize the value of feedback, demonstrate its applications in specific learning situations, and explain how implementing it is beneficial in improving academic performance. This notion can be reinforced by effectively **modeling** how to receive and apply feedback to enhance student understanding of the process. Feedback must always be constructive and highlight students' strengths to help them identify specific areas for improvement. By **checking** students' understanding of feedback frequently, the teacher ensures they know how to productively apply it for enhanced learning. This includes encouraging students to **respond** to given feedback by contributing their thoughts and asking for clarification as necessary. In addition, students are more likely to internalize and effectively apply feedback that is **timely** and provided throughout instruction rather than at the end. Providing feedback in this way allows students to utilize it in guiding their own learning. This allows students to establish personal connections between feedback and their learning that strengthen their understanding and promote academic success.

Teaching Students to Use Self-Assessment

Developing students' **self-assessment** capabilities provides them with a sense of self-sufficiency for guiding and enhancing their own learning. To facilitate this, the teacher must establish a supportive **classroom environment** in which students feel comfortable and empowered to take risks and objectively evaluate their own progress as they seek areas for improvement. **Modeling** strategies for utilizing self-assessment to enhance learning and explaining its significance in supporting continued success are valuable strategies in enabling students to assess their own progress to guide and improve their learning. By guiding students with **open-ended questions** as they engage in learning, the teacher encourages students to assess their own progress and demonstrates how to implement effective questioning to seek areas for improvement within their own work. The teacher should include multiple outlets for self-assessment to facilitate the development of this skill, including **reflection** opportunities that enable students to evaluate their own understanding and guide their development as they engage in learning.

SIGNIFICANCE OF SELF-ASSESSMENT IN FACILITATING GROWTH AND ACHIEVEMENT

When students are able to objectively assess their own progress, they are equipped with the tools necessary to continuously seek areas for improvement that guide and enhance their learning. This empowers students with a sense of **ownership** and responsibility over their learning as they monitor their own performance to refine their skills for enhanced growth and achievement. Self-assessment and monitoring strengthen students' **personal connections** to their work, as they are able to relate their learning to their own prior knowledge and frames of reference. This ultimately makes learning more relevant, thus increasing motivation, productivity, and achievement. Students who regularly self-assess their work develop the independence necessary for engaging in **self-directed** learning, thus establishing a foundation for continued growth and success. In addition, continuously seeking areas for improvement allows students to develop a sense of confidence to take risks in their learning, as they understand how to overcome obstacles as they progress.

DEVELOPMENT OF REAL-WORLD LIFE SKILLS FOR FUTURE SUCCESS

The ability to effectively apply feedback and self-assessment for enhanced learning prepares students with the life skills necessary for future success in academic and real-world situations. Developing this skill instills within students the notion that there is always room for improvement in their performance. In addition, it helps develop their understanding of the characteristics of quality, helps them overcome learning obstacles, and builds the **self-motivation** required to take initiative. Students who frequently employ feedback and self-assessment have a strong sense of **independence** in enhancing their own learning. In addition, this skill provides students with the **self-awareness** necessary to recognize their strengths and weaknesses, thus making them more inclined to continuously seek areas for increased understanding and improvement for maximized achievement. Students' communication and cooperation skills are enhanced when they learn to properly use feedback and self-assessment, as it develops their ability to appreciate constructive criticism and internalize multiple perspectives as they work to improve their performance.

SELF-ASSESSMENT THAT ENCOURAGES EVALUATION OF LEARNING AND IMPROVEMENT

Providing multiple strategies for self-assessment throughout instruction develops students' abilities to monitor and evaluate their performance for continuous improvement. Self-assessment strategies can be formal or informal and can occur on an individual or whole-class basis. Teaching students how to set **SMART goals** (specific, measurable, attainable, relevant, time-bound) enables them to set learning goals, determine a path to achieve them, and reflect upon their performance to seek areas for improvement as they progress. Implementing strategies for students to indicate their level of comprehension is valuable in encouraging reflection on their own understanding and areas for improvement as they progress through the learning process. Such strategies include open-ended **questioning** to encourage reflection, color-coded **response cards** to signify understanding, or **whole-class activities** such as four corners. Graphic organizer activities such as **KWL charts** are beneficial in prompting students to consider prior knowledge and reflect on their progress after a lesson. This facilitates students in forming personal connections and determining areas in which they can extend and improve upon their learning. **Reflection** opportunities, such as exit tickets or learning logs, are also valuable for encouraging self-assessment, as they prompt students to consider areas in which they excelled and areas in which there is potential room for improvement.

Review Video: SMART Goals
Visit mometrix.com/academy and enter code: 100378

Characteristics of SMART Goals

S	**Specific**	The goal is clearly stated and narrow in scope. Details of the goal, including who, what, where, when, why, and how much, are explicitly outlined.
M	**Measurable**	The goal includes a quantifiable method of measuring progress toward achievement, such as reading twenty-five books in a year.
A	**Attainable**	The goal is challenging yet realistic and within the realm of the individual's current abilities and skills.
R	**Relevant**	The goal is meaningful to the individual and contributes toward personal improvement and long-term goals.
T	**Time-bound**	The goal sets a specific timeline for achievement. This helps the individual monitor progress and hold personal accountability.

Skilled Questioning to Support Learning

Higher-Level Questioning

Higher-level questioning that prompts students to **analyze**, **evaluate**, and **create** responses and solutions fosters effective student discussions by encouraging students to consider information beyond basic recollection. When students are asked to **explain**, **justify**, **predict**, and **provide examples**, they are encouraged to actively participate in learning, thus enhancing discussion. In addition, higher-level questioning increases the effectiveness of student discussion by promoting the use of higher-order and critical thinking skills to **consider alternatives**, **compare**, **contrast**, **discuss hypothetically**, and **develop** creative solutions to problems. Higher-level questioning encourages students to elaborate on their thinking and learning, thus allowing for productive discussions that strengthen the learning experience.

Impact of Student Discussions on Overall Learning Experience

Student discussion is a valuable instructional strategy for deepening and enhancing the overall learning experience. When students have the opportunity to discuss new concepts in their own words, it increases their ability to internalize and retain information. Effective student discussions prompt students to relate information to their own experiences and create personal connections that enhance learning by making it relevant and meaningful. Likewise, in listening to and interacting with their peers, students gain insight on differing perspectives and can build on one another's background knowledge to increase understanding. Incorporating effective discussions into instruction also produces an interesting and engaging learning environment by encouraging active student participation. When students are asked to inquire and consider information on a complex level, explain and elaborate on their reasoning, and think critically about situations, they are given an active role that serves to deepen and enhance the learning experience.

Impact of Skilled Questioning and Discussion

Encouraging Exploration of Content and Learning

Skilled questioning and discussion are essential components in enhancing learning, and they contribute to establishing an engaging learning environment that promotes the exploration of content material beyond basic knowledge. By challenging students during discussions based upon their abilities through specific questioning, the teacher effectively prompts students to think critically about instructional content, devise new solutions to problems, and implement higher-order thinking skills, which require further exploration of content material. Effective discussions encourage students to examine the nuances of subject matter and reflect upon others' perspectives to build upon their understanding. Furthermore, when students are provided with effective questions to promote interesting and engaging discussions, they become motivated to actively participate in their learning and explore instructional content on a deeper level.

Extending Students' Knowledge on Instructional Content

The implementation of skilled questioning when leading effective discussions is valuable in extending students' knowledge of instructional content. Skilled questioning activates higher-order thinking skills, as it prompts students to consider ideas and information on a more complex level. When teachers skillfully craft questions on content material during discussions, they are able to extend students' knowledge on the instructional topic by creating specific, increasingly complex questions that build on students' capabilities. Effective questions during discussions also increase students' knowledge on content material by motivating them to seek further information and thoughtfully consider their answers to elaborate on and provide examples for their reasoning. Additionally, skilled questioning and discussions foster active participation in learning, giving students the opportunity to build and reflect upon the knowledge and experiences of others. This ultimately increases their understanding of the instructional content by allowing them to integrate their frame of reference with others' perspectives.

Fostering Active Inquiry

An interesting and engaging environment is necessary in fostering active curiosity and inquiry for learning among students. Through skilled questioning and effective student discussions, the teacher creates an atmosphere in which students must actively engage and participate throughout the learning process, thus providing them with a sense of self-motivation for active inquiry. In addition, skilled questioning challenges students to utilize higher-order thinking skills that require them to inquire about a discussion topic beyond basic information and seek new information to thoughtfully consider and elaborate on their responses. In the discussion setting, students are also engaged and encouraged to ask each other questions to deepen understanding. Effective questioning and student discussions enhance learning and productivity by creating an engaging, **inquiry-based** environment that provides students with a sense of ownership over their learning as they seek new information.

Developing Higher-Order Thinking Skills

Skillful questioning when leading student discussions is an effective method of developing **higher-order thinking** skills to strengthen understanding and enhance the learning experience. In thoughtfully proposing questions that challenge students based on their abilities, the teacher establishes a foundation of knowledge to build upon with increasingly rigorous and skilled questioning. When students are asked to apply their learning to **analyze**, **evaluate**, and **create**, higher-order thinking skills are developed in that students must think deeply and critically about ideas, information, and situations beyond the basic recall of information. Effective questioning in discussions prompts students to think more complexly and synthesize previously learned information to craft and support new ideas, responses, and solutions. Students are thus required to take more time to evaluate their responses carefully, consider alternatives and differing perspectives of their classmates, and create personal connections by applying their own experiences to their learning.

Increasing Problem-Solving Skills

Incorporating skilled questions into class discussions fosters the development of problem-solving skills by eliciting students' critical thinking abilities to devise creative solutions. By asking complex, open-ended questions that prompt students to **hypothesize**, **predict**, and **consider alternative** methods of solving a problem, the teacher creates an engaging learning environment that promotes curiosity, exploration, and inquiry. Such questioning effectively develops problem-solving skills by increasing student motivation for seeking new solutions and analyzing their results. Thoughtfully crafted questions encourage students to **synthesize** and **apply** their own experiences and previously learned information when devising a solution to a problem. In addition, in proposing skilled questions when leading discussions, the teacher fosters students' abilities to apply knowledge, understanding, and reasoning methods from one learning context to another, thus developing real-world problem-solving skills. Effective class discussions encourage students to collaborate to build upon one another's experiences and knowledge when seeking solutions. This demonstrates the validity of multiple approaches to situations and develops students' overall problem-solving abilities.

Promoting Positive, Supportive Interactions to Enhance the Learning Experience

In facilitating effective class discussions, the teacher must propose skillful questions that encourage positive and supportive interactions to ensure that all students feel respected when contributing. To achieve this, the teacher must lead discussions with open-ended questions that emphasize the validity of multiple responses and accompany students' responses with follow-up questions. Such skilled questioning fosters **prosocial** interactions by creating a safe and respectful learning environment that encourages students to collaborate, actively participate in discussion with one another, and appreciate varying perspectives. In addition, skillful questioning and effective discussions include appropriate wait time between questions and responses. This promotes supportive interactions by allowing students the opportunity to process their responses and by demonstrating the importance of active listening. In emphasizing this, students ultimately feel respected in their ideas and empowered to add to the discussion. When teachers effectively lead student discussions with thoughtfully crafted questions, they enhance the overall learning experience by creating a welcoming, respectful learning environment in which students feel confident to take risks and explore new ideas through discussion.

Significance of Appropriate Wait Time in Effective Student Discussions

Appropriate wait time is an integral component in leading effective student discussions. When students are given a few seconds after questioning to consider their responses, they are able to effectively process and synthesize information to formulate and elaborate on their ideas. Wait time during discussions leads to more thoughtful responses, as students are given time to consider their learning on a more complex level. In addition, providing time between questions and discussion allows students to process one another's responses to contribute more effectively to the conversation and enhance the overall learning experience.

Bloom's Taxonomy (1956)

Bloom's taxonomy is a framework for categorizing learning objectives with increasing levels of complexity to promote the development of higher-order thinking skills. Measures of ability are organized into **knowledge**, **comprehension**, and **application** as lower-level benchmarks and **analysis**, **synthesis**, and **evaluation** as higher-level targets. Lower-level objectives are intended to build and evaluate student comprehension and ability to ultimately achieve higher-level targets intended to deepen understanding and develop higher-order thinking skills. Bloom's taxonomy is integral in engaging in skilled questioning. This model assists teachers in developing specific, increasingly-challenging questions, activities, and assessments that establish a foundation of knowledge and build upon it for the development of higher-order thinking skills. In addition, it provides an outline for identifying students' cognitive abilities and allows the teacher to effectively develop appropriate questions that build and enhance understanding to foster success in learning.

Review Video: Bloom's Taxonomy
Visit mometrix.com/academy and enter code: 755020

Bloom's Taxonomy

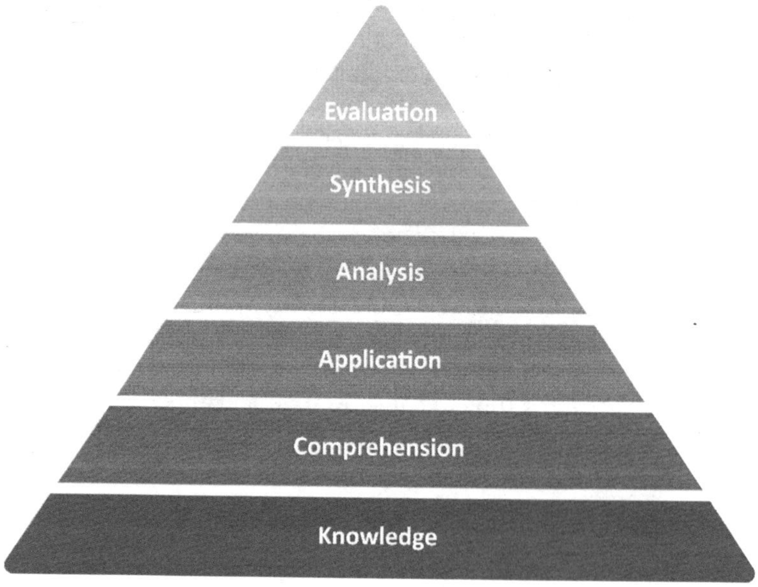

The Revised Bloom's Taxonomy (2001)

In 2001, a group of educators sought to update the original Bloom's taxonomy to better meet the needs of a 21st century audience. The revised version was not actually produced by Benjamin Bloom, who passed away in 1999, but was developed primarily by Anderson and Krathwohl. Many resources use the term "Bloom's Taxonomy" to refer to both, interchangeably. The major differences between the original and the revised versions of the taxonomy include a reordering of two of the tiers as well as a modification of the names of the levels to be more action-oriented. Instead of using nouns, the revised version uses verbs that describe the types of tasks that are associated with each level of thinking. Teachers are encouraged to use task stem words associated with each level to help produce curriculum leading to higher-order thinking.

Assessment Methodology

Assessment Methods

Effective teaching requires multiple methods of assessment to evaluate student comprehension and instructional effectiveness. Assessments are typically categorized as diagnostic, formative, summative, and benchmark and are applicable at varying stages of instruction. **Diagnostic** assessments are administered before instruction and indicate students' prior knowledge and areas of misunderstanding to determine the path of instruction. **Formative** assessments occur continuously to measure student engagement, comprehension, and instructional effectiveness. These assessments indicate instructional strategies that require adjustment to meet students' needs in facilitating successful learning and include strategies like checking for understanding, observations, total participation activities, and exit tickets. **Summative** assessments are given at the end of a lesson or unit to evaluate student progress in reaching learning targets and identify areas of misconception for reteaching. Such assessments can be given in the form of exams and quizzes or be project-based activities in which students demonstrate their learning through hands-on, personalized methods. Additionally, portfolios serve as valuable summative assessments in allowing students to demonstrate their progress over time and provide insight regarding individual achievement. **Benchmark** assessments occur less frequently and encompass large portions of curriculum. These assessments are intended to evaluate the progress of groups of students in achieving state and district academic standards.

Assessment Types

- **Diagnostic:** These assessments can either be formal or informal and are intended to provide teachers with information regarding students' level of understanding prior to beginning a unit of instruction. Examples include pretests, KWL charts, anticipation guides, and brainstorming activities. Digital resources, such as online polls, surveys, and quizzes are also valuable resources for gathering diagnostic feedback.
- **Formative:** These assessments occur throughout instruction to provide the teacher with feedback regarding student understanding. Examples include warm-up and closure activities, checking frequently for understanding, student reflection activities, and providing students with color-coded cards to indicate their level of understanding. Short quizzes and total participation activities, such as four corners, are also valuable formative assessments. Numerous digital resources, including polls, surveys, and review games, are also beneficial in providing teachers with formative feedback to indicate instructional effectiveness.
- **Summative:** Summative assessments are intended to indicate students' levels of mastery and progress toward reaching academic learning standards. These assessments may take the form of written or digital exams and include multiple choice, short answer, or long answer questions. Examples also include projects, final essays, presentations, or portfolios to demonstrate student progress over time.
- **Benchmark:** Benchmark assessments measure students' progress in achieving academic standards. These assessments are typically standardized to ensure uniformity, objectivity, and accuracy. Benchmark assessments are typically given as a written multiple choice or short answer exam, or as a digital exam in which students answer questions on the computer.

Review Video: Formative and Summative Assessments
Visit mometrix.com/academy and enter code: 804991

Determining Appropriate Assessment Strategies

As varying assessment methods provide different information regarding student performance and achievement, the teacher must consider the most applicable and effective assessment strategy in each stage of instruction. This includes determining the **desired outcomes** of assessment as well as the information the teacher intends to ascertain and how they will apply the results to further instruction. **Age-** and **grade-level-**appropriateness must be considered when selecting which assessment strategies will enable students to successfully demonstrate their learning. Additionally, the teacher must be cognizant of students' individual differences and learning needs to determine which assessment model is most **accommodating** and reflective of their progress. It is also important that teachers consider the practicality of assessment strategies and methods they will use to implement the assessment for maximized feedback regarding individual and whole-class progress in achieving learning goals.

Assessments That Reflect Real-World Applications

Assessments that reflect **real-world applications** enhance relevancy and students' ability to establish personal connections to learning that deepen understanding. Implementing such assessments provides authenticity and enhances engagement by defining a clear and practical purpose for learning. These assessments often allow for hands-on opportunities for demonstrating learning and can be adjusted to accommodate students' varying learning styles and needs while measuring individual progress; however, assessments that focus on real-world applications can be subjective, thus making it difficult to extract concrete data and quantify student progress to guide future instructional decisions. In addition, teachers may have difficulty analyzing assessment results on a large scale and comparing student performance with other schools and districts, as individual assessments may vary.

Diagnostic Tests

Diagnostic tests are integral to planning and delivering effective instruction. These tests are typically administered prior to beginning a unit or lesson and provide valuable feedback for guiding and planning instruction. Diagnostic tests provide **preliminary information** regarding students' levels of understanding and prior knowledge. This serves as a baseline for instructional planning that connects and builds upon students' background knowledge and experiences to enhance success in learning. Diagnostic tests allow the teacher to identify and clarify areas of student misconception prior to engaging in instruction to ensure continued comprehension and avoid the need for remediation. They indicate areas of student strength and need as well as individual instructional aids that may need to be incorporated into lessons to support student achievement. In addition, these tests enable the teacher to determine which instructional strategies, activities, groupings, and materials will be most valuable in maximizing engagement and learning. Diagnostic tests can be **formal** or **informal** and include pre-tests, pre-reading activities, surveys, vocabulary inventories, and graphic organizers (such as KWL charts). These tests are used to assess student understanding prior to engaging in learning. Diagnostic tests are generally not graded, as there is little expectation that all students in a class possess the same baseline of proficiency at the start of a unit.

Formative Assessments

Formative assessments are any assessments that take place in the **middle of a unit of instruction**. The goals of formative assessments are to help teachers understand where a student is in his or her progress toward **mastering** the current unit's content and to provide the students with **ongoing feedback** throughout the unit. The advantage of relying heavily on formative assessments in instruction is that it allows the teacher to continuously **check for comprehension** and adjust instruction as needed to ensure that the whole class is adequately prepared to proceed at the end of the unit. To understand formative assessments well, teachers need to understand that any interaction that can provide information about the student's comprehension is a type of formative assessment which can be used to inform future instruction.

Formative assessments are often a mixture of formal and informal assessments. **Formal formative assessments** often include classwork, homework, and quizzes. Examples of **informal formative assessments** include simple comprehension checks during instruction, class-wide discussions of the current topic, and exit slips, which are written questions posed by teachers at the end of class, which helps the teacher quickly review which students are struggling with the concepts.

Summative Assessments

Summative assessment refers to an evaluation at the end of a discrete unit of instruction, such as the end of a course, unit, or semester. Classic examples of summative assessments include end-of-course assessments, final exams, or even qualifying standardized tests such as the SAT or ACT. Most summative assessments are created to measure student mastery of particular **academic standards**. Whereas formative assessment generally informs current instruction, summative assessments are used to objectively demonstrate that each individual has achieved adequate mastery of the standards in question. If a student has not met the benchmark, he or she may need extra instruction or may need to repeat the course.

These assessments usually take the form of **tests** or formal portfolios with rubrics and clearly defined goals. Summative assessments are usually high-stakes, heavily-weighted, and they should always be formally graded. These types of assessments often feature a narrower range of question types, such as multiple choice, short answer, and essay questions to help with systematic grading.

Project-based assessments are beneficial in evaluating achievement, as they incorporate several elements of instruction and highlight real-world applications of learning. This allows students to demonstrate understanding through a hands-on, individualized approach that reinforces connections to learning and increases retainment. **Portfolios** of student work over time serve as a valuable method for assessing individual progress toward reaching learning targets. Summative assessments provide insight regarding overall instructional effectiveness and are necessary for guiding future instruction in subsequent years but are not usually used to modify current instruction.

Review Video: Assessment Reliability and Validity
Visit mometrix.com/academy and enter code: 424680

Benchmark Assessments

Benchmark assessments are intended to quantify, evaluate, and compare individual and groups of students' achievement of school-wide, district, and state **academic standards.** They are typically administered in specific intervals throughout the school year and encompass entire or large units of curriculum to determine student mastery and readiness for academic advancement. Benchmark assessments provide data that enable the teacher to determine students' progress toward reaching academic goals to guide current and continued instruction. This data can be utilized by the school and individual teachers to create learning goals and objectives aligned with academic standards. It can also be used to plan instructional strategies, activities, and assessments to support students in achieving these academic standards. In addition, benchmark assessments provide feedback regarding understanding and the potential need for remediation to allow the teacher to instill necessary supports in future instruction that prepare students for success in achieving learning targets.

Alignment of Assessments with Instructional Goals and Objectives

To effectively monitor student progress, assessments must align with **instructional goals** and **objectives.** This allows the teacher to determine whether students are advancing at an appropriate pace to achieve state and district academic standards. When assessments are aligned with specific learning targets, the teacher ensures that students are learning relevant material to establish a foundation of knowledge necessary for growth and academic achievement. To achieve this, teachers must determine which instructional goals and objectives their students must achieve and derive instruction, content, and activities from these specifications. Instruction must reflect and reinforce learning targets, and the teacher must select the most effective strategies for addressing students' needs as they work to achieve them. Assessments must be reflective of content instruction to ensure they are aligned with learning goals and objectives, as well as to enable the teacher to evaluate student progress in mastering them. The teacher must clearly communicate learning goals and objectives throughout all stages of instruction to provide students with clarity on expectations. This establishes a clear purpose and focus for learning that enhances relevancy and strengthens connections to support student achievement.

Clearly Communicating Assessment Criteria and Standards

Students must be clear on the purpose of learning throughout all stages of instruction to enhance understanding and facilitate success. When assessment **criteria** and **standards** are clearly communicated, the purpose of learning is established, and students are able to effectively connect instructional activities to learning goals and criteria for assessment. Communicating assessment criteria and standards provides students with clarity on tasks and learning goals they are expected to accomplish as they prepare themselves for assessment. This allows for more **focused instruction** and engagement in learning, as it enhances relevancy and student motivation. Utilizing appropriate forms of **rubrics** is an effective strategy in specifying assessment criteria and standards, as it informs students about learning goals they are working toward, the quality of work they are expected to achieve, and skills they must master to succeed on the assessment. Rubrics indicate to students exactly how they will be evaluated, thus supporting their understanding and focus as they engage in learning to promote academic success.

Rubrics for Communicating Standards

The following are varying styles of rubrics that can be used to communicate criteria and standards:

- **Analytic:** Analytic rubrics break down criteria for an assignment into several categories and provide an explanation of the varying levels of performance in each one. This style of rubric is beneficial for detailing the characteristics of quality work as well as providing students with feedback regarding specific components of their performance. Analytic rubrics are most effective when used for summative assessments, such as long-term projects or essays.
- **Holistic:** Holistic rubrics evaluate the quality of the student's assignment as a whole rather than scoring individual components. Students' scores are determined based upon their performance across multiple performance indicators. This style of rubric is beneficial for providing a comprehensive evaluation but limits the amount of feedback that students receive regarding their performance in specific areas.
- **Single-point:** Single-point rubrics outline criteria for assignments into several categories. Rather than providing a numeric score to each category, however, the teacher provides written feedback regarding the students' strengths and ways in which they can improve their performance. This style of rubric is beneficial in providing student-centered feedback that focuses on their overall progress.
- **Checklist:** Checklists typically outline a set of criteria that is scored using a binary approach based upon completion of each component. This style increases the efficiency of grading assignments and is often easy for students to comprehend but does not provide detailed feedback. This method of grading should generally be reserved for shorter assignments.

Communicating High Academic Expectations in Assessments

The attitudes and behaviors exhibited by the teacher are highly influential on students' attitudes toward learning. Teachers demonstrate belief in students' abilities to be successful in learning when they communicate **high academic expectations**. This promotes students' **self-concept** and establishes a **growth mindset** to create confident, empowered learners that are motivated to achieve. High expectations for assessments and reaching academic standards communicates to students the quality of work that is expected of them and encourages them to overcome obstacles as they engage in learning. When communicating expectations for student achievement, it is important that the teacher is aware of students' individual learning needs to provide the necessary support that establishes equitable opportunities for success in meeting assessment criteria and standards. Setting high expectations through assessment criteria and standards while supporting students in their learning enhances overall achievement and establishes a foundation for continuous academic success.

Effective Communication and Impact on Student Learning

Communicating high academic expectations enhances students' self-concept and increases personal motivation for success in learning. To maximize student achievement, it is important that the teacher set high academic expectations that are **clearly** communicated through **age-appropriate** terms and consistently reinforced. Expectations must be reflected through learning goals and objectives and must be **visible** at all times to ensure student awareness. Teachers must be **specific** in communicating what they want students to accomplish and clearly detail necessary steps for achievement while assuming the role of facilitator to guide learning and provide support. Providing constructive **feedback** throughout instruction is integral in reminding students of academic expectations and ensuring they are making adequate progress toward reaching learning goals. When high academic expectations are communicated and reinforced, students are empowered with a sense of confidence and self-responsibility for their own learning that promotes their desire to learn. This ultimately enhances achievement and equips them with the tools necessary for future academic success.

Analyzing and Interpreting Assessment Data

Teachers can utilize multiple techniques to effectively analyze and interpret assessment data. This typically involves creating charts and graphs outlining different data subsets. They can list each learning standard that was assessed, determine how many students overall demonstrated proficiency on the standard, and identify individual students who did not demonstrate proficiency on each standard. This information can be used to differentiate instruction. Additionally, they can track individual student performance and progress on each standard over time.

Teachers can take note of overall patterns and trends in assessment data. For example, they can determine if any subgroups of students did not meet expectations. They can consider whether the data confirms or challenges any existing beliefs, implications this may have on instructional planning and what, if any, conclusions can be drawn from this data.

Analyzing and interpreting assessment data may raise new questions for educators, so they can also determine if additional data collection is needed.

Using Assessment Data to Differentiate Instruction for Individual Learners

By analyzing and interpreting assessment data, teachers can determine if there are any specific learning standards that need to be retaught to their entire classes. This may be necessary if the data shows that all students struggled in these specific areas. Teachers may consider reteaching these standards using different methods if the initial methods were unsuccessful.

Teachers can also form groups of students who did not demonstrate proficiency on the same learning standards. Targeted instruction can be planned for these groups to help them make progress in these areas. Interventions can also be planned for individual students who did not show proficiency in certain areas. If interventions have already been in place and have not led to increased learning outcomes, the interventions may be redesigned. If interventions have been in place and assessment data now shows proficiency, the interventions may be discontinued.

If assessment data shows that certain students have met or exceeded expectations in certain areas, enrichment activities can be planned to challenge these students and meet their learning needs.

Aligning Assessments with Instructional Goals and Objectives

Assessments that are congruent to instructional goals and objectives provide a **clear purpose** for learning that enhances student understanding and motivation. When learning targets are reflected in assessments, instructional activities and materials become more **relevant**, as they are derived from these specifications. Such clarity in purpose allows for more focus and productivity as students engage in instruction and fosters connections that strengthen overall understanding for maximized success in learning. Aligning assessments with instructional goals and objectives ensures that students are learning material that is relevant to the curriculum and academic standards to ensure **preparedness** as they advance in their academic careers. In addition, it enables the teacher to evaluate and monitor student progress to determine whether they are progressing at an ideal pace for achieving academic standards. With this information, the teacher can effectively modify instruction as necessary to support students' needs in reaching desired learning outcomes.

Norm-Referenced Tests

On **norm-referenced tests**, students' performances are compared to the performances of sample groups of similar students. Norm-referenced tests identify students who score above and below the average. To ensure reliability, the tests must be given in a standardized manner to all students.

Norm-referenced tests usually cover a broad range of skills, such as the entire grade-level curriculum for a subject. They typically contain a few questions per skill. Whereas scores in component areas of the tests may be calculated, usually overall test scores are reported. Scores are often reported using percentile ranks, which indicate what percentage of test takers scored lower than the student being assessed. For example, a student's score in the 75th percentile means the student scored better than 75% of other test takers. Other times, scores may be reported using grade-level equivalency.

One advantage of norm-referenced tests is their objectivity. They also allow educators to compare large groups of students at once. This may be helpful for making decisions regarding class placements and groupings. A disadvantage of norm-referenced tests is that they only indicate how well students perform in comparison to one another. They do not indicate whether or not students have mastered certain skills.

Criterion-Referenced Tests

Criterion-referenced tests measure how well students perform on certain skills or standards. The goal of these tests is to indicate whether or not students have mastered certain skills and which skills require additional instruction. Scores are typically reported using the percentage of questions answered correctly or students' performance levels. Performance levels are outlined using terms such as *below expectations, met expectations,* and *exceeded expectations.*

One advantage of criterion-referenced tests is that they provide teachers with useful information to guide instruction. They can identify which specific skills students have mastered and which skills need additional practice. Teachers can use this information to plan whole-class, small-group, and individualized instruction. Analyzing results of criterion-referenced tests over time can also help teachers track student progress on certain skills. A disadvantage of criterion-referenced tests is that they do not allow educators to compare students' performances to samples of their peers.

Ways That Standardized Test Results Are Reported

- **Raw scores** are sometimes reported and indicate how many questions students answered correctly on a test. By themselves, they do not provide much useful information. They do not indicate how students performed in comparison to other students or to grade-level expectations.
- **Grade-level equivalents** are also sometimes reported. A grade-level equivalent score of 3.4 indicates that a student performed as well as an average third grader in the fourth month of school. It can indicate whether a student is performing above or below grade-level expectations, but it does not indicate that the student should be moved to a different grade level.
- **Standard scores** are used to compare students' performances on tests to standardized samples of their peers. Standard deviation refers to the amount that a set of scores differs from the mean score on a test.
- **Percentile ranks** are used on criterion-referenced tests to indicate what percentage of test takers scored lower than the student whose score is being reported.
- **Cutoff scores** refer to predetermined scores students must obtain in order to be considered proficient in certain areas. Scores below the cutoff level indicate improvement is needed and may result in interventions or instructional changes.

Formal and Informal Assessments

Assessments are any method a teacher uses to gather information about student comprehension of curriculum, including improvised questions for the class and highly-structured tests. **Formal assessments** are assessments that have **clearly defined standards and methodology** and which are applied consistently to all students. Formal tests should be objective and scrutinized for validity and reliability since they tend to carry higher weight for the student. Summative assessments, such as end-of-unit tests, lend themselves to being formal tests because it is necessary that a teacher test the comprehension of all students in a consistent and thorough way.

Although formal assessments can provide useful data about student performance and progress, they can be costly and time-consuming to implement. Administering formal assessments often interrupts classroom instruction and may cause testing anxiety.

Informal assessments are assessments that do not adhere to formal objectives, and they do not have to be administered consistently to all students. As a result, they do not have to be scored or recorded as a grade and generally act as a **subjective measure** of class comprehension. Informal assessments can be as simple as asking the students to raise their hands if they are ready to proceed to the next step or asking a particular question of an individual student.

Informal assessments do not provide objective data for analysis, but they can be implemented quickly and inexpensively. Informal assessments can also be incorporated into regular classroom instruction and activities, making them more authentic and less stressful for students.

Using Various Assessments

The goal of **assessment** in education is to gather data that, when evaluated, can be used to further student learning and achievement. **Standardized tests** are helpful for placement purposes and to reflect student progress toward goals set by a school district or state. If a textbook is chosen to align with district learning standards, the textbook assessments can provide teachers with convenient, small-scale, regular checks of student knowledge against the target standard.

In order be effective, teachers must know where their students are in the learning process. Teachers use a multitude of **formal and informal assessment methods** to do this. Posing differentiated discussion questions is an example of an informal assessment method that allows teachers to gauge individual student progress rather than their standing in relation to a universal benchmark.

Effective teachers employ a variety of assessments, as different formats assess different skills, promote different learning experiences, and appeal to different learners. A portfolio is an example of an assessment that gauges student progress in multiple skills and through multiple media. Teachers can use authentic or performance-based assessments to stimulate student interest and provide visible connections between language-learning and the real world.

Assessment Reliability

Assessment reliability refers to how well an assessment is constructed and is made up of a variety of measures. An assessment is generally considered **reliable** if it yields similar results across multiple administrations of the assessment. A test should perform similarly with different test administrators, graders, test-takers, and over multiple iterations. Factors that affect reliability include the day-to-day wellbeing of the student (students can sometimes underperform), the physical environment of the test, the way it is administered, and the subjectivity of the scorer (with written-response assessments).

Perhaps the most important threat to assessment reliability is the nature of the **exam questions** themselves. An assessment question is designed to test knowledge of a certain construct. A question is reliable in this sense if students who understand the content answer the question correctly. Statisticians look for patterns in student marks, both within the single test and over multiple tests, as a way of measuring reliability. Teachers should watch out for circumstances in which a student or students answer correctly a series of questions about a given concept (demonstrating their understanding) but then answer a related question incorrectly. The latter question may be an unreliable indicator of concept knowledge.

Measures of Assessment Reliability

- **Test-retest reliability** refers to an assessment's consistency of results with the same test-taker over multiple retests. If one student shows inconsistent results over time, the test is not considered to have test-retest reliability.
- **Intertester reliability** refers to an assessment's consistency of results between multiple test-takers at the same level. Students at similar levels of proficiency should show similar results.
- **Inter-rater reliability** refers to an assessment's consistency of results between different administrators of the test. This plays an especially critical role in tests with interactive or subjective responses, such as Likert-scales, cloze tests, and short answer tests. Different raters of the same test need to have a consistent means of evaluating the test-takers' performance. Clear rubrics can help keep two or more raters consistent in scoring.
- **Intra-rater reliability** refers to an assessment's consistency of results with one rater over time. One test rater should be able to score different students objectively to rate subjective test formats fairly.
- **Parallel-forms reliability** refers to an assessment's consistency between multiple different forms. For instance, end-of-course assessments may have many distinctive test forms, with different questions or question orders. If the different forms of a test do not provide the same results, the test is said to be lacking in parallel-forms reliability.
- **Internal consistency reliability** refers to the consistency of results of similar questions on a particular assessment. If there are two or more questions targeted at the same standard and at the same level, they should show the same results across each question.

Assessment Validity

Assessment validity is a measure of the relevancy that an assessment has to the skill or ability being evaluated and the degree to which students' performance is representative of their mastery of the topic of assessment. In other words, a teacher should ask how well an assessment's results correlate to what it is looking to assess. Assessments should be evaluated for validity on both the **individual question** level and as a **test overall**. This can be especially helpful in refining tests for future classes. The overall validity of an assessment is determined by several types of validity measures.

An assessment is considered **valid** if it measures what it is intended to measure. One common error that can reduce the validity of a test (or a question on a test) occurs if the instructions are written at a reading level the students can't understand. In this case, it is not valid to take the student's failed answer as a true indication of his or her knowledge of the subject. Factors internal to the student might also affect exam validity: anxiety and a lack of self-esteem often lower assessments results, reducing their validity as a measure of student knowledge.

An assessment has content validity if it includes all the **relevant aspects** of the subject being tested—if it is comprehensive, in other words. An assessment has **predictive validity** if a score on the test is an accurate predictor of future success in the same domain. For example, SAT exams purport to have validity in predicting student success in a college. An assessment has construct validity if it accurately measures student knowledge of the subject being tested.

Measures of Assessment Validity

- **Face validity** refers to the initial impression of whether an assessment seems to be fit for the task. As this method is subjective to interpretation and unquantifiable, it should not be used singularly as a measurement of validity.
- **Construct validity** asks if an assessment actually assesses what it is intended to assess. Some topics are more straightforward, such as assessing if a student can perform two-digit multiplication. This can be directly tested, which gives the assessment a strong content validity. Other measures, such as a person's overall happiness, must be measured indirectly. If an assessment asserted that a person is generally happy if he or she smiles frequently, it would be fair to question the construct validity of that assessment because smiling is unlikely to be a consistent measure of all peoples' general happiness.

- **Content validity** indicates whether the assessment is comprehensive of all aspects of the content being assessed. If a test leaves out an important topic, then the teacher will not have a full picture as a result of the assessment.
- **Criterion validity** refers to whether the results of an assessment can be used to **predict** a related value, known as **criterion**. An example of this is the hypothesis that IQ tests would predict a person's success later in life, but many critics believe that IQ tests are not valid predictors of success because intelligence is not the only predictor of success in life. IQ tests have shown validity toward predicting academic success, however. The measure of an assessment's criterion validity depends on how closely related the criterion is.
- **Discriminant validity** refers to how well an assessment tests only that which it is intended to test and successfully discriminates one piece of information from another. For instance, a student who is exceptional in mathematics should not be able to put that information into use on a science test and gain an unfair advantage. If the student is able to score well due to his or her mathematics knowledge, the science test did not adequately discriminate science knowledge from mathematics knowledge.
- **Convergent validity** is related to discriminant validity, but takes into account that two measures may be distinct but correlated. For instance, a personality test should distinguish self-esteem from extraversion so that they can be measured independently, but if an assessment has convergent validity, it should show a correlation between related measures.

Practicality

An assessment is **practical** if it uses an appropriate amount of human and budgetary resources. A practical exam doesn't take very long to design or score, nor does it take students very long to complete in relation to other learning objectives and priorities. Teachers often need to balance a desire to construct comprehensive or content-valid tests with a need for practicality: lengthy exams consume large amounts of instruction time and may return unreliable results if students become tired and lose focus.

Assessment Bias

An assessment is considered biased if it disadvantages a certain group of students, such as students of a certain gender, race, cultural background, or socioeconomic class. A **content bias** exists when the subject matter of a question or assessment is familiar to one group and not another. For example, a reading comprehension passage that discusses an event in American history would be biased against students new to the country. An **attitudinal bias** exists when a teacher has a pre-conceived idea about the likely success of an assessment of a particular individual or group. A **method bias** arises when the format of an assessment is unfamiliar to a given group of students. **Language bias** occurs when an assessment utilizes idioms, collocations, or cultural references unfamiliar to a group of students. Finally, **translation bias** may arise when educators attempt to translate content-area assessments into a student's native language—rough or hurried translations often result in a loss of nuance important for accurate assessment.

Authentic Assessments

An authentic assessment is an assessment designed to closely resemble something that a student does, or will do, in the real world. For example, students will never encounter a multiple-choice test requiring them to choose the right tense of a verb, but they will encounter contexts in which they have to write a narration of an event that has antecedents and consequents spread out in time—like narrating their version of what caused a traffic accident. The latter is an example of a potential **authentic assessment**.

Well-designed authentic assessments require a student to exercise **advanced cognitive skills** (e.g., solving problems, integrating information, performing deductions), integrate **background knowledge**, and confront **ambiguity**. Research has demonstrated that mere language proficiency is not predictive of future language success—learning how to utilize knowledge in a complex context is an essential additional skill.

The terms "authentic" and "performance-based" are often used interchangeably when describing assessments; however, a performance-based assessment doesn't necessarily have to be grounded in a possible authentic experience.

Performance-Based Assessments

A performance-based assessment is one in which students demonstrate their learning by performing a **task** rather than by answering questions in a traditional test format. Proponents of **performance-based assessments** argue that they lead students to use **high-level cognitive skills** since they focus on how to put their knowledge to use and plan a sequence of stages in an activity or presentation. They also allow students more opportunities to individualize their presentations or responses based on preferred learning styles. Research suggests that students welcome the chance to put their knowledge to use in real-world scenarios.

Advocates of performance-based assessments suggest that they avoid many of the problems of language or cultural bias present in traditional assessments, allowing more accurate assessment of how well students learned the underlying concepts. In discussions regarding English as a second language, they argue that performance assessments come closer to replicating what should be the true goal of language learning—the effective use of language in real contexts—than do more traditional exams. Critics point out that performance assessments are difficult and time-consuming for teachers to construct and for students to perform. Finally, performative assessments are difficult to grade in the absence of a well-constructed and detailed rubric.

Technology-Based Assessments

Technology-based assessments provide teachers with multiple resources for evaluating student progress to guide instruction. They are applicable in most formal and informal instructional settings and can be utilized as formative and summative assessments. Technology-based assessments simplify and enhance the efficiency of determining comprehension and instructional effectiveness, as they quickly present the teacher with information regarding student progress. This data enables the teacher to make necessary adjustments to facilitate student learning and growth. Implementing this assessment format simplifies the process of aligning them to school and district academic standards. This establishes objectivity and uniformity for comparing results and progress among students. It also helps ensure that all students are held to the same academic expectations. While technology-based assessments are beneficial, there are some shortcomings to consider. This format may not be entirely effective for all learning styles in demonstrating understanding, as individualization in technology-based assessment can be limited. These assessments may not illustrate individual students' growth over time but rather their mastery of an academic standard, thus hindering the ability to evaluate overall achievement. As technology-based evaluation limits hands-on opportunities, the real-world application and relevancy of the assessment may be unapparent to students.

Advantages and Disadvantages of Technology-Based Assessments

Technology-based assessments can have many advantages. They can be given to large numbers of students at once, limited only by the amounts of technological equipment schools possess. Many types of technology-based assessments are instantly scored, and feedback is provided quickly. Students are sometimes able to view their results and feedback at the conclusion of their testing sessions. Data can be quickly compiled and reported in easy-to-understand formats. Technology-based assessments can also often track student progress over time.

Technology-based assessments can have some disadvantages as well. Glitches and system errors can interfere with the assessment process or score reporting. Students must also have the necessary prerequisite technological skills to take the assessments, or the results may not measure the content they are designed to measure. For example, if students take timed, computer-based writing tests, they should have proficient typing skills. Otherwise, they may perform poorly on the tests despite strong writing abilities. Other prerequisite skills include knowing how to use a keyboard and mouse and understanding how to locate necessary information on the screen.

Portfolio Assessments

A **portfolio** is a collection of student work in multiple forms and media gathered over time. Teachers may assess the portfolio both for evidence of progress over time or in its end state as a demonstration of the achievement of certain proficiency levels.

One advantage of **portfolio assessments** is their breadth. Unlike traditional assessments, which focus on one or two language skills, portfolios may contain work in multiple forms, such as writing samples, pictures, and graphs designed for content courses, video and audio clips, student reflections, teacher observations, and student exams. A second advantage is that they allow a student to develop work in authentic contexts, including in other classrooms and at home.

In order for portfolios to function as an objective assessment tool, teachers should negotiate with students in advance of what genres of work will be included and outline a grading rubric that makes clear what will be assessed, such as linguistic proficiency, use of English in academic contexts, and demonstrated use of target cognitive skills.

Curriculum-Based Assessments

Curriculum-based assessments, also known as **curriculum-based measurements (CBM)**, are short, frequent assessments designed to measure student progress toward meeting curriculum **benchmarks**.

Teachers implement CBMs by designing **probes**, or short assessments that target specific skills. For example, a teacher might design a spelling probe, administered weekly, that requires students to spell 10 unfamiliar but level-appropriate words. The data from these assessments can be tracked over time to measure student progress toward defined grade-level goals.

CBM has several clear advantages. If structured well, the probes have high reliability and validity. Furthermore, they provide clear and objective evidence of student progress—a welcome outcome for students and parents who often grapple with less-clear and subjective evidence. Used correctly, CBMs also motivate students and provide them with evidence of their own progress; however, while CBMs are helpful in identifying areas of student weaknesses, they do not identify the causes of those weaknesses or provide teachers with strategies for improving instruction.

Textbook Assessments

Textbook assessments are the assessments provided at the end of a chapter or unit in an approved textbook. **Textbook assessments** present several advantages for a teacher: they are already made; they are likely to be accurate representations of the chapter or unit materials; and, if the textbook has been prescribed or recommended by the state, it is likely to correspond closely to Common Core or other tested standards.

Textbook assessments can be limiting for students who lag in the comprehension of academic English or whose preferred learning style is not verbal. While textbooks may come with DVDs or recommended audio links, ESOL teachers will likely need to supplement these assessment materials with some of their own findings. Finally, textbook assessments are unlikely to represent the range of assessment types used in the modern classroom, such as a portfolio or performance-based assessments.

Peer Assessment

A peer assessment is when students grade one another's work based on a teacher-provided framework. **Peer assessments** are promoted as a means of saving teacher time and building student metacognitive skills. They are typically used as **formative** rather than summative assessments, given concerns about the reliability of student scoring and the tensions that can result if student scores contribute to overall grades. Peer assessments are used most often to grade essay-type written work or presentations. Proponents point out that peer assessments require students to apply metacognition, build cooperative work and interpersonal skills, and broaden the sense that the student is accountable to peers and not just the teacher. Even advocates of the practice agree that students need detailed rubrics in order to succeed. Critics often argue that low-performing students have little to offer high-performing students in terms of valuable feedback—and this disparity may be more pronounced in ESOL classrooms or special education environments than in mainstream ones. One way to overcome this weakness is for the teacher to lead the evaluation exercise, guiding the students through a point-by-point framework of evaluation.

The Role of Assessment in Education

Roles of Assessment

Instructional Planning for Individuals and Groups

Effective assessments provide valuable feedback to teachers on how to design and adjust instruction for individuals and groups. Both **formative** and **summative** assessments give insight into student understanding and needs before and after content material is taught. Assessment provides the information necessary to effectively design instruction based on students' individual needs. **Diagnostic** assessments provide teachers with pertinent information about students' individual background knowledge, experiences, and learning needs, thus allowing them to understand students' skills and abilities to focus and plan future instruction accordingly. Additionally, assessments provide teachers with feedback on student progress and areas of individual need that drive instructional planning in allowing teachers to more effectively plan curriculum that is tailored to students' individual needs, skills, and abilities. Assessments inform future instruction through highlighting concepts that students are not understanding for reteaching. Furthermore, it allows them to group students more effectively in future planning to provide scaffolding and ensure that all students are supported in achieving academic standards.

Providing Teacher Accountability and Evaluating Teacher Effectiveness

Teachers are responsible for ensuring that all students are properly supported in achieving lesson objectives, instructional goals, and state academic standards. Thus, they are responsible for effectively designing and implementing instruction, lessons, and activities that are tailored to meet individual students' needs as they work to achieve learning outcomes. Assessments provide feedback regarding student mastery of academic standards and are reflective of the effectiveness of the instructional practices and strategies implemented to support them in their achievement. Consequently, student achievement on assessments reflects and measures the effectiveness of the teacher in designing instructional materials that meet individual students' needs, foster engagement and understanding, and facilitate desired learning outcomes. When teachers are evaluated based on student assessment results, they are held accountable for developing effective instruction and identifying areas for improvement in their teaching practice.

Methods and Applications for Analyzing Students' Strengths and Needs

Instructional assessment takes many forms, and each method has different applications and provides distinct feedback for analyzing students' strengths and needs. All forms of assessment should be incorporated in order to develop comprehensive instruction that is tailored to students' individual strengths and needs. **Formative assessments** are an informal, ongoing method of measuring student understanding throughout a lesson. They are valuable in allowing the teacher to adjust and adapt instructional practices and strategies to individual student needs as necessary as they move through a lesson. **Summative assessments** generally occur at the end of a lesson or unit and are intended to measure student achievement of a particular objective or instructional goal. These assessments allow teachers to identify students' individual strengths and needs, and they influence future instruction by highlighting areas of understanding or misconception for reteaching. **Standardized assessments** reflect student mastery of state academic standards and illustrate whether students have met academic benchmarks for their grade level. The results of these assessments can be applied to identify students' strengths and needs to determine the starting point of future instruction and proper grouping of students based on skills, needs, and abilities.

Use of State Standards and Assessments

Instruction Development

Effective instruction is driven by state standards and assessment. State academic standards serve as a framework for grade-level academic benchmarks that students are expected to achieve during the school year. From these, teachers derive instructional goals and objectives and determine instruction, activities, and materials that will support students in academic achievement. Additionally, teachers use state standards as assessment criteria to monitor student progress and evaluate how successfully students are reaching them. These assessments provide feedback to teachers that influences future instruction by helping teachers identify areas of misconception that require reteaching or individual student needs. State standardized assessments influence the development of instruction in that student achievement on these assessments indicates their level of success in meeting academic targets. They highlight areas of strength and need among students, providing teachers with a framework for effectively designing instruction to address these needs and support students in meeting academic goals.

Evaluating Student Progress, Strengths, and Needs

State and classroom assessments provide data that allow the teacher to effectively analyze whole-class and individual student performance in meeting learning targets to determine further instructional planning. Whole-class achievement on assessments is indicative of the effectiveness of learning objectives, instructional strategies, and lesson activities in supporting students' achievement of academic standards. Whole-class assessments also provide insight on areas for improvement and reteaching. Individually, in analyzing where students fall on a bell curve for assessment, teachers can effectively identify specific strengths and needs of students to determine instructional planning. This information indicates student progress and where they may need additional support, which allows teachers to better meet students' individual needs in planning future instruction by implementing strategies which are tailored to their skills and abilities.

Materials and Resources

Materials and Resources That Enhance Student Learning and Engagement

Instructional Materials and Resources

The careful selection of instructional materials and resources for lesson plans is an integral component of enhancing student engagement and the overall learning experience. Lesson materials should be relevant to students' interests so as to facilitate personal connections to learning and ultimately, deepen understanding. In building positive relationships with students by educating themselves on students' backgrounds and interests, teachers can effectively locate and implement varied instructional materials and resources that are relevant to students and foster motivation for learning. Additionally, interactive materials, such as manipulatives or other hands-on learning resources, enhance learning and engagement through encouraging participation. Similarly, cooperative learning materials encourage student participation and engagement through fostering collaboration. Teachers can also enhance learning experiences through incorporating authentic materials that are relevant to instruction such as maps, brochures, historical documents, or similar materials that enhance student engagement and learning.

Technological Resources

Technology is integrated in nearly every aspect of life as a tool to enhance and assist in daily activities. This notion also applies in the classroom, as technological resources are an excellent method of increasing student engagement and interest, supporting students in their individual learning needs, and enhancing learning. The use of computers, tablets, smartphones, and other technological resources serve to improve understanding of classroom instruction, foster relevancy and personal connections, and scaffold instruction to address diverse learning styles and needs. Additionally, teachers have myriad digital resources available in the form of interactive websites, videos clips, and apps that can be implemented to enrich lessons and increase development across all subject areas. Often, these resources accommodate students' individual learning needs through providing increasingly challenging activities based on individual skill level, and the teacher can utilize these resources to tailor instruction to address individual student needs. Technological resources can also add authenticity to learning experiences, making them more engaging and enhancing student learning. Virtual field trips or science experiments can provide real-world connections to instruction by recreating authentic learning experiences without students having to leave the classroom.

Community Resources

Community resources are beneficial in enriching instruction to foster engagement and enhance student learning. They provide students the opportunity to connect and apply what they learn in the classroom with the real world. This ultimately makes learning more authentic, as students are able to see the relevancy of what they are learning. This enhances learning by making it more engaging. Through field trips, teachers can incorporate community resources such as museums, art exhibits, science centers, and even local areas such as parks or historical sites into curriculum to accompany material learned in class. Additionally, if access to field trips is limited, teachers can take advantage of community outreach programs that bring learning experiences to classrooms. Reaching out to members of the community that are relevant to topics being covered in class, such as scientists or local historians, can be beneficial in allowing students to understand how what they are learning is applicable outside of the classroom. Locating and implementing community resources enhances student learning and engagement through making learning authentic, relevant, and applicable in the real world.

Developmentally Appropriate Materials and Resources

To create engaging and effective learning experiences, instructional materials and resources must be developmentally appropriate. Teachers must have a solid understanding of the general cognitive, physical, social, and emotional developmental levels of their students as well as individual differences in skills and abilities to properly select developmentally appropriate materials. The age and developmental level appropriateness of instructional resources can be determined by considering the material's size, height, and level of difficulty for students. Whether materials accommodate individual differences in skill level, ability, or interest can be determined by their versatility. If a resource can be used in multiple ways, it will appeal to a variety of learning needs and interests and support development across domains. Developmentally appropriate materials are reflective and considerate of students' diversities. Teachers can determine this by using their knowledge of students' backgrounds to select materials that incorporate and are sensitive to their students' cultural differences to support development by fostering personal connections to learning.

Instructional Technologies

Current Technology, Systems, and Operations

Terms and Concepts

As technology resources advance, it is important that the teacher understands basic terms and is informed on recent developments. **Hardware** refers to the physical components of technology systems and operations, including computers, keyboards, mice, monitors, and projectors. Recently, tablets, smart boards, and smart phones have been incorporated into classrooms as well. **Software**, such as word processors, internet browsers, games, applications, and social media, are programs run within the computer and are valuable resources in planning, delivering, and evaluating instruction. **Input devices** allow users to enter information into the computer to complete tasks or display information. These devices include the keyboard, mouse, microphone, camera, and touch screen. **Output devices**, such as screens, speakers, headphones, and printers display information in a comprehensible format as well as communicate with users or other devices. A **network** is a group of computers or devices that communicate with one another. In education, networks allow multiple schools within a district to communicate, enable colleagues to share resources, and provide internet access for locating information. **Basic design** principles, in regard to instruction, refers to the components of creating content that is visually appealing, clear, and accurate.

Electronic Information

Effectively Locating on Networks and Application in Instruction

The ability to proficiently utilize networks for harnessing electronic information enhances the planning, organization, delivery, and evaluation of instruction. The **internet** is perhaps the most common network that teachers employ when locating information to apply to their practice; therefore, teachers must know how to efficiently navigate this resource to maximize productivity and instructional effectiveness. Several **search engines** are available that enable teachers to locate and acquire a multitude of information to apply it to all aspects of instruction. To properly use a search engine, teachers must consider the information they are seeking and determine specific key terms that will garner the best results. Search results must then be filtered for accuracy, credibility, and relevancy before integrating them into the instructional process. Once the desired information is located, teachers can refine their search by utilizing results to locate additional or more detailed information. Additionally, schools within the same district are often connected on a common network, thus allowing teachers to utilize it for sharing and locating information and resources to apply to the planning, organization, delivery, and evaluation of instruction. Once information is sufficiently compiled and reviewed, teachers can determine where it is most applicable and beneficial in enhancing the instructional process.

Secondary Storage and Remote Devices

Secondary storage devices are useful tools for preserving and reinforcing files and data. Secondary storage can either exist as **hardware devices**, such as USB or external hard drives, or **remote devices**, including a cloud or online repository. The procedures for accessing information on secondary storage devices are dependent on the nature of the device. Remote devices allow the user to retrieve stored files from any location by using a web browser to access a file storing service or by using the file explorer feature on a computer. They also allow the user to easily share information within the files with others. Information on hardware secondary storage devices is only retrievable when the device is connected to the computer, as this gives the user access to the information stored on the device through the file explorer. Once the information is accessible, the user can then manipulate it to acquire, analyze, and evaluate electronic information. The user can then save any changes made to the information and continue to store it in the secondary device.

Utilizing Online Help and Documentation

Employing the assistance of online resources and documents when acquiring, analyzing, and evaluating electronic information enhances the teacher's ability to create and provide accurate, valid, and relevant instruction. **Online resources**, including electronic communities, tutorials, forums, chat services, and consultations, are valuable in educating the teacher on effective practices for locating, refining, and determining the credibility, relevancy, and usefulness of electronic information to integrate into instruction. In addition, these resources are beneficial in helping the teacher understand how to access, analyze, and evaluate digital information to incorporate into instruction using secure procedures that protect their own and students' safety and privacy. **Online documents** in the form of PDFs, articles, or journals allow the teacher to research and gather information to utilize as reference tools for effectively acquiring, analyzing, and evaluating electronic information. When teachers utilize online resources and documentation to improve their knowledge and effectiveness in the acquisition, analysis, and evaluation of electronic information, they ensure students receive high-quality instruction that safely facilitates success in learning.

Evaluating Electronic Information

The availability of digital information and resources has been transformative in enhancing teaching and learning. While it is a valuable tool, there are several considerations the teacher must make when evaluating the merits of electronic information. All material found online must be determined as **accurate**, **reliable**, and **valid** prior to integrating it into the instructional process. This is achieved by assessing multiple sources related to a given topic to ensure that the information provided is factual. In addition, the teacher must evaluate the **credibility** and expertise of the creator to ascertain the legitimacy of their content. Electronic information must be current, relevant to desired learning outcomes, and comprehensible to effectively engage and support students in the learning process. Digital material must also be **culturally sensitive** and representative of multiple perspectives to prevent bias, as this is imperative in creating an inclusive learning environment that encourages students to consider information from varying points of view. Evaluating electronic information prior to utilizing it is integral to planning, organizing, and delivering effective instruction, as it ensures students are provided with high-quality materials for successful learning.

Relevant Tools and Procedures for Synthesizing Knowledge and Information

Utilizing the proper technology resources and tools for the synthesis of knowledge and information serves to increase overall efficiency and effectiveness when planning, organizing, delivering, and evaluating instruction. Such tools as **word processing programs**, **slide shows**, and other **multimedia presentations** allow the teacher to synthesize various pieces of information and knowledge within one location, thus allowing them to compile multiple resources for lesson planning, organization, and delivery of instruction. Additionally, these tools often allow for collaboration, as multiple individuals can contribute to the compilation of knowledge and resources. When analyzing and evaluating instruction, **spreadsheet** documents are beneficial for combining several elements of related information to examine results and make informed decisions regarding how to proceed with instruction. Similarly, **graphic tools**, including charts, diagrams, and tables, enable the teacher to identify trends and correlations related to their instructional process in order to recognize areas for improvement or adjustment to meet students' learning needs.

Solutions in Problem-Solving and Project-Based Situations

Implementing task-appropriate technology resources throughout the instructional process improves one's ability to create and modify solutions in problem-solving and project-based situations. To effectively apply these tools, the teacher must evaluate the aspects of the given task or problem to determine which digital resource, such as a **word processing** document, **spreadsheet**, **graph**, or **database**, will be most useful in creating a solution or product. These tools encompass a multitude of features that allow the user to navigate, manipulate, and devise solutions within them that can be modified as the information or the nature of the task evolves or as necessary. The vast availability of technology resources provides the user with multiple methods to engage in problem-solving and project-based learning activities. This ultimately enhances productivity when creating solutions and products as well as efficiency when modifying them.

Tools and Procedures for Evaluating Results

Technology resources for quantifying data and evaluating results enhance the teacher's ability to plan, organize, and deliver instruction. When teachers determine the nature of the information they are seeking, they can effectively choose task-appropriate tools such as **spreadsheets**, **databases**, or **graphs** to enter data and evaluate results for application in instruction. These resources enable teachers to organize multiple data sets in relation to one another in a relevant, logical manner to accurately evaluate results, identify correlations, and make informed instructional decisions based upon their findings. The features within these tools allow teachers to modify information as desired results change or as necessary. Properly implementing task-appropriate tools and procedures for evaluating results supports teachers in determining instructional effectiveness, comprehension, and student needs to make adjustments as necessary, thus enhancing the learning experience.

Electronic Communities

Collaboration with colleagues is an integral component of developing and refining one's instructional practice. Electronic communities provide teachers from different locations and levels of experience the opportunity to interact with one another as learners, initiators, and contributors within the realm of education. In this space, teachers can develop their knowledge and skills in planning, organizing, delivering, and evaluating instruction by participating in discussions with other educators, as these communities provide access to multiple perspectives, experiences, and authentic insights. This enables teachers to build upon one another's strengths and abilities to improve their overall practice. Additionally, electronic communities serve as a space in which teachers can share and work together in creating instructional resources, materials, lesson plans, and ideas. Collaborating in online communities enhances the efficiency and quality of the instructional process, as teachers can borrow relevant materials from one another to enrich their curriculum, and multiple individuals can participate in the development of instructional materials by contributing their unique ideas and perspectives.

Productivity Tools for Collaborating and Communicating Information

Digital productivity tools increase the efficiency of collaboration and communication in the classroom to enhance instruction. Resources, such as **slideshows**, **multimedia presentations**, and **word processing applications**, allow students to upload, edit, and collaborate on assignments in real-time for more productive and interactive learning. In addition, these tools allow the teacher to review and communicate immediate feedback on assignments as students work to ensure understanding and allow them to make necessary changes before moving on. When delivering instruction, digital productivity tools enhance efficiency by enabling the compilation of multiple pieces of information in a centralized resource for presentation. These tools are also valuable in communicating updates and pertinent information to teachers, students, and families. Whole-class participation apps provide the teacher with immediate feedback on student understanding that enables them to adapt and improve instruction as necessary to meet students' needs. Through **newsletters**, **digital applications**, and **social media platforms**, teachers can distribute learning materials and quickly communicate important dates, events, and assignments to students and families for enhanced instruction.

Methods for Publishing Information

Publishing information through a variety of methods ensures clear, efficient, and consistent communication for successful teaching and learning. In the classroom, publishing information through several mediums enables the teacher to deliver multifaceted content that reinforces and enhances instruction by addressing the needs of varying learning styles to ensure comprehension. When delivering pertinent information regarding classroom updates, events, or assignments to students and families, utilizing multiple means of publication ensures accessibility and efficiency of communication for all recipients. **Printed publication** materials, including handouts, flyers, pamphlets, or newsletters, enable the teacher to provide students and families with hard copies of important information and updates. **Digital publication** outlets allow for immediate communication and modification of information, including displaying information on a monitor, slide show, internet documents, classroom website, and social media platforms. Additionally, several digital applications are available that allow students and families to join a digitally connected group to receive immediate communication updates from the teacher regarding important classroom information.

Consistent Knowledge on Current Technologies

When teachers are knowledgeable on current technologies and their application in the classroom, they are more equipped to effectively plan, organize, deliver, and evaluate instruction. Teachers must consistently educate themselves on new technologies to incorporate into their practice to foster student engagement and success in learning. By participating in **continuing education** in the form of professional development trainings, technology courses, workshops, and conferences, teachers can stay informed on new and relevant digital resources to enhance instruction. Additionally, teachers can **collaborate** with colleagues or mentors either in person or through electronic communities to share information and gain insight on current technologies and how to implement them in the classroom. **Self-education** is a valuable tool for learning about technological developments and how to utilize them in instruction. When teachers take initiative to conduct their own research about recent advancements and personally engage with new digital resources, they can determine how to effectively incorporate them into instruction to enhance teaching and learning.

Technology Use in the Classroom

Significance of Technology in Instruction

Rapid advancements in technology systems and operations require the teacher to actively educate themselves on new developments to effectively plan, organize, deliver, and evaluate instruction. Most students are **digital natives**, meaning they have grown up accustomed to using technology in their daily lives and are familiar with its functions. As such, the teacher must be proficient with current technology and how to effectively incorporate it into daily instruction to create a relevant, interesting, and engaging learning environment. Understanding how to utilize and implement new technology resources improves a teacher's effectiveness in planning, organizing, and delivering differentiated instruction, as it enables them to derive material from a multitude of resources that appeal to students' individual needs and interests. In addition, it improves the teacher's ability to collaborate with other teachers for instructional planning and communicate with students, families, and colleagues. This ultimately enhances the learning experience by providing individualized, student-centered, and interactive instruction to promote engagement and support academic success. Additionally, understanding the functions of current technology systems and operations enhances the planning, organization, and evaluation of instruction by enabling the teacher to effectively utilize relevant digital productivity tools.

Incorporation into Daily Classroom Activities

Numerous educational technology resources are available to enhance all aspects of daily instruction. Digital tools can be highly beneficial in increasing student engagement, participation, and understanding, as well as addressing a variety of learning needs. Technology resources such as presentation slides, video clips, or audio books, can be used to introduce new topics or supplement instruction. Teachers can also create an **online classroom** in which they deliver instruction as well as provide students opportunities to collaborate in a digital workspace, ask questions, participate in discussions, turn in assignments, and receive feedback. Online activities such as WebQuests or digital scavenger hunts are valuable in allowing students to explore new concepts or research information while interacting with authentic digital resources. Teachers can also incorporate **total participation activities** to conduct formative assessments using technology resources, such as online surveys, polls, or games (such as word clustering games). In addition, students can prepare for assessments by utilizing resources such as online flashcards, quizzes, or review games. **Educational experiences** can also be supplemented using technology resources. For example, digital science experiments can reinforce concepts learned in the classroom. Additionally, virtual field trips allow students to explore locations they may otherwise be unable to visit.

Safe and Appropriate Use of Technology

Issues That May Be Encountered

Technology provides valuable learning tools, yet the teacher must be mindful of issues that may arise regarding safety and appropriateness when planning, organizing, delivering, and evaluating instruction. When using the internet, social media, and digital resources, students may be vulnerable to inappropriate or unsafe content. The teacher must assess all digital material when planning and organizing instruction to ensure that content, advertisements, and search engine results are **safe**, **instructionally applicable**, and respectful of **students' privacy**. Student misuse of technology is a common issue that may be exacerbated when students are permitted to bring their own devices to class. **Misuse** includes using technology for off-task activities, accessing inappropriate websites, apps, or social media, and engaging in cyberbullying. It is important that the teacher establish clear expectations for the use of personal devices and take proper measures to block access to non-instructional material to ensure students engage with technology appropriately. Students may encounter individuals online that subject them to harmful or inappropriate communication. In addition to ensuring that students remain on task, the teacher must frequently monitor students' technology use to ensure they are not engaging with individuals or materials that may ask them to divulge personal details or compromise their safety.

Importance of Educating Students on Appropriate Technology Use

Educating students on appropriate technology use establishes a focused, engaged, and safe learning environment. When teachers **model** and **instruct** students on appropriate and responsible practices, they develop an awareness of the immediate and future implications of their online behavior. This ultimately teaches students to make informed decisions that protect their safety and privacy when using digital resources both within and outside of the classroom. Establishing clear procedures and expectations for technology discourages misuse, as it helps ensure that students are focused, on task, and engage appropriately with technology as a learning tool to enhance instruction. In addition, it teaches students how to interact with others online safely and responsibly using proper **digital citizenship**. It also teaches students how to respond if they encounter inappropriate content or behavior. When the teacher effectively educates students on proper technology use, it becomes an efficient and valuable instructional resource that enhances the overall learning experience.

Privacy Guidelines

To establish a safe learning environment in which all students are protected, it is imperative that teachers consistently adhere to strict privacy guidelines. Teachers must ensure that all of their actions and practices within and outside of the classroom align with **FERPA** as well as state and district laws regarding student privacy. Additionally, teachers must be well informed on and follow the privacy policies of their individual schools. Students' **personal information**, including grade histories, attendance and discipline records, medical histories, special needs, addresses, birthdays, and any other sensitive details must remain confidential. In an increasingly digital learning environment, it is important that teachers make sure photographs, video recordings, or names of students are not shared online or on social media without proper consent. When students interact with digital resources in the classroom, their data is often collected and recorded, so teachers must be cognizant of what information is shared, select technology resources appropriately, and instruct students not to divulge any personal information about themselves online. Following strict privacy guidelines is necessary in protecting all students' rights to confidentiality.

Copyright Laws

When creating, planning, and delivering instruction, teachers must consider copyright laws before selecting or distributing materials and resources to ensure they do not infringe upon the creator's rights. While teachers are often given flexibility regarding the **Copyright Law** under the **Fair Use Doctrine**, they must be mindful to ensure that accessing, copying, and utilizing unpurchased materials, content, resources, or images falls under this doctrine to avoid copyright infringement. Teachers must make certain that all resources are used explicitly for instructional purposes and avoid reproducing and distributing entire works for individual student use. Teachers should, instead, copy or display excerpts. To avoid potential copyright infringement when planning and delivering instruction, teachers can either ask creators for permission to use their work or ask their schools, districts, or students to purchase the material. Teachers can further protect themselves by citing the source of all retrieved and distributed content. Utilizing free instructional material that is not covered under the Copyright Law, including facts and resources within the **public domain** or **Creative Commons**, as well as government records, pictures, and maps, allows teachers to avoid copyright infringement when creating, planning, and delivering instruction.

Fair Use Doctrine, Public Domain, and Creative Commons

Fair Use Doctrine	• The Fair Use Doctrine allows educators to use, reproduce, and redistribute copyrighted materials for educational purposes so long as they adhere to specified guidelines. These guidelines are typically categorized as: • **Purpose**: Materials must be used for educational, nonprofit purposes to achieve a specific learning objective. • **Nature**: The nature of the work refers to the type of copyrighted work being reproduced (fictional/nonfictional, consumable) • **Amount**: Reproduction and redistribution must be limited to a small portion of the creator's work, such as an excerpt from a book. • **Effect**: Reproduction and redistribution may not interfere with the creator's ability to substantially profit from his or her work in the future.
Public Domain	Materials in the public domain are not protected under copyright laws and are free for use, reproduction, or redistribution. This includes government or historical documents, speeches, ideas, or facts and works published before March 1, 1989 that do not have an official copyright license. Copyrighted works in the United States enter the public domain 70 years after the death of the original creator.
Creative Commons	Creative Commons is an organization in which creators can reserve partial copyrights to their original works while relinquishing others to allow for public use, reproduction, and redistribution. This organization is intended to provide educators with access to learning materials, resources, and original works to incorporate into their classroom.

Acceptable Use Policies

Acceptable use policies are integral to establishing a classroom environment in which all students and staff engage with technology safely and appropriately. An acceptable use policy is an **agreement** between students, families, the school, and the district to ensure users are **accountable** for their use of technology and online behavior. These policies outline specific guidelines and **expectations** to make users aware of safe and responsible practices regarding technology use in the classroom and help to prevent inappropriate behavior by defining clear **consequences** for violating the terms. In addition, acceptable use policies are beneficial in informing students, staff, and families of the actions taken to protect students' privacy and safety when using technology in the classroom, such as blocking access to inappropriate or non-instructional websites. When acceptable use policies are successfully implemented and followed, students, teachers, and families are protected while interacting with digital materials in the classroom, ensuring a safe and appropriate learning environment.

Review Video: Benefits of Technology in the Classroom
Visit mometrix.com/academy and enter code: 536375

Digital Etiquette

Digital etiquette refers to a set of guidelines for **appropriate** and **responsible** interaction with technology and individuals online. These guidelines emphasize the importance of engaging with individuals online politely and respectfully in a considerate manner, just as they would in face-to-face communication. This includes using appropriate language, respecting others' opinions, and avoiding engaging in harmful interactions or content online. In addition, digital etiquette outlines how to adjust communication styles based on one's audience to ensure proper and professional interactions. Digital etiquette also defines proper measures for protecting oneself and others when engaging online. This includes avoiding potentially harmful situations such as providing personal information about oneself or others, communicating with individuals whom one does not know, and carefully considering the present and future implications of one's online behavior. As a teacher, following and instilling these guidelines in students is integral to establishing a positive learning environment in which students safely and responsibly interact with technology. Digital etiquette provides teachers and students with a framework for acceptable technology use and online behavior that is necessary for success in an increasingly digital world.

Effective Incorporation of Technology in Instruction Process

To enhance the quality of the overall instructional process, teachers must thoughtfully consider a variety of aspects regarding which technology resources will be most valuable in increasing efficiency and effectiveness. Teachers must determine **desired learning outcomes** and evaluate which technologies will be most beneficial in planning, organizing, delivering, and evaluating instruction. They must evaluate the **efficacy** of the resource in supporting students as they achieve learning targets. This includes ensuring that technology resources are current, relevant, and effective in enhancing the delivery of comprehensible and engaging instruction. When determining which technologies to implement for student use, teachers must assess the **developmental appropriateness** of the technologies as well as whether the resources are **adaptable** to individual differences, learning needs, and interests. Additionally, it is important that teachers ensure that technology resources foster **interaction** and **active learning** among students so as to support curiosity and engagement in learning. As **equity** issues regarding technology may exist within the classroom, the teacher must consider what supports may need to be implemented to properly support students in achieving learning targets. Students' safety and privacy when utilizing technology is paramount; therefore, the teacher must be certain that selected digital resources protect students from harmful content.

Developmentally Appropriate Selection of Technology for Instruction

Student learning and achievement is maximized when the teacher applies knowledge of **developmentally appropriate** practices, activities, and materials to selecting technology resources that enhance instruction. Teachers must understand the characteristics and needs of developmental stages, including age-related and individual learning differences across domains. This knowledge enables the teacher to implement technology that supports achievement when planning and delivering instruction. Effectively applying this knowledge requires the teacher to incorporate digital resources that provide **age** and **individually appropriate** challenges to facilitate developmental growth. This includes integrating technology that supports instruction by stimulating engagement, curiosity, and exploration. Developmentally appropriate technology provides appropriate levels of difficulty, interaction, and active learning opportunities based upon students' developmental stage while accommodating individual needs, interests, and abilities. Additionally, in developmentally appropriate practice, the teacher integrates technology resources to accompany instructional activities for a length of time that is beneficial to students relative to their developmental stage to maximize learning benefits.

Integrating Technology to Promote Creativity and Innovation

The availability of digital resources allows the teacher to provide students with multiple opportunities to develop their creativity and innovation in all areas of instruction. When integrated to accompany learning, technology is highly beneficial in allowing students to navigate new ways to **construct knowledge**, **generate ideas**, and **create products**. Effectively incorporating technology for these purposes requires the teacher to consider the instructional topic, specific skills they intend to develop, desired learning outcomes, and students' individual needs and interests. This knowledge enables the teacher to determine which digital resources are most engaging, applicable, and beneficial in providing a learning environment that enhances creativity and innovation among students. For example, digital storytelling resources are effective in enhancing creative writing in language arts, virtual labs can enhance science instruction, and digital drawing apps can enrich artistic creativity for creating new ideas and products. During instruction, assuming the role of facilitator while allowing flexibility for appropriate student choice is an effective strategy for allowing the expression of creativity as students manipulate digital tools for the development of knowledge, ideas, and products. It is important to note, however, that technology in the classroom should be used intentionally to enhance, rather than replace, instruction.

The effective integration of technology into instruction is invaluable in promoting creative thinking and innovation among students when constructing and generating knowledge, new ideas, and products. With the vast array of available technology for instructional use, the teacher can select from a multitude of resources on a variety of topics to enhance instruction and accommodate students' varying learning styles, needs, and interests. The incorporation of technology facilitates the creative and innovative process while promoting **critical thinking** and **problem-solving** abilities by allowing students to explore, manipulate, and learn the functions of digital tools in a way that is relevant to them. This encourages students to employ **higher-order thinking** skills as they make connections between the capabilities of digital resources and their application in solving problems and creating new ideas and products. Using technology to support instruction increases engagement and enhances the overall learning experience. Students' understanding is deepened as they construct knowledge using technology resources.

Equity Issues in the Classroom Related to the Use of Technology

The integration of technology to enhance learning is a valuable and increasingly prevalent component of instruction; however, equity issues related to the use of technology pose significant impacts on teaching and learning. Schools in **rural** or **socioeconomically disadvantaged** districts may lack the necessary funding to provide all students with technology devices for classroom use. Economically underprivileged students may lack internet access, computers, and digital devices at home or access to a public library, thus impeding their ability to complete assignments outside of class that require technology use. During instructional activities that require students to bring personal digital devices for participation, students without their own devices face inequity that hinders their ability to engage in learning. In addition, students who lack access to digital resources often face challenges in the classroom, as they may not have developed the same knowledge regarding technology use and functions as classmates with more experience. Equity issues related to technology access and use can negatively impact academic achievement. It is imperative that teachers are mindful of potential inequities that exist within their classrooms when planning instruction to properly address them and support student success.

Identifying and Addressing Issues

As technology becomes increasingly integrated into daily life, inequities among students are more apparent and pose significant impacts to achievement. Identifying disparities related to technology is integral to applying equitable practices to ensure that students are supported. To properly identify digital equity issues, teachers must recognize some of the **causal factors**, including socioeconomic status, race, and geographic location, and determine the presence of these factors in their districts. Additionally, teachers must be aware of individual students' backgrounds and needs to identify potential inequities regarding technology. Applying **equitable practices** to address these issues ensures all students have equal academic opportunities. It cannot be assumed that all students have devices or access to computers and the internet at home, so teachers should avoid requiring technology use outside of the classroom when possible. If the school is financially able, students can be issued equipment such as devices and hotspots to establish equity. Teachers can also provide alternative, paper assignments that achieve the same outcomes as the technology-based version if school devices are unavailable. In the classroom, teachers can provide time during, before, and after the school day for technology use as well as provide available school-issued devices for activities.

Effectively Addressing Equity Issues

Access to technology and familiarity with its functions is vital for success in the modern-day classroom. Implementing appropriate measures for addressing inequities among students regarding technology use is imperative in supporting and facilitating academic achievement. By consciously applying **equitable practices**, teachers and staff ensure that all students are provided with the necessary support for access to technology and digital resources for instructional use. In addition, promptly identifying and addressing equity issues ensures that students are able to keep pace with their peers in regard to understanding how to utilize digital resources to maximize their learning. Applying equitable practices to support students that lack access to technology helps close the achievement gap by providing all students with equal opportunities for academic achievement.

Chapter Quiz

Ready to see how well you retained what you just read? Scan the QR code to go directly to the chapter quiz interface for this study guide. If you're using a computer, simply visit the online resources page at **mometrix.com/resources719/texespprte370** and click the Chapter Quizzes link.

Knowledge of Students and Student Learning

Overview of Human Developmental Theories

Issues of Human Development

Historically, there have been a number of arguments that theories of human development seek to address. These ideas generally lie on a spectrum but are often essential concepts involved in developmental theories. For instance, the nature vs. nurture debate is a key concept involved in behaviorist camps of development, insisting that a substantial portion of a child's development may be attributed to his or her social environment.

- **Universality vs. context specificity**: Universality implies that all individuals will develop in the same way, no matter what culture they live in. Context specificity implies that development will be influenced by the culture in which the individual lives.
- **Assumptions about human nature** (three doctrines: original sin, innate purity, and tabula rasa):
  - Original sin says that children are inherently bad and must be taught to be good.
  - Innate purity says that children are inherently good.
  - Tabula rasa says that children are born as "blank slates" without good or bad tendencies and can be taught right and wrong.
- **Behavioral consistency**: Children either behave in the same manner no matter what the situation or setting or they change their behavior depending on the setting and who is interacting with them.
- **Nature vs. nurture**: Nature refers to the genetic influences on development. Nurture refers to the environmental and social influences on development.
- **Continuity vs. discontinuity**: Continuity states that development progresses at a steady rate and that the effects of change are cumulative. Discontinuity states that development progresses in a stair-step fashion and that the effects of early development have no bearing on later development.
- **Passivity vs. activity**: Passivity refers to development being influenced by outside forces. Activity refers to development influenced by the child him or herself and how he or she responds to external forces.
- **Critical vs. sensitive period**: The critical period is the window of time when the child will be able to acquire new skills and behaviors. The sensitive period refers to a flexible time period when a child will be receptive to learning new skills, even if it is later than the norm.

Theoretical Schools of Thought on Human Development

- **Behaviorist Theory** – This philosophy discusses development in terms of conditioning. As children interact with their environments, they learn what behaviors result in rewards or punishments and develop patterns of behaviors as a result. This school of thought lies heavily within the nurture side of the nature/nurture debate, arguing that children's personalities and behaviors are a product of their environments.
- **Constructivist Theory** – This philosophy describes the process of learning as one in which individuals build or construct their understanding from their prior knowledge and experiences in an environment. In constructivist thought, individuals can synthesize their old information to generate new ideas. This school of thought is similar to behaviorism in that the social environment plays a large role in learning. Constructivism, however, places greater emphasis on the individual's active role in the learning process, such as the ability to generate ideas about something an individual has not experienced directly.

- **Ecological Systems Theory** – This philosophy focuses on the social environments in and throughout a person's life. Ecological systems theorists attempt to account for all of the complexities of various aspects of a person's life, starting with close relationships, such as family and friends, and zooming out into broader social contexts, including interactions with school, communities, and media. Alongside these various social levels, ecological systems discuss the roles of ethnicity, geography, and socioeconomic status in development across a person's lifespan.
- **Maturationist Theory** – This philosophy largely focuses on the natural disposition of a child to learn. Maturationists lean heavily into the nature side of the nature/nurture argument and say that humans are predisposed to learning and development. As a result, maturationists propose that early development should only be passively supported.
- **Psychoanalytic Theory** – Psychoanalytic theorists generally argue that beneath the conscious interaction with the world, individuals have underlying, subconscious thoughts that affect their active emotions and behaviors. These subconscious thoughts are built from previous experiences, including developmental milestones and past traumas. These subconscious thoughts interact with conscious thoughts to form a person's desires, personality, attitudes, and habits.

Freud's Psychosexual Developmental Theory

Sigmund Freud was a neurologist who founded the psychoanalytic school of thought. He described the distinction between the conscious and unconscious mind and the effects of the unconscious mind on personality and behavior. He also developed a concept of stages of development, in which an individual encounters various conflicts or crises, called psychosexual stages of development. The way in which an individual handles these crises was thought to shape the individual's personality over the course of life. This general formula heavily influenced other psychoanalytic theories.

Erikson's Psychosocial Developmental Theory

Erik Erikson's psychosocial development theory was an expansion and revision of Freud's psychosexual stages. Erikson describes eight stages in which an individual is presented with a crisis, such as an infant learning to trust or mistrust his or her parents to provide. The choice to trust or mistrust is not binary, but is on a spectrum. According to the theory, the individual's resolution of the crisis largely carries through the rest of his or her life. Handling each of the eight conflicts well theoretically leads to a healthy development of personality. The conflicts are spaced out throughout life, beginning at infancy and ending at death.

Kohlberg's Stages of Moral Development

Kohlberg's stages of moral development are heavily influenced by Erikson's stages. He describes three larger levels of moral development with substages. In the first level, the **preconventional level**, morality is fully externally controlled by authorities and is motivated by the avoidance of punishment and pursuit of rewards. In the second level, the **conventional level**, the focus shifts to laws, social factors, and the pursuit of being seen by others as good or nice. In the third and final level, the **postconventional** or **principled level**, the individual looks beyond laws and social obligations to more complex situational considerations. A person in this stage might consider that a law may not always be the best for individuals or society and that a particular situation may warrant breaking the rule for the true good.

George Herbert Mead's Play and Game Stage Development Theory

George Herbert Mead was a sociologist and psychologist who described learning by stepping into **social roles.** According to his theory, children first interact with the world by imitating and playing by themselves. While engaged in this play, a child can experiment with concepts. Mead describes this development in terms of three stages characterized by increasing complexity of play. A child in the **preparatory stage** can **play** pretend and learn cooking concepts by pretending to cook. As a child develops socially, he or she learns to step in and out of increasingly abstract and complex **roles** and includes more interaction. This is known as the **play stage,** including early interactive roles. For instance, children may play "cops and robbers," which are more symbolically significant roles because they are not natural roles for children to play in society. As social understanding develops, children enter the **game stage,** in which the child can understand his or her own role and the roles of others in a game. In this stage, children can participate in more complex activities with highly structured rules. An example of a complex game is baseball, in which each individual playing has a unique and complex role to play. These stages are thought to contribute to an individual's ability to understand complex social roles in adulthood.

Ivan Pavlov

Ivan Pavlov was a predecessor to the behaviorist school and is credited with being the first to observe the process of classical conditioning, also known as Pavlovian conditioning. Pavlov observed that dogs would begin salivating at the sound of a bell because they were conditioned to expect food when they heard a bell ring. According to classical conditioning, by introducing a neutral stimulus (such as a bell) to a naturally significant stimulus (such as the sight of food), the neutral stimulus will begin to create a conditioned response on its own.

John B. Watson

Watson is credited as the founder of behaviorism and worked to expand the knowledge base of conditioning. He is famous for his experiments, including highly unethical experiments such as the "Little Albert" experiment in which he used classical conditioning to cause an infant to fear animals that he was unfamiliar with. Watson proposed that psychology should focus only on observable behaviors.

B.F. Skinner

Skinner expanded on Watson's work in behaviorism. His primary contributions to behaviorism included studying the effect of **reinforcement** and **punishment** on particular behaviors. He noted that stimuli can be either additive or subtractive and may be used to either increase or decrease behavior frequency and strengths.

Lev Vygotsky

Vygotsky's sociocultural theory describes development as a social process in which individuals mediate knowledge through social interactions and can learn by interacting with and watching others. Vygotsky's ideas have been widely adopted in the field of education, most notably his theory of the **zone of proximal development**. This theory describes three levels of an individual's ability to do tasks, including completely incapable of performing a task, capable with assistance, and independently capable. As an individual's experience grows, he or she should progress from dependent and less capable to more capable and independent.

Review Video: Instructional Scaffolding
Visit mometrix.com/academy and enter code: 989759

Bandura's Social Learning Theory

Albert Bandura's social learning theory argues against some of the behaviorist thoughts that a person has to experience stimulus and response to learn behaviors and, instead, posits that an individual can learn from other people's social interactions. Bandura would say that most learning takes place from observing and predicting social behavior, not through direct experience. This becomes a more efficient system for learning because people are able to learn information more synthetically.

Bowlby's Attachment Theory

Bowlby's attachment theory describes the impact that early connections have on lifelong development. Working from an evolutionary framework, Bowlby described how infants are predisposed to be attached to their caregivers because this increases chance of survival. According to Bowlby's theory, infants are predisposed to stay close to known caregivers and use them as a frame of reference to help with learning what is socially acceptable and what is safe.

Piaget's Cognitive Development Theory

Piaget's theory of cognitive development describes how as individuals develop, their cognitive processes are able to become more complex and abstract. In the early stages, an infant may be able to recognize an item, such as a glass of water, on sight only. As that individual grows, he or she is able to think, compare, and eventually develop abstract thoughts about that concept. According to Piaget, this development takes place in all individuals in predictable stages.

Maslow's Hierarchy of Needs

Maslow defined human motivation in terms of needs and wants. His **hierarchy of needs** is classically portrayed as a pyramid sitting on its base divided into horizontal layers. He theorized that, as humans fulfill the needs of one layer, their motivation turns to the layer above. The layers consist of (from bottom to top):

- **Physiological**: The need for air, fluid, food, shelter, warmth, and sleep
- **Safety**: A safe place to live, a steady job, a society with rules and laws, protection from harm, and insurance or savings for the future
- **Love/belonging**: A network consisting of a significant other, family, friends, co-workers, religion, and community
- **Esteem or self-respect**: The knowledge that you are a person who is successful and worthy of esteem, attention, status, and admiration
- **Self-actualization**: The acceptance of your life, choices, and situation in life and the empathetic acceptance of others, as well as the feeling of independence and the joy of being able to express yourself freely and competently

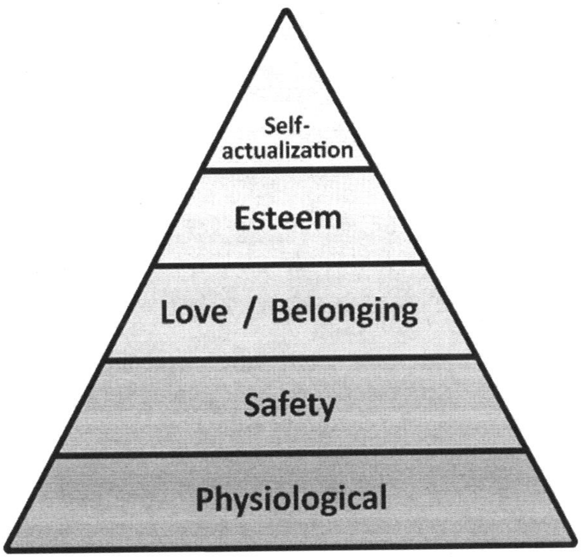

Review Video: Maslow's Hierarchy of Needs
Visit mometrix.com/academy and enter code: 461825

Cognitive Development

Piaget's Theory of Cognitive Development

Jean Piaget's theory of cognitive development consists of four stages that a child moves through throughout life. The four stages are the **sensorimotor stage** (birth-2 years), **preoperational stage** (2-7 years), **concrete operational stage** (7-11 years), and **formal operational stage** (12 years and beyond). Piaget believed that the way children think changes as they pass through these stages. In the **sensorimotor stage**, infants exist in the present moment and investigate their world for the first time through their senses, reflexes, and actions. Key skills infants acquire during this stage include object permanence and self-recognition. In the **preoperational stage**, children learn to express ideas symbolically, including through language and pretend play. Markers of this stage include engaging in animism, egocentrism, and the inability to understand conservation (the knowledge that the quantity of something does not change when its appearance does). In the **concrete operational stage**, children develop logical thought and begin understanding conservation. The **formal operational stage** brings the ability to think abstractly and hypothetically. Piaget believed that children learn through experimenting and building upon knowledge from experiences. He asserted that educators should be highly qualified and trained to create experiences that support development in each of these stages.

Review Video: Piaget's Cognitive Development Theory
Visit mometrix.com/academy and enter code: 100376

Skills Typically Acquired at Each Stage of Cognitive Development

- **Sensorimotor:** Children in the sensorimotor stage gain an increasing awareness of their bodies and the world around them and acquire a wide range of skills as they mature from infancy to toddlerhood. Early skills at this stage include sucking, tasting, smiling, basic vocalizations, and **gross motor skills** such as kicking and grasping. These skills increase in complexity over time and come to include abilities such as throwing and dropping objects, crawling, walking, and using simple words or phrases to communicate. As children near the end of this stage, they are typically able to exhibit skills such as stacking, basic problem solving, planning methods to achieve a task, and attempting to engage in daily routines, such as dressing themselves or brushing their hair.
- **Preoperational:** This stage is marked by significant leaps in **cognition** and **gross motor skills**. Children in the preoperational stage are able to use increasingly complex language to communicate, and they develop skills like jumping, running, and climbing as they gain increasing control over their bodies. Preoperational children begin learning the basic categorization of alike objects, such as animals, flowers, or foods. This stage is also characterized by the development of pretend play and includes skills such as creating imaginary friends, role playing, and using toys or objects to symbolize something else, such as using a box as a pretend house.
- **Concrete operational:** In this stage, children begin developing **logical reasoning** skills that allow them to perform increasingly complex tasks. Concrete operational children are able to distinguish subcategories, including types of animals, foods, or flowers, and can organize items in ascending or descending order based upon characteristics like height, weight, or size. Children at this stage develop the understanding that altering the appearance of an object or substance does not change the amount of it. A classic example of this is the understanding that liquid transferred from one container to another retains its volume. This concept is known as **conservation**.
- **Formal operational:** The formal operational stage is characterized by the development of **abstract** and **hypothetical** cognitive skills. Children at this stage are able to solve increasingly complex math equations, hypothesize and strategically devise a plan for engaging in science experiments, and develop creative solutions to problems. They are also able to theorize potential outcomes to hypothetical situations as well as consider the nuances of differing values, beliefs, morals, and ethics.

Substages of the Sensorimotor Stage

Piaget's sensorimotor stage is divided into six substages. In each, infants develop new skills for representing and interacting with their world. In the first substage, infants interact **reflexively** and involuntarily to stimuli in the form of muscle jerking when startled, sucking, and gripping. Subsequent stages are circular, or repetitive, in nature and are based on interactions with the self and, increasingly, the environment. **Primary circular reactions**, or intentionally repeated actions, comprise the second substage. Infants notice their actions and sounds and purposefully repeat them, but these actions do not extend past the infant's body. Interaction with the environment begins in the third substage as infants engage in **secondary circular reactions**. Here, infants learn that they can interact with and manipulate objects within their environment to create an effect, such as a sound from pressing a button. They then repeat the action and experience joy in this ability. In the fourth substage, secondary circular reactions become coordinated as infants begin planning movements and actions to create an effect. **Tertiary circular reactions** allow for exploration in the fifth substage, as infants start experimenting with cause and effect. In the sixth substage, infants begin engaging in **representational thought** and recall information from memory.

Examples of Primary, Secondary, and Tertiary Circular Reactions

The following are some common examples of primary, secondary, and tertiary circular reactions:

- **Primary:** Primary circular reactions are repeated **bodily** actions that the infant finds enjoyable. Such actions include thumb sucking, placing hands or feet in the mouth, kicking, and making basic vocalizations.
- **Secondary:** Secondary circular reactions refer to repeated enjoyable interactions between the infant and objects within their **environment** in order to elicit a specific response. Such actions include grasping objects, rattling toys, hitting buttons to hear specific sounds, banging two objects together, or reaching out to touch various items.
- **Tertiary:** Tertiary circular reactions are intentional and planned actions using objects within the environment to **achieve a particular outcome**. Examples include stacking blocks and knocking them down, taking toys out of a bin and putting them back, or engaging in a repeated behavior to gauge a caretaker's reaction each time.

Defining Characteristics of the Preoperational Stage of Development

The preoperational stage of development refers to the stage before a child can exercise operational thought and is associated with several defining characteristics including **pretend play**, **animism**, and **egocentrism**. As children learn to think and express themselves symbolically, they engage in pretend play as a means of organizing, understanding, and representing the world around them as they experience it. During this stage, children do not understand the difference between inanimate and animate objects and thus demonstrate animism, or the attribution of lifelike qualities to inanimate objects. Egocentrism refers to the child's inability to understand the distinction between him or herself and others and, consequentially, the inability to understand the thoughts, perspectives, and feelings of others. During the preoperational stage, the brain is not developed enough to understand **conservation**, which is the understanding that the quantity of something does not change just because its appearance changes. Thus, children in this stage exhibit **centration**, or the focusing on only one aspect of something at a time. Additionally, children struggle with **classification** during this stage, as they are not cognitively developed enough to understand that an object can be classified in multiple ways.

Milestones Achieved During the Concrete Operational Stage of Development

The concrete operational stage marks the beginning of a child's ability to think logically about the concrete world. In this stage, children develop many of the skills they lacked in the preoperational phase. For example, egocentrism fades as children in this stage begin to develop empathy and understand others' perspectives. Additionally, they develop an understanding of conservation, or the idea that the quantity of something does not change with its appearance. Children in this stage begin to learn to classify objects in more than one way and can categorize them based on a variety of characteristics. This allows them to practice **seriation**, or the arranging of objects based on quantitative measures.

Development of Cognitive Abilities in the Formal Operational Stage

In the formal operational stage, children can think beyond the concrete world and in terms of abstract thoughts and hypothetical situations. They develop the ability to consider various outcomes of events and can think more creatively about solutions to problems than in previous stages. This advanced cognitive ability contributes to the development of personal identity. In considering abstract and hypothetical ideas, children begin to formulate opinions and develop personal stances on intangible concepts, thus establishing individual character. The formal operational stage continues to develop through adulthood as individuals gain knowledge and experience.

Lev Vygotsky's Theory of Cognitive Development

Lev Vygotsky's theory on cognitive development is heavily rooted in a **sociocultural** perspective. He argued that the most important factors for a child's cognitive development reside in the cultural context in which the child grows up and social interactions that they have with adults, mentors, and more advanced peers. He believed that children learn best from the people around them, as their social interactions, even basic ones such as smiling, waving, or facial expressions, foster the beginning of more complex cognitive development. He is well-known for his concept of the **Zone of Proximal Development (ZPD)**, which is the gap between what a child can do independently and what the child can do with assistance from a more advanced individual or a collaborator. He believed that children could move through the ZPD and complete increasingly complicated tasks when receiving assistance from more cognitively advanced mentors. According to Vygotsky, children develop the most when passing through the ZPD. Vygotsky's contributions are heavily embedded in modern education and often take the form of teacher-led instruction and scaffolding to assist learners as they move through the ZPD.

Zone of Proximal Development

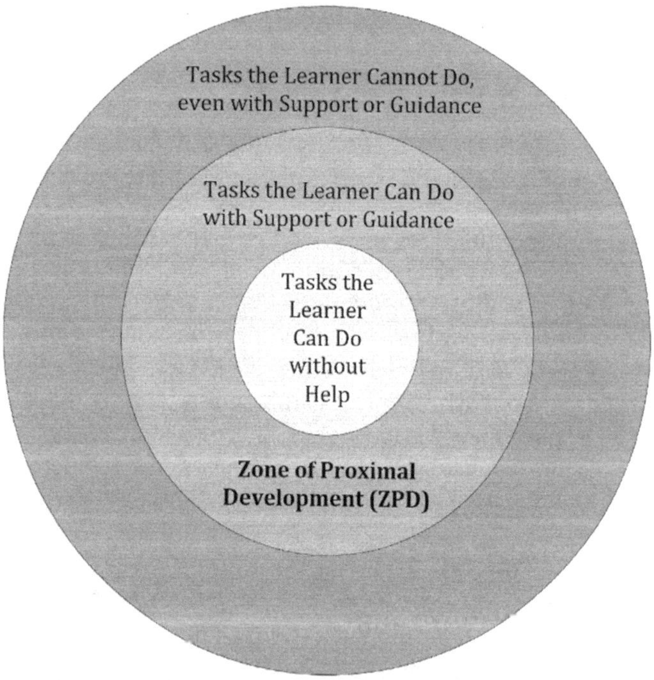

Review Video: Zone of Proximal Development (ZPD)
Visit mometrix.com/academy and enter code: 555594

Social and Emotional Development

Erik Erikson's Eight Stages of Psychosocial Development

Erik Erikson defined eight predetermined stages of psychosocial development from birth to late adulthood in which an individual encounters a crisis that must be resolved to successfully transition to the next stage. The first is **trust vs. mistrust** (0-18 months), where the infant learns that the world is safe and that caregivers can be trusted to tend to his or her basic needs. The next stage is **autonomy vs. shame** (18 months-3 years), where children learn to control their actions and establish independence. In the **initiative vs. guilt stage** (3-5 years), children acquire a sense of purpose and initiative through social interactions. Next, children enter the **industry vs. inferiority stage** (6-11 years), where they develop mastery and pride in completing a task. The next stage is **identity vs. role confusion** (12-18 years), in which children explore and develop characteristics that will comprise their identities and determine their roles in society. The sixth stage is **intimacy vs. isolation** (19-40 years), where one forms relationships by sharing the identity developed in the previous stage with others. **Generativity vs. stagnation** (40-65 years) occurs in middle adulthood and focuses on contributing to society's next generation through finding one's life purpose. The last stage is **ego integrity vs. despair** (65 to death), in which one reflects on the productivity and success of his or her life.

Expected Behaviors at Each Stage of Psychosocial Development

Stage	Examples of expected behaviors
Trust vs. mistrust	In this stage, the infant's primary goal is ensuring the fulfillment of his or her **basic needs**. Infants will cry or make other vocalizations to indicate to caregivers when they want something, such as to be fed or picked up. Separation anxiety from parents is also typical during this stage.
Autonomy vs. shame	Children in this stage begin attempting to perform daily tasks **independently**, such as making food, dressing themselves, bathing, or combing their hair. As children in this stage begin to realize they have a separate identity, they often begin attempting to assert themselves to parents and caregivers.
Initiative vs. guilt	Children at this stage often begin actively engaging and playing with other children. In play settings, these children will often assume **leadership roles** among a group of peers, create new games or activities, and devise their own rules for them. The initiative vs. guilt stage is also characterized by the development of feelings of sadness or guilt when making a mistake or hurting another's feelings.
Industry vs. inferiority	In this stage, children begin attempting to master concepts or skills with the intention of seeking **approval** and **acceptance** from others, particularly those older than themselves, in order to secure a feeling of competency. Children in this stage often become more involved in striving to succeed academically, extracurricular activities, and competitive sports.
Identity vs. role confusion	This stage is characterized by experimentation and uncertainty as young adolescents strive to establish an **independent identity**. Typical behaviors include interacting with new peer groups, trying new styles of dress, engaging in new activities, and considering new beliefs, values, and morals. As young adolescents in this stage are impressionable, they may potentially engage in risky or rebellious behavior as a result of peer pressure.
Intimacy vs. isolation	Individuals in this stage have typically established their identities and are ready to seek **long-term relationships**. This stage marks the development of a social network composed of close friends and long-term romantic partners.

Stage	Examples of expected behaviors
Generativity vs. stagnation	During this stage, individuals begin engaging in **productive** activities to benefit others and elicit personal fulfillment. Such activities include advancing in a career, parenting, or participating in community service projects.
Integrity vs. despair	This stage occurs at the end of one's life and is characterized by **reflection** upon lifetime accomplishments and positive contributions to society. Doing so allows the individual to assess whether his or her purpose was fulfilled and begin accepting death.

Incorporating Life Skills into Curriculum

In addition to academic achievement, the ultimate goal of education is to develop the whole child and provide a successful transition to independence and adulthood. Incorporating valuable life skills, such as decision-making, goal setting, organization, self-direction, and workplace communication, in early childhood through grade 12 is vital in ensuring students become productive contributors to society. Furthermore, the implementation of these life skills in early childhood is integral in allowing children to successfully progress in independence and maturity. The acquisition of such skills instills in students the self-motivation and ability to set goals, make decisions on how to effectively organize and manage time to complete them, and overcome obstacles. Additionally, teaching students to apply these skills promotes effective communication when working with others toward a goal. Through incorporating life skills into curriculum, teachers instill a growth mindset and foster self-empowered, confident lifelong learners with the necessary tools to navigate real-life situations and achieve success as they transition to adulthood. In the classroom, activities that promote leadership skills, cooperative learning, goal setting, self-monitoring, and social interaction foster an increasing sense of independence as children develop.

External Environmental Factors on Social and Emotional Development

Social and emotional development is heavily influenced by a child's home environment. Children learn social and emotional skills such as self-regulation, self-awareness, coping, and relationship building through modeling from parents and caregivers. A positive and supportive home environment is integral for proper social and emotional development. External factors, including lack of affection and attention, parental divorce, and homelessness, pose profound negative impacts on this development. In terms of social development, such external factors could lead to attachment or abandonment issues as well as distrust. Furthermore, children exposed to negative environmental factors could struggle in forging relationships, cooperating, and following societal rules. Emotionally, negative impacts on development cause aggression, poor self-regulation, insecurity, anxiety, isolation, and depression. Since developmental domains are interconnected, the impacts that external factors have on social and emotional development ultimately damage cognitive and physical development. Underdeveloped social skills impair cognitive development because the inability to properly interact with peers impedes the ability to learn from them. Additionally, inadequate emotional skills can inhibit concentration and understanding in school, thus inhibiting cognitive development. Physically, struggling to interact with others leads to impaired development of gross and fine motor skills as well as large muscle development that would be achieved through play.

Physical Development

Physical Changes Occurring in Early Childhood Through Adolescence

Early Childhood

As children pass through stages of development from early childhood through middle childhood and adolescence, they experience significant physical changes. Children in early childhood experience rapid growth in height and weight as they transition away from physical characteristics of infancy. In this stage, children begin to gain independence as they develop and improve upon gross and fine motor skills. Throughout early childhood, children develop the ability to walk and run, and as they mature through this stage, they learn to throw, catch, climb, and hop. Of the locomotive skills listed, walking comes first, running and climbing can develop simultaneously, and hopping or jumping comes last. They improve in their fine motor skills and learn to hold and manipulate small objects such as zippers and buttons and can grasp writing utensils to create shapes, letters, and drawings with increasing accuracy.

Middle Childhood

Physical growth varies for individual children in middle childhood, as some children begin experiencing prepubescent bodily changes. Children in middle childhood experience further improvements and refinements of gross and fine motor skills and coordination. Significant physical and appearance changes occur in adolescence as children enter puberty. These changes often occur quickly, resulting in a period of awkwardness and lack of coordination as adolescents adjust to this rapid development.

Impact of External Factors on Physical Development

As children pass through physical development stages from early childhood to adolescence, it is important that environmental factors are supportive of proper growth and health. Physical development can be hindered by external factors, such as poor nutrition, lack of sleep, prenatal exposure to drugs, and abuse, as these can cause significant and long-lasting negative consequences. Exposure to such factors can lead to stunted physical growth, impaired brain development and function, poor bone and muscle development, and obesity. Furthermore, the negative impacts from such external factors ultimately impedes cognitive, social, and emotional development. Impaired brain development and function negatively affect cognitive development by impacting the ability to concentrate and grasp new concepts. In terms of emotional development, physical impairments due to external factors can cause a child to become depressed, withdrawn, aggressive, prone to low self-esteem, and unable to self-regulate. Improper physical growth and health impacts social development in that physical limitations could hinder a child's ability to properly interact with and play with others. Impacted brain development and function can limit a child's ability to understand social cues and norms.

Language Development

Stages of Language Development

The first stage of language development and acquisition, the **pre-linguistic stage**, occurs during an infant's first year of life. It is characterized by the development of gestures, making eye contact, and sounds like cooing and crying. The **holophrase** or **one-word sentence stage** develops in infants between 10 and 13 months of age. In this stage, young children use one-word sentences to communicate meaning in language. The **two-word sentence stage** typically develops by the time a child is 18 months old. Each two-word sentence usually contains a noun or a verb and a modifier, such as "big balloon" or "green grass." Children in this stage use their two-word sentences to communicate wants and needs. **Multiple-word sentences** form by the time a child is two to two and a half years old. In this stage, children begin forming sentences with subjects and predicates, such as "tree is tall" or "rope is long." Grammatical errors are present, but children in this stage begin demonstrating how to use words in appropriate context. Children ages two and a half to three years typically begin using more **complex grammatical structures**. They begin to include grammatical structures that were not present before, such as conjunctions and prepositions. By the age of five or six, children reach a stage of **adult-like language development**. They begin to use words in appropriate context and can move words around in sentences while maintaining appropriate sentence structure. Language development and acquisition has a wide range of what is considered normal development. Some children do not attempt to speak for up to two years and then may experience an explosion of language development at a later time. In these cases, children often emerge from their silent stage with equivalent language development to babies who were more expressive early on. A child who does not speak after two years, however, may be exhibiting signs of a developmental delay.

Oral Language Development

Oral language development begins well before students enter educational environments. It is learned first without formal instruction, with **environmental factors** being a heavy influence. Children tend to develop their own linguistic rules as a result of genetic disposition, their environments, and how their individual thinking processes develop. Oral language refers to both speaking and listening. Components of oral language development include phonology, syntax, semantics, morphology, and pragmatics. **Phonology** refers to the production and recognition of sounds. **Morphology** refers to how words are formed from smaller pieces, called morphemes. **Semantics** refers to the meaning of words and phrases and has overlap with morphology and syntax, as morphemes and word order can both change the meaning of words. Semantic studies generally focus on learning and understanding vocabulary. **Syntax** refers to how words and morphemes are combined to make up meaningful phrases. In English, word order is the primary way that many components of grammar are communicated. Finally, **pragmatics** refers to the practical application of language based on various social situations. For instance, a college student is likely to use different vocabulary, complexity, and formality of language when speaking with a professor than when speaking with his or her peer group. Each of these five components of language are applied in oral language. Awareness and application of these components develops over time as students gain experience and education in language use. **Oral language development** can be nurtured by caregivers and teachers well before children enter educational environments. Caregivers and teachers can promote oral language development by providing environments full of language development opportunities. Additionally, teaching children how conversation works, encouraging interaction among children, and demonstrating good listening and speaking skills are good strategies for nurturing oral language development.

> **Review Video: Components of Oral Language Development**
> Visit mometrix.com/academy and enter code: 480589

Helping Students Develop Oral Language Abilities

Children pick up oral language skills in their home environments and build upon these skills as they grow. Early language development is influenced by a combination of genetic disposition, environment, and individual thinking processes. Children with **oral language acquisition difficulties** often experience difficulties in their

literacy skills, so activities that promote good oral language skills also improve literacy skills. **Strategies** that help students develop oral language abilities include developing appropriate speaking and listening skills; providing instruction that emphasizes vocabulary development; providing students with opportunities to communicate wants, needs, ideas, and information; creating language learning environments; and promoting auditory memory. Developing appropriate speaking and listening skills includes teaching turn-taking, awareness of social norms, and basic rules for speaking and listening. Emphasizing **vocabulary development** is a strategy that familiarizes early learners with word meanings. Providing students with opportunities to **communicate** is beneficial for developing early social skills. Teachers can create **language learning environments** by promoting literacy in their classrooms with word walls, reading circles, or other strategies that introduce language skills to students. Promoting **auditory memory** means teaching students to listen to, process, and recall information.

Review Video: Types of Vocabulary Learning (Broad and Specific)
Visit mometrix.com/academy and enter code: 258753

Helping Students Monitor Errors in Oral Language

Oral language is the primary way people communicate and express their knowledge, ideas, and feelings. As oral language generally develops, their **speaking and listening skills** become more refined. This refinement of a person's language is called fluency, which can be broken down into the subdisciplines of language, reading, writing, speaking, and listening. **Speaking fluency** usually describes the components of rate, accuracy, and prosody. **Rate** describes how fast a person can speak, and **prosody** describes the inflection and expressions that a person puts into speech. **Accuracy** describes how often a person makes an error in language production. In early stages of language development, individuals generally do not have enough language knowledge to be able to monitor their own speech production for errors and require input from others to notice and correct their mistakes. As an individual becomes more proficient, he or she will be able to monitor his or her own language usage and make corrections to help improve fluency. In the classroom, the teacher needs to be an active component of language monitoring to help facilitate growth. Teachers can monitor **oral language errors** with progress-monitoring strategies. Teachers can also help students monitor their own **oral language development** as they progress through the reading curriculum. Students can monitor their oral language by listening to spoken words in their school and home environments, learning and practicing self-correction skills, and participating in reading comprehension and writing activities. Students can also monitor oral language errors by learning oral language rules for phonics, semantics, syntax, and pragmatics. These rules typically generalize to developing appropriate oral language skills.

Expressive and Receptive Language

Expressive language refers to the aspects of language that an individual produces, generally referring to writing and speaking. **Receptive language** refers to the aspects of language that an individual encounters or receives and generally refers to reading and listening. Both expressive and receptive language are needed for communication from one person to another.

	Expressive	Receptive
Written	Writing	Reading
Oral	Speaking	Listening

Expressive Language Skills

Expressive language skills include the ability to use vocabulary, sentences, gestures, and writing. People with good **expressive language skills** can label objects in their environments, put words in sentences, use appropriate grammar, demonstrate comprehension verbally by retelling stories, and more. This type of language is important because it allows people to express feelings, wants, needs, thoughts, ideas, and individual points of view. Strong expressive language skills include pragmatic knowledge, such as using gestures and facial expressions or using appropriate vocabulary for the listener or reader and soft skills, such as checks for comprehension, use of analogies, and grouping of ideas to help with clarity. Well-expressed language should be relatively easy for someone else to comprehend.

Receptive Language Skills

Receptive language refers to a person's ability to perceive and understand language. Good receptive language skills involve gathering information from the environment and processing it into meaning. People with good **receptive language skills** perceive gestures, sounds, words, and written information well. Receptive language is important for developing appropriate communication skills. Instruction that targets receptive language skills can include tasks that require sustained attention and focus, recognizing emotions and gestures, and listening and reading comprehension. Games that challenge the players to communicate carefully, such as charades or catchphrase, can be a great way to target receptive language skills. As one student tries to accurately express an idea with words or gestures, the rest of the class must exercise their receptive language skills. Lastly, focusing on **social skills and play skills instruction** encourages opportunities for children to interact with their peers or adults. This fosters receptive language skills and targets deficits in these skills.

Stages of Literacy Development

The development of literacy in young children is separated into five stages. Names and ranges of these stages sometimes vary slightly, but the stage milestones are similar. Stage 1 is the **Emergent Reader stage**. In this stage, children ages 6 months to 6 years demonstrate skills like pretend reading, recognizing letters of the alphabet, retelling stories, and printing their names. Stage 2 is the **Novice/Early Reader stage** (ages 6–7 years). Children begin to understand the relationships between letters and sounds and written and spoken words, and they read texts containing high-frequency words. Children in this stage should develop orthographic conventions and semantic knowledge. In Stage 3, the **Decoding Reader stage**, children ages 7–9 develop decoding skills in order to read simple stories. They also demonstrate increased fluency. Stage 4 (ages 8–15 years) is called the **Fluent, Comprehending/Transitional Reader stage**. In this stage, fourth to eighth graders read to learn new ideas and information. In Stage 5, the **Expert/Fluent Reader stage**, children ages

16 years and older read more complex information. They also read expository and narrative texts with multiple viewpoints.

Review Video: Stages of Reading Development
Visit mometrix.com/academy and enter code: 121184

Relationship between Language Development and Early Literacy Skills

Language development and early literacy skills are interconnected. **Language concepts** begin and develop shortly after birth with infant/parent interactions, cooing, and then babbling. These are the earliest attempts at language acquisition for infants. Young children begin interacting with written and spoken words before they enter their grade school years. Before they enter formal classrooms, children begin to make **connections** between speaking and listening and reading and writing. Children with strong speaking and listening skills demonstrate strong literacy skills in early grade school. The development of **phonological awareness** is connected to early literacy skills. Children with good phonological awareness recognize that words are made up of different speech sounds. For example, children with appropriate phonological awareness can break words (e.g., "bat" into separate speech sounds, "b-a-t"). Examples of phonological awareness include rhyming (when the ending parts of words have the same or similar sounds) and alliteration (when words all have the same beginning sound). Success with phonological awareness (oral language) activities depends on adequate development of speech and language skills.

Promoting Literacy During the Early Stages of Literacy Development

Teachers and parents can implement strategies at different stages of literacy development in order to build **good reading skills** in children with and without disabilities. During the **Emergent Reader stage**, teachers and parents can introduce children to the conventions of reading with picture books. They can model turning the pages, reading from left to right, and other reading conventions. Book reading at this stage helps children begin to identify letters, letter sounds, and simple words. Repetitive reading of familiar texts also helps children begin to make predictions about what they are reading. During the **Novice/Early Reader** and **Decoding Reader stages**, parents and teachers can help children form the building blocks of decoding and fluency skills by reading for meaning and emphasizing letter-sound relationships, visual cues, and language patterns. In these stages, increasing familiarity with sight words is essential. In the **Fluent, Comprehending/Transitional Reader stage**, children should be encouraged to read book series, as the shared characters, settings, and plots help develop their comprehension skills. At this stage, a good reading rate (fluency) is an indicator of comprehension skills. **Expert/Fluent readers** can independently read multiple texts and comprehend their meanings. Teachers and parents can begin exposing children to a variety of fiction and non-fiction texts before this stage in order to promote good fluency skills.

Review Video: Phonics (Encoding and Decoding)
Visit mometrix.com/academy and enter code: 821361

Review Video: Fluency
Visit mometrix.com/academy and enter code: 531179

Managing Developmental Transitions

Developmental Changes Experienced in Early Adolescence

Early adolescence is a time of considerable development in all domains. Physically, children enter pubert, and must learn to deal with its emotional, social, and academic impacts. Consequently, children at this stage are impressionable and begin developing habits that influence success as they transition to adulthood. Thus, early adolescents have specific developmental needs, and an accommodating approach to instruction is required. As the goal of education is providing the necessary skills to successfully transition into adulthood and increasing independence, it must be recognized that the shift from elementary to high school is drastic, and high school curriculum is not developmentally appropriate for early adolescence. The shift from elementary to high school is stressful and may negatively impact a child's attitude toward acquiring necessary life skills for success. Thus, middle-level education is integral in providing a developmentally responsive curriculum that eases this transition yet allows for increasing personal and academic independence. Middle-level education considers the physical developmental changes of early adolescents and fosters cognitive, social, and emotional growth through engaging instruction that encourages self-direction, responsibility, and positive social relationships. Middle-level curriculum instills skills such as organization, time management, and goal setting that promote success in high school and, ultimately, adulthood.

Risks Faced by Students When Experiencing Challenges

As students experience rapid physical, cognitive, emotional, and social developments in later childhood, adolescence, and young adulthood, they encounter challenges while developing habits, beliefs, and relationships that will shape their identities and future decisions. Such challenges as self-image, changing physical appearance, eating disorders, rebelliousness, identity formation, and educational and career decisions pose emotional, social, behavioral, and academic risks with long-term consequences if not addressed. Students may respond to challenges by engaging in risky behavior or developing social and emotional issues, such as depression, anxiety, or aggression. Such challenges may induce apathy toward academics and extracurricular activities and declining academic performance. These risks threaten the successful transition to adulthood and success throughout life in that they potentially hinder the educational and career choices that would lead to a successful future. Early intervention is imperative to support students facing challenges, as this can help prevent the consequences associated with them. Some supports include fostering and encouraging positive social relationships with peers and mentors, encouraging participation in extracurricular activities within the school and community, providing access to guidance counselors, and providing adequate health education to help students understand the challenges they are facing as they develop.

Indicators and Negative Impacts of Risky Behaviors in Students

The likelihood that students will engage in risky behaviors, such as drug and alcohol use, gang involvement, or other dangerous activities, increases as they approach adolescence. Such behaviors pose serious negative consequences on development and learning. Cognitively, risky behaviors harm brain function and development and lead to trouble sleeping, focusing, and learning. Socially, these students may have trouble maintaining positive relationships and are more likely to associate with others engaging in the same behaviors. Emotionally, these behaviors could cause depression, anxiety, and low self-esteem. Physically, negative impacts include injury, illness, or long-term health consequences. Furthermore, risky behaviors are detrimental to learning. Students participating in these behaviors have trouble focusing and grasping new concepts. They may also become apathetic toward academics. It is important to recognize indicators of risky behavior to intervene as early as possible and prevent long-term negative consequences. Indicators include being withdrawn, poor grades, poor appearance, bad hygiene, poor sleeping and eating habits, and a lack of interest in academics or extracurricular activities. Schools and communities must do their best to prevent students from engaging in risky behaviors through encouraging positive social relationships, participation in extracurricular activities, providing access to guidance counselors, and providing access to proper health education.

Roles of Peers, Acceptance, and Conformity During Adolescent Development

Adolescence is an insecure and impressionable time as students navigate rapid physical, emotional, social, and cognitive development. This stage introduces an increased sense of **independence** as adolescents begin developing the opinions, beliefs, values, and social relationships that will comprise their identities and establish the foundations for their futures as they transition to adulthood. Social relationships are a vital part of identity formation during this stage, as adolescents engage with different peer groups, norms, and expectations, and seek acceptance in desired crowds. Adolescents will often conform their behaviors to the social norms of a desired peer group for fear of rejection; thus, the nature of the peer group has significant implications for teaching and learning. Involvement with unhealthy peer groups may lead to engaging in risky behaviors in search of social acceptance and a disinterest in learning and academic success. In contrast, association with healthy peer groups fosters the development of positive and supportive social relationships that encourage constructive behavior. Consequently, engaging in healthy peer groups increases the likelihood that the adolescent will be interested in academic involvement, achievement, and success.

Developmental Delays

Developmental Differences Encountered and Strategies to Address Them

Cognitive, physical, social, and emotional milestones through which children pass as they mature are approximate, and development in any domain depends on the individual child as well as countless environmental factors that comprise each child's unique situation; therefore, a teacher will encounter multiple variations in cognitive, physical, social, and emotional development in students that pose significant implications for instructional planning. Cognitively, a teacher will encounter several intelligences and learning styles. Teachers will encounter students with various learning disabilities, gifted and talented students, or English Language Learners. Physically, students grow and develop at individual rates, and teachers will encounter students with varying physical abilities or limitations. Social developmental differences vary as well and are heavily influenced by environmental factors. Variances in social cues, norms, relationship building, and communication are based on a child's culture and environment. Emotional development, such as self-regulation and coping, are also impacted by environment. Such an array of differences requires a teacher to be trained to recognize the prior knowledge and learning needs of his or her students in order to effectively teach to those differences. Strategies to achieve this include adjusting curriculum, activities, and assessments to match individual student needs, providing necessary scaffolds, and differentiating instruction to access learners of all abilities.

Effect of Developmental Delays on Learning Experiences and Assessments

Developmental delays in any domain pose significant potential impacts on learning experiences and assessments through affecting comprehension and participation. A delay in cognitive development could impact information processing times, information retention, and the ability to understand complex ideas, thus hindering comprehension and ultimately impacting the willingness to participate. A student with a physical developmental delay may struggle with fine and gross motor skills that prevent effective participation in class activities that would improve comprehension of new instruction. Students with social developmental delays may have difficulty properly expressing a need for assistance, thus potentially discouraging participation and overall comprehension. Furthermore, students with social or emotional developmental delays may be withdrawn, depressed, anxious, or have behavioral issues that impede their self-motivation and ability to focus, thus affecting comprehension and willingness to participate. These potential impacts can have long-lasting consequences on students' overall learning experiences, and early recognition is imperative for instilling the proper accommodations for each student.

Accommodations to Assist Students with Developmental Delays

In order to create an equitable and inclusive environment, the teacher must have an understanding of the developmental characteristics of each student. Furthermore, the teacher must be able to use this knowledge to make the proper accommodations to the curriculum, instruction, and assessments in such a way that addresses individual needs and abilities across the domains of development. Modifications should be specific to the student and his or her individual needs and should provide the necessary support to allow for success in learning. Such accommodations may include scaffolding to break instruction into smaller, more manageable pieces, extended work time for assignments and assessments, shorter work periods with frequent breaks, reduced ratio of students to teacher, individualized instruction, and preferential seating based on the student's need for proximity. Additionally, students may require accommodations to address physical developmental delays, including scribes, text to speech for assignments, or enlarged fonts. Providing accommodations to address individual needs in the four areas of development allows for the teacher to effectively assess student progress and ultimately allows for success in learning.

Recognizing Signs of Developmental Delays or Impairments

Although each child develops at a different pace, there are often indicators that a student is not developing at a similar rate as his or her peers. Developmental delays or impairments can be cognitive, physical, emotional, or social. Some common indicators of developmental delays include lower-than-average assessment scores, difficulty concentrating and retaining new information, difficulty socializing or communicating with others, limited vocabulary compared to others in the same age group, clumsiness, and difficulty holding small objects. Delays can be difficult to detect, but a teacher can recognize signs through observing students and analyzing their progress across subject areas compared to their peers. Early recognition and detection are beneficial in early intervention and developing treatment plans for these students that can improve their progress both inside and outside of the classroom.

Developmentally Appropriate Practices

Developmentally Appropriate Practice

Developmentally appropriate practice **(DAP)** is an approach to teaching grounded in theories of child development. It is derived from the belief that children are naturally curious learners who feel encouraged to take initiative in their own learning when provided a stimulating environment. This approach allows for a great deal of choice in learning experiences. The teacher's role is to facilitate active learning by creating developmentally appropriate activities based on the awareness of similarities between children in various developmental stages and the knowledge that each child develops at a different rate. With this knowledge, the teacher can then adjust the curriculum, activities, and assessments to fit the needs of individual students based on an awareness of age, cultural, social, and individual expectations.

Creating Instruction Tailored to Cognitive Development

A developmentally responsive teacher understands that the needs of students change as they mature through the stages of cognitive development. Furthermore, an effective teacher uses this knowledge to plan instruction that coincides with each developmental level. The early childhood teacher understands the needs and abilities of preoperational children and designs instruction that focuses on interacting with the world around them through hands-on activities and pretend play. Such activities foster exploration of the environment, roles, and connections. Developmentally responsive elementary school teachers are aware of the logical thinking patterns that occur during the concrete operational stage. Thus, they create instruction that allows children to interact with tangible materials to help them draw logical conclusions about their environment and understand abstract ideas. As children reach adolescence, a developmentally responsive teacher understands the increased ability to think abstractly, hypothetically, and reflectively in the formal operational stage. They use this knowledge to create instruction that encourages discussion, debate, creative problem solving, and opportunities to develop opinions, beliefs, and values.

Cognitive Development

Importance in Design of Appropriate Learning Experiences That Facilitate Growth

Teachers must understand their students' cognitive developmental abilities relative to their grade levels in order to create effective, engaging learning experiences that facilitate growth. This understanding allows teachers to develop age-appropriate instruction, activities, and assessments that challenge students based on their skills and abilities while remaining attainable. In knowing how students in a given grade level think and learn, the teacher can develop instruction that effectively facilitates learning and growth, such as creating opportunities for purposeful play with young children, opportunities for middle-school aged students to engage in logical problem solving, or activities that promote the development of abstract thinking and reasoning with adolescents. In addition, understanding students' cognitive abilities of each developmental level allow the teacher to better understand the nuances that exist within them, as students ultimately develop at their own pace and have individual learning needs.

Impact on Teaching and Learning

Students' thinking and learning develops as they mature and their thought processes and worldviews change. Consequently, teaching and learning must adapt to accommodate these changes and facilitate growth. In the early years of cognitive development, children learn through interacting with the surrounding environment using their physical senses and engage in independent play. To facilitate this, young children need learning experiences that stimulate their development through exploration. As children reach early elementary school, they begin to think symbolically and play with others. Purposeful play and interaction with learning materials becomes an important part of learning at this stage. Teachers should act as facilitators and provide multiple opportunities for children to engage in purposeful, self-directed play with interactive materials as they learn to categorize the world around them. By later childhood, children think concretely and logically, thus needing hands-on learning experiences that provide opportunities for classification, experimentation, and problem-solving skills to facilitate their level of cognition and promote development. As children reach adolescence, they are increasingly able to think abstractly and consider hypothetical situations beyond what is concretely present. To enhance learning, teachers must provide opportunities for exploring different perspectives, values, and synthesizing information to engage in creative problem solving.

Appropriate Instructional Activities

The following are some examples of appropriate instructional activities for early childhood, middle-level, and high school students:

- **Early childhood:** Activities that allow for exploration, play, and movement while teaching young children to function and cooperate in a group setting are most valuable in early childhood classrooms. **Movement activities** such as dancing, jumping rope, using outdoor play equipment, and structured and unstructured play are beneficial in developing gross motor skills and teaching young children to properly interact with others. **Whole-group** activities such as circle time, class songs, and read-aloud sessions are also valuable in teaching young children appropriate communication skills within a group. **Thematic learning stations**, such as a science center, dramatic play area, library corner, block area, art center, and technology center, allow young children to explore their own interests on a variety of topics while developing creative and imaginative skills. **Sensory play** stations that include items like a sand box or water table are beneficial in further developing motor skills and allowing young children to explore and experiment with a variety of textures. Young children also require opportunities for quiet activities, such as nap time, self-selected reading, or meditation throughout the day in order to process information, reflect, and rest after active movement.
- **Middle-level**: Students at this age are best supported by the implementation of **hands-on** learning activities that develop **logical reasoning** and **collaboration** skills. Collaborative activities used for this purpose include science experiments, mathematical word problems, the use of manipulatives, and projects that allow opportunities for building, creating, disassembling, and exploring. Social and emotional learning activities are also important in developing middle school students' skills in these domains. Incorporating class meetings, community building activities, and self-reflection activities is valuable for teaching social and emotional skills. In addition, cooperative learning opportunities should be implemented frequently across subject areas to further develop students' abilities to work productively with others. Examples include literacy circles, creating teams for class review games, or group presentations.

- **High school:** Instructional activities for high school students should be designed to foster the development of **abstract** and **hypothetical** thinking abilities while preparing them to become productive members of society as they enter adulthood. Activities such as debates, class discussions, and mock trials are beneficial in providing high school students the opportunity to employ abstract reasoning, consider solutions to hypothetical situations, and develop empathy for opposing viewpoints. Assignments that require students to engage in the research process are valuable opportunities for developing higher-order thinking skills, as they encourage students to analyze, compare, and interpret information as well as seek evidence to support their claims. In addition, incorporating activities that benefit the community, such as fundraisers or food and clothing drives, are beneficial in teaching high school students the importance of positively contributing to society.

Developmentally Appropriate Learning Experiences and Assessments

Effective developmentally appropriate instruction requires careful consideration when planning to ensure that students' individual needs across domains are supported to facilitate growth and a positive learning experience. The teacher must consider the developmental stage of their students based upon their age group as well as students' individual differences. With this knowledge in mind, teachers must ensure that they provide an inclusive learning environment that fosters growth and development by creating challenging yet attainable activities based on students' needs. Likewise, teachers must evaluate whether learning experiences and assessments are appropriate for the age, development, culture, and learning differences of the students. Learning experiences must provide opportunities for hands-on, cooperative, and self-directed learning, exploration, and participation to allow students to interact with their environment and build experiences. Additionally, lessons and activities should be flexible in nature to allow for inquiry and build upon students' prior experiences. Effective and developmentally appropriate assessments are aimed at monitoring student progress and allow for flexibility based on students' learning differences. They should be intended to provide feedback to the teacher on how to better adapt instruction to meet students' individual needs and foster developmental growth.

Development of Life Skills and Attitudes in Middle School-Age Children

Middle school-age children are at a pivotal development point in which they experience rapid and profound change. In this transition, they often demonstrate characteristics of younger and older children. They are at a critical stage for developing the beliefs, attitudes, and habits that will be the foundation for their futures. Teachers must understand the implications of these changes and design instruction that addresses students' learning needs and facilitates the development of important life skills such as working and getting along with others, appreciating diversity, and committing to continued schooling. Cooperative learning and team building strategies instill the importance of working together positively to solve problems, building on one another's strengths, and valuing the perspectives of others. These strategies also teach students to appreciate diversity through encouraging them to work with peers with different backgrounds and experiences. Additionally, teachers can teach students to embrace diversity through creating a culturally responsive classroom environment that models acceptance and incorporates elements of students' differences into instruction to demonstrate the value of diverse perspectives. Teachers promote positive attitudes toward academics that encourage a commitment to continued schooling by teaching organization, time management, and goal-setting skills that instill a growth mindset and provide a foundation for success.

Impact of Student Characteristics on Teaching and Learning

Young Children

The developmental level of young children is characterized by defining attributes that impact teaching and learning and for which several considerations must be made to design and implement effective instruction. As the attention span of young children is limited, the teacher must think about how to effectively act as a facilitator for learning more often than directly instructing students. **Direct instruction** must be delivered in small, manageable chunks to accommodate students' attention spans and ensure they retain and understand new concepts. Thus, the teacher must evaluate which elements of the curriculum require structured learning while allowing for flexibility within instruction to accommodate student inquiry. Young children also need frequent **movement**, **physical activity**, and **social interaction**, as they learn and build experiences concretely through moving, playing, interacting with, and exploring their environment. To create a learning environment that accommodates these characteristics, the teacher must consider the physical arrangement of the classroom and whether it adequately allows for movement. Additionally, teachers must incorporate **structured** and **unstructured activities** that foster and promote exploration, inquiry, play, cooperative learning, and hands-on interactions with the learning environment. With these considerations in mind, the teacher enhances students' learning experiences by tailoring instruction to their developmental characteristics.

Middle School-Age Children

As middle school-age children transition from childhood to adolescence, they experience vast changes across all developmental domains. Consequently, they exhibit characteristics that affect teaching and learning that require careful consideration when adapting instruction to their unique learning needs. While these students require increasing independence as they mature, they still need a structured, predictable environment to ease the transition into high school. The teacher must create a balance between fostering independence and growth while providing a schedule and routine. Opportunities for self-directed learning and student choice as well as strategies for self-assessment and reflection foster autonomy and self-responsibility over learning while the teacher facilitates and monitors progress. Strategies to teach effective organizational and time management skills further promote independence and prepare students for success upon entering high school. As middle school-age students develop, the importance of peers becomes increasingly prevalent because they begin to search for their identities and shape their own values and beliefs. Teachers must ensure to provide opportunities for cooperative and small group learning to facilitate students' social development while considering the importance of promoting positive peer relationships at this impressionable developmental level.

Adolescent Children

The developmental changes that occur in adolescence result in distinct characteristics as students in this age group transition into young adulthood. During this stage, students are discovering their identities, values, and beliefs and begin to explore long-term career and life choices. As they navigate their development and shape the people they will become, social relationships come to be increasingly important. Teachers must consider the impact of these characteristics when developing instruction to effectively address the unique needs of this age group and establish foundational attitudes, habits, and skills necessary for success in life. Effective instruction encourages adolescents to consider different perspectives, morals, and values to broaden their worldviews and foster the development of their own beliefs. Lessons and activities should allow for exploration of personal interests, skills, and abilities as students shape their personalities and begin to consider long-term life goals. Moreover, teachers should incorporate strategies that assist adolescents in setting goals to successfully foster a growth mindset and provide a foundation for success. Additionally, as socialization is highly influential at this stage, teachers must consider the importance of incorporating cooperative learning strategies and opportunities for socialization within instruction to encourage healthy peer relationships and foster positive identity development.

Interconnection of Developmental Domains

Developmental domains are deeply interconnected. If one area of a child's development is negatively impacted, it is likely to pose negative consequences on other developmental areas. Proper physical development, for example, is key to developing cognitively, socially, and emotionally because physical development allows children to acquire the necessary gross and fine motor skills to explore and experiment with the world around them and interact with others. Physical development includes development of the brain. Factors such as poor nutrition, sleep, or prenatal exposure to drugs potentially hinder brain development. Consequentially, this may result in cognitive delays and, ultimately, lead to social or emotional developmental delays through negatively impacting the child's ability to interact with others, build relationships, emotionally regulate, or communicate effectively.

Review Video: Early Childhood Developmental Domains
Visit mometrix.com/academy and enter code: 100380

Factors to Consider When Selecting Materials for Learning and Play

To plan meaningful, integrated, and active learning and play experiences, the teacher must have a deep understanding of both the developmental stage of the students and an understanding of students' individual needs. With this knowledge in mind, there are several factors that the teacher must consider when choosing materials that support active learning, play experiences, and the development of the whole child. Materials should be adaptable in use to facilitate development in multiple areas. Versatility is also important in fostering imagination and creativity. Teachers must consider how the chosen materials will support the understanding of concepts covered in instruction as well as how they will support conceptual, perceptual, and language development. Furthermore, teachers must ensure that materials are age-appropriate and stimulating and that they encourage active participation both independently and cooperatively.

Characteristics of a Developmentally Responsive Classroom

A developmentally responsive classroom is one in which the teacher understands the cognitive, physical, social, and emotional developmental stages of students while recognizing nuances and individual developmental differences within these stages. Teachers must understand that developmental domains are interconnected, Teachers must effectively respond to unique developmental differences by designing a learner-centered curriculum and classroom environment that caters to each student's abilities, needs, and developmental levels to develop the whole child. The developmentally responsive classroom is engaging, supportive, and provides challenging learning opportunities based on individual learner abilities. There are several factors teachers must consider in the developmentally responsive classroom when planning an appropriate, engaging, and challenging learning experience. Teachers must have a deep understanding of which teaching strategies will most effectively appeal to students of varying developmental levels and be prepared to teach content in multiple ways. Furthermore, teachers must consider how to plan and organize activities, lessons, breaks, and the overall classroom environment. This includes considering how to arrange the classroom, which activity areas to include, spacing, and classroom equipment. The developmentally responsive classroom should promote positivity and productivity through creating a supportive yet challenging learning atmosphere that welcomes and respects differences, thus encouraging students' curiosity and excitement for learning.

Factors that Impact Student Learning

Home and Community Factors that Impact Student Learning

Students are exposed to multiple social and cultural factors from their homes and communities that significantly impact learning, so it is imperative that the teacher is conscious of these factors to effectively adapt instruction and assessment to enhance students' learning. Students are often held to different academic and behavioral expectations by their parents depending on their social and cultural backgrounds. These expectations affect self-motivation, engagement, and academic performance. When adapting instruction and assessment, teachers must ensure that all students are held to high expectations while providing individual students with the necessary supports for success. Teachers must also consider the availability of community resources that offer support and enhance learning, as this differs among social and cultural groups. Students from low sociocultural backgrounds may lack quality resources such as libraries, tutoring, or after-school activities, so teachers must adapt to include time outside of instruction for completing assignments, additional support, and use of school resources. Community problems pose obstacles that hinder students' motivation, self-concept, and attitude toward learning. It is important that teachers establish a safe, welcoming, and engaging classroom while providing the necessary academic and behavioral supports to foster equity and promote a growth mindset.

Self-Directed Learning

In a **self-directed learning** environment, students are given a sense of agency that enhances self-motivation and feelings of ownership and responsibility for their own learning. By choosing what and how they learn based on their individual interests, learning styles, and preferences, students have the ability to explore and inquire freely, thus increasing their natural curiosity and motivation to do so. In choosing their own learning, students determine their own learning goals, thus creating a sense of ownership and self-responsibility. This sentiment is also increased when students can tailor their learning according to their own needs and challenge themselves based on their skills and abilities. Furthermore, when students achieve self-decided goals, they develop a sense of ownership over their learning. In order to foster a self-guided environment in which students are fully engaged in their own learning, teachers must adopt a facilitator role in instruction and offer support when necessary. Instruction and assessment must allow multiple opportunities for student choice in how learning is determined and demonstrated. By providing opportunities for self-evaluation and reflection, teachers further facilitate self-motivation, ownership, and responsibility over students' own learning through encouraging them to make personal connections, reflect on accomplishments, and seek areas for self-improvement.

Teacher Roles in Student Learning

The teacher's role is multifaceted in nature, and teachers must often adopt multiple roles within a single lesson to effectively facilitate learning and accommodate individual students' needs. The role of the **lecturer**, **model**, and **facilitator** are applicable to different learning situations and have varying impacts on learning. As the lecturer, the teacher delivers direct instruction to students. This role is most appropriate when introducing a new concept, providing instructions for an upcoming activity, or reviewing material. In addition, teachers can effectively communicate new skills, ideas, and thought processes through modeling to students, as this is a highly influential method of instruction. When teachers serve as facilitators, they guide students in learning while offering support, scaffolding, and assistance when necessary. This role is effective in active and open-ended learning situations in which students are encouraged to explore, practice, and engage in creative problem solving. Through this method, teachers allow students to adopt a self-directed approach that encourages ownership over their own learning, thus creating an engaging, empowering learning experience.

Impact of Student Roles on Learning

Students adopt multiple roles in the learning process, and teachers must be cognizant of individual learning styles and specific learning situations to determine which role is most applicable and effective for enhancing learning. As **active learners**, students participate and interact throughout the learning process. In this role, students are encouraged to implement higher-order thinking skills through exploration, inquiry, and problem solving, thus creating an engaging learning environment that promotes the retainment of information. This role is particularly effective in learning situations in which students are practicing new skills, testing hypotheses, and exploring new concepts. The opportunity to actively participate in learning allows them to better internalize new information and formulate creative solutions to problems. Active learning also occurs in effectively designed collaborative learning situations. As **group participants**, students can build upon one another's skills, abilities, and experiences to solve problems, explore new information, and understand new perspectives to enhance the overall learning experience. When students are learning new skills, behaviors, or thought processes, they often adopt the role of the observer. Modeling is an influential instructional strategy. In **observing** the teacher or another more experienced individual, students learn to utilize and implement new information in learning situations.

Gardner's Theory of Multiple Intelligences

When determining instruction, activities, and assessment, teachers must consider and incorporate students' various approaches to learning. Every student learns differently and has unique needs, so teachers must ensure that auditory, visual, kinesthetic, and tactile learning styles are addressed in all areas of curriculum to maximize students' learning potential. Through incorporating multiple modalities using Howard Gardner's **theory of multiple intelligences** as a framework, teachers can design content and activities that deliver instruction in a variety of ways simultaneously (visual-spatial, linguistic, musical, naturalistic, interpersonal, intrapersonal, logical-mathematical, bodily-kinesthetic). Through this approach, student understanding is reinforced, and each student is provided the opportunity to learn in the way that best suits their individual needs. By differentiating instruction with these modalities, teachers can incorporate several strategies simultaneously when teaching a concept, such as independent practice, cooperative learning, music, art, problem solving, and movement. Opportunities for student choice in learning further allows the integration of multiple modalities in instruction, as it lets students decide the method of learning that is best tailored to their individual learning style and needs.

Review Video: Teaching Through Multiple Modalities
Visit mometrix.com/academy and enter code: 100371

Howard Gardner's Theory of Multiple Intelligences

Visual/Spatial	Prefers visual representations, able to visualize with the mind's eye, excels in activities that incorporate drawing, building, creative expression, and manipulatives.
Logical-Mathematical	Prefers activities that require order, analysis, and problem-solving using logical reasoning. Excels in solving math equations, conducting science experiments, puzzles, and analyzing data.
Verbal-Linguistic	Prefers learning through reading, writing, speaking, and listening. Often skilled in acquiring foreign languages. Excels in activities that incorporate discussion, debate, oral presentations, and written assignments.
Bodily-Kinesthetic	Prefers hands-on learning experiences that involve movement and physical interaction with the learning environment. Excels in activities that involve sports, dance, building, and hands-on projects.
Interpersonal	Prefers learning opportunities that involve communicating and collaborating with others. Excels in partner, small group, and whole group learning activities.
Intrapersonal	Prefers to learn and work independently. Usually possesses a strong sense of self-awareness. Excels in activities that allow for independent, self-paced learning and self-reflection.
Musical	Learns best when music is incorporated into instruction. Prefers using songs, mnemonic devices, and rhythms to learn concepts and retain information.
Naturalistic	Learns best when opportunities to connect with nature are incorporated into instruction. Prefers activities such as nature walks, identifying and classifying elements of nature, and working outside.

MULTIPLE LITERACIES

Multiple literacies are part of modern learning and business. To be successful, people must effectively process and share different types of information using **multiple forms of media**. Teachers must devote instructional time to teaching students the skills they need to succeed in this technology-rich environment.

Teaching multiple literacies requires a mixture of explicit instruction, guided practice, and opportunities for application. For example, teachers need to teach students to find supporting details in digital texts. They may explicitly teach this skill during mini lessons by modeling how they highlight key phrases. Teachers may then ask students to highlight key phrases in digital texts independently while they observe and provide feedback. Students may then be given multiple opportunities to apply this skill throughout the year to complete projects and assignments.

Teachers should also provide opportunities for students to interact with texts of all types and communicate using different media. They can offer choices in projects and assignments as long as instructional objectives are met. This method allows students to pursue their own interests and leads to increased engagement and ownership over learning.

CHARACTERISTICS OF AUDITORY LEARNERS

Auditory learners easily gather and process information through listening. For example, they may determine main ideas from lectures, assess subtle details from speakers' tones during conversations, and follow oral directions to complete multistep tasks. Auditory learners often enjoy speaking as well, and they may frequently participate in class discussions and conversations.

Teachers can implement many instructional strategies to support auditory learners. They can incorporate read-alouds, discussions, and lectures into classroom activities. They can provide audio versions of textbooks and storybooks. They can also record lectures so that students can listen to them later to prepare for assignments and assessments. Teachers can allow students to interview others to gather information, and they can introduce songs, chants, and rhymes to assist with memorization. When designing projects and assessments, teachers can allow students to complete oral reports or presentations. Additionally, they can allow students to think through problems out loud and offer verbal feedback. Directions can also be given orally.

Characteristics of Visual Learners

Visual learners easily gather and process information by observing. They may learn by seeing written words, photographs, models, or any other visual representations of information. For example, they may locate words signaling the main ideas of written texts, summarize events detailed in illustrations, or complete new tasks after seeing the steps modeled.

Teachers can implement many instructional strategies to support visual learners. They can encourage visual learners to take notes when reading new texts or learning new concepts. Notes can consist of words, pictures, or combinations of both. Teachers can also provide written directions to complete tasks, or they can visually model the steps. Additionally, teachers can use photos, realistic objects, diagrams, and other visual materials when introducing new concepts to learners. They can provide graphic organizers to help learners visualize the connections among concepts. When reading aloud, teachers can also share and discuss the illustrations. When teachers are designing projects and assessments, they can allow students to present their learning through multimedia presentations, models, or other visual means.

Characteristics of Kinesthetic Learners

Kinesthetic learners learn best by doing. They benefit from watching people model how to do things and being given opportunities to do things themselves. They also benefit from opportunities to be active within the classroom.

Teachers can implement many instructional strategies to support kinesthetic learners. They can consider active ways for students to learn and practice new concepts. For example, first-grade students can trace sight words in chalk and hop along the letters, helping them memorize the spellings. Students of all ages can complete science experiments that allow them to mix, measure, and complete other scientific tasks. During math lessons on comparing and ordering numbers, students can form human number lines and discuss the processes they used.

Classroom arrangements and routines are also important for kinesthetic learners. Teachers can consider flexible seating arrangements and opportunities to move throughout the classroom to accommodate these students' needs.

Characteristics of Tactile Learners

Tactile learning is sometimes viewed as a synonym of kinesthetic learning, but there are some key differences. Kinesthetic learning refers to active learning by doing, and **tactile learning** refers to learning through **physical touch**. Tactile learners benefit from frequent opportunities to feel and manipulate items during instruction.

Teachers can implement many instructional strategies to support tactile learners. For example, early childhood students can trace letter cards made of different textures. Students can be given opportunities to spell words in rice, sand, or other textured materials. Manipulating letter tiles can also be used during word work activities. When completing science activities, students can feel objects and describe their textures. During math activities, students can use manipulatives to explore concepts and solve problems. When teachers are designing projects and assessments, they can also allow students to present their learning using models constructed from types of artistic materials.

Using Instructional Strategies That Address All Learning Modalities

Teachers should consider all learning modalities and accommodate auditory, visual, kinesthetic, and tactile learners within the classroom. This is important for several reasons, including the possibility that each student may display preferences for multiple modalities. Additionally, students can benefit from having information presented in multiple ways. For example, students may learn how to complete new tasks by watching their teachers model the steps; however, if given opportunities to practice the steps themselves, students may be better able to remember and apply them in the future.

Teachers need to consider the specifics of each concept they are teaching when determining which **modalities** to address during instruction. For example, it is difficult to teach letter formation using only oral directions. Students benefit from seeing the process teachers use to form each letter and from having opportunities to practice forming the letters independently. When teaching rhyming, auditory instruction is important. All modalities play a role in learning.

Classrooms are also made up of **diverse students** who prefer different modalities. To meet the needs of all learners, teachers can offer instructional choices and present information in multiple ways. For example, teachers can offer print and auditory versions of texts. Directions can be provided in written form and spoken verbally. Teachers can also offer project choices that allow students to present their learning in oral, written, or visual form.

Role of Play in Learning and Development

Characteristics of the Developmental Play Stages

As children develop, so do their styles of play. Developmental play stages are divided into five primary phases: **solitary play** (birth–2 years), **onlooker play** (2 years), **parallel play** (2–3 years), **associative play** (3–4 years), and **cooperative play** (4 years and beyond). During the **solitary play** stage, children play alone and are uninterested in playing with others or what other children around them are doing. When they reach the **onlooker play** stage, children will watch other children play but will not actively engage in playing with others. In **parallel play**, children do not play with one another but will often play next to each other and will use similar materials. They may be curious about what other children are doing and may copy them. Children begin to intentionally play with others in the **associative play** stage, but the play is unorganized and still largely individual in its goals. In **cooperative play**, children begin to intentionally play and share materials in organized groups, often with a common purpose or goal when playing.

Parallel Play

Cooperative Play

Purposes and Benefits of Play in Early Childhood Education

Purposeful play is an integral part of learning and development in the early childhood classroom. Its purpose is to aid and allow children to incorporate all aspects of development and thus provides cognitive, social, emotional, and physical benefits. Purposeful play deepens children's understanding of new concepts through allowing them to explore and experiment in the world around them using imagination and creativity. Integrating purposeful play into the early childhood classroom is beneficial because it allows children to construct and build on knowledge through experiences and helps develop divergent and convergent thinking.

The socialization children get from play strengthens their language skills through speaking to one another, using new vocabulary, and listening to others. Purposeful play strengthens physical-motor development, as it calls for children to move their bodies in games, running, jumping, etc. Play is necessary for building important emotional and social skills that are necessary for being a successful member of society later in life.

Diverse Student Populations

Understanding Students' Diverse Backgrounds and Needs

Self-Education

Educating oneself on students' diverse backgrounds and needs enhances one's overall understanding of their students and creates a culturally sensitive, accepting classroom environment tailored to students' individual needs. There are several avenues through which teachers should educate themselves in an effort to build an accepting and respectful classroom climate. Communication is key for learning about diversities; thus, it is important for teachers to foster and maintain positive communications with students' families to deepen understanding of cultures, beliefs, lifestyles, and needs that exist within their classrooms. This could include learning some language of students with different cultural backgrounds, attending family nights at school, or participating in social events within their students' communities to integrate themselves into the culture. Furthermore, teachers can learn more about their students' backgrounds and needs through gaining an understanding of student differences, incorporating these diversities into the curriculum, and encouraging students to participate in learning by sharing aspects of their lives with the class.

Teaching, Learning, and Classroom Climate Benefits

A deep understanding of students' diverse backgrounds and needs provides multiple benefits for teaching, learning, and overall classroom climate. Knowledge of students' diversities allows teachers to understand the individual needs and abilities of their students and tailor instruction accordingly to maximize student development and achievement. Additionally, it allows teachers to know which authentic materials to incorporate in lessons and instructions to best create an engaging, relevant, and respectful learning experience that fosters student interest in learning and promotes success. Furthermore, by enhancing understanding of students' diverse backgrounds and needs, teachers consequently begin to model an attitude of inclusivity, acceptance, and respect for differences, which is then reflected by students and achieves a positive, welcoming classroom climate that promotes diversity.

Implications for Teaching, Learning, and Assessment in Diverse Classrooms

In any classroom, a teacher will encounter a wide range of variances among individual students that inevitably will influence teaching, learning, and assessment. Diversities in ethnicity, gender, language background, and learning exceptionality will likely exist simultaneously in a single classroom. Educators must be prepared to teach to these diversities while concurrently teaching students the value and importance of diversity. The curriculum and classroom environment must be adjusted to meet individual student needs and create an **inclusive**, **respectful**, and **equitable** environment that welcomes differences and allows for success in learning. This begins with the teacher developing an understanding of the unique diversities that exist within their students and using this knowledge to **differentiate** curriculum, materials, activities, and assessments in such a way that students of all needs, interests, backgrounds, and abilities feel encouraged and included. Furthermore, the teacher must understand how to instill appropriate supports to accommodate the diverse needs of students and how to modify the classroom environment in such a way that is reflective of the diversity of the students.

Considerations for Teaching in Diverse Classrooms

Ethnically Diverse Classrooms

As society becomes increasingly diverse, teachers will certainly encounter classrooms with students of multiple ethnicities. Thus, to create an accepting and respectful classroom environment that allows for success in learning for all students, there are several factors to consider. Teachers must educate themselves on the various ethnicities within their classroom. This includes being mindful of the **social norms, values, beliefs, traditions,** and **lifestyles** of different ethnic groups and learning to communicate with students and families in a respectful, culturally sensitive manner. Additionally, teachers must make a conscious effort to incorporate aspects of each ethnicity into the curriculum, activities, and classroom environment to create an inclusive atmosphere that teaches the acceptance, respect for, and celebration of differences. Teachers must be **culturally competent** and ensure that all materials are accurate, relevant, authentic, and portray the different ethnicities within the classroom in a respectful, unbiased manner. Furthermore, teachers must consider how their own ethnicity impacts their teaching style and interactions with students, how they may be perceived by other ethnic groups, and how to respond in a manner that fosters respect and inclusivity.

Gender-Diverse Classrooms

When approaching a gender-diverse classroom, teachers need to consider their perceptions and expectations of different genders as well as their interactions with different genders. Teachers should also consider how the classroom environment and materials portray gender differences. Teachers must work to eliminate possible stereotypical beliefs so that all students feel respected, accepted, and encouraged to participate. Furthermore, teachers must consider how their behavior acts as a model for how students perceive gender roles and should act in a way that eliminates gender divisiveness. Teachers should use gender-neutral language when addressing students and ensure that all students receive equal attention. Teachers must maintain equal academic and behavioral expectations between genders and be sure to equally praise and discipline students so that neither gender feels superior or inferior to another. Regarding curriculum and classroom materials, teachers must ensure that the classroom environment encourages equal participation in, access to, and choice of all activities and procedures. Activities and materials should provide equal opportunities and foster collaboration between genders. Furthermore, teachers must ensure that curriculum materials avoid gender stereotypes and highlight each gender equally in order to create an accepting and respectful learning environment that provides equal opportunities for students of all genders to develop their individual identities and abilities.

Linguistically Diverse Classrooms

In a **linguistically diverse** classroom, teachers must consider how to effectively demonstrate value for students' native languages while simultaneously supporting the development of necessary language skills to thrive in the school setting. By accepting and encouraging students to use their native languages, teachers can establish an inclusive learning environment that celebrates linguistic differences and encourages students to want to build upon their language skills. Through this, teachers create an equitable learning environment that allows for academic success. To develop English language skills, teachers must first consider each student's language ability, level of exposure to English prior to entering the classroom, and the level of language learning support each student has at home. Teachers can then implement effective instructional strategies and supports to modify curriculum in a way that addresses students' language needs. Teachers must also consider the implications of the classroom environment on language acquisition. By creating an atmosphere that encourages language acquisition through **literacy-rich resources** and **cooperative learning**, teachers promote the use of language skills and ultimately provide opportunities for success for all students.

Linguistic Supports and Instructional Strategies for English Language Proficiency

Incorporating a variety of linguistic aids and instructional strategies is beneficial in supporting ELL students of varying levels of English language proficiency. **Visual representations** to accompany instruction, such as posters, charts, pictures, slide shows, videos, tables, or anchor charts, are valuable in providing clarification and reference while promoting vocabulary acquisition. When delivering instruction, **body language** such as hand gestures, eye contact, and movement to mimic verbal directions and explanations can provide clarification to enhance understanding. These students may also require **translation devices** for clarification, an interpreter to help with understanding instructions and new concepts, alternate assignments with simplified language, or **individualized instruction** from an ESL teacher. Frequently checking for understanding and providing clarification as necessary throughout instruction are necessary to ensuring ELL students understand learning materials, instructions, and assessments. In addition, creating a print- and literacy-rich environment is valuable in promoting English language acquisition. This can be done by including word walls for new vocabulary, reading materials that vary in complexity, labels, and opportunities for speaking, reading, and writing within instruction.

LEARNING DISABILITIES AND OTHER EXCEPTIONALITIES

In a classroom where learning disabilities and exceptionalities are present, teachers must consider accommodations for students of various learning needs while fostering an atmosphere of respect and acceptance. Teachers must understand the individual learning needs of each student and differentiate instruction accordingly to create an equitable and inclusive learning atmosphere. For **learning disabled** students, teachers must consider accommodations that allow for inclusion in all areas of curriculum and instruction. Such considerations may include extended work time, individualized instruction, and cooperative learning activities to ensure that learning disabled students are provided the necessary supports to achieve academic success. For students with other exceptionalities, such as **gifted and talented** students, teachers need to consider ways to provide challenging and stimulating opportunities for expansion and enrichment of curriculum. Furthermore, teachers must be aware of their own interactions with students in order to demonstrate and encourage respect and acceptance among students. By providing supports for individual student success, teachers can effectively highlight students' strengths and teach students to accept and celebrate differences in learning abilities.

Educating Students about Diversity

GOALS OF TEACHING DIVERSITY IN THE CLASSROOM

Teaching diversity in the classroom aims to establish a welcoming and inclusive classroom environment that encourages academic achievement and whole-child development. Diversity education works to develop students' understanding, acceptance, and respect for others' perspectives while instilling the concept that people are ultimately more alike than different and that diversity should be celebrated. Teaching the importance of differences creates a positive, inclusive classroom atmosphere in which all students feel respected, safe, and valued by their teacher and peers. Such an environment promotes academic achievement among students in that it encourages participation in learning and builds the self-esteem necessary for positive growth and development. Furthermore, teaching diversity has a significant role in **whole-child development** in that it instills the ability to understand and respect multiple frames of reference, thus increasing the child's ability to problem solve, cooperate with others, and develop a broader global perspective. Additionally, it allows for the development of cultural competency and ultimately creates accepting and respectful contributors to society.

Review Video: Multiculturalism/Celebrating All Cultures
Visit mometrix.com/academy and enter code: 708545

RECOGNIZING AND ELIMINATING PERSONAL BIASES

Personal biases are often subtle and unconscious, yet it is essential that teachers work to recognize and eliminate them to create an accepting and respectful classroom environment. Personal biases may negatively impact teaching style, interactions with students, student learning, and self-esteem. In eliminating personal bias, teachers ensure that they establish an inclusive classroom environment where each student is treated fairly. Furthermore, students' beliefs toward diversity are influenced by the attitudes and behaviors modeled by their teacher; therefore, eradicating personal bias is vital in positively influencing students to accept and respect differences. To eliminate personal bias, teachers must **reflect** on their own culture's attitudes toward diversity as well as how these attitudes influence their interactions toward other groups, and work to make positive changes. Teachers must **educate** themselves on the diversities among their students and work to deepen their understanding of different groups through **communicating** with families, **integrating** themselves into students' communities, and participating in **professional development** that focuses on **cultural competency** and the importance of teaching diversity. Through making positive changes against personal biases, teachers foster a classroom environment that promotes diversity and empowers all students to be successful.

Impact of Diverse Cultural Climate in the Classroom

Creating a diverse cultural climate in the classroom results in an empowering and engaging learning environment that facilitates academic success. An atmosphere that respects and accepts differences fosters a sense of inclusivity and welcoming among teachers and students, which allows students to feel comfortable with differences, safe in their own identities, and comfortable to engage in learning. This fosters a positive attitude toward learning that promotes academic achievement. Additionally, when students accept one another's differences in a diverse cultural climate, they are better able to work together and adopt creative problem-solving solutions through others' perspectives, which results in success in learning. Furthermore, a successfully diverse cultural climate reflects the diversity of the students within it, which ultimately creates a more engaging and relevant academic environment that sparks motivation and curiosity toward learning. Learning environments that reflect students' diversity create a sense of unity and belonging in the classroom and positively contribute to success in learning through building students' self-esteem and self-concept to empower them in believing they can achieve academic success.

Authentic Classroom Materials

Authentic classroom materials are artifacts from various cultures, events, or periods of time. These items enhance the relevancy of instruction by promoting students' real-world connection to learning and may also be used to incorporate students' backgrounds and experiences into the classroom to increase engagement. Such materials include magazines, newspapers, advertisements, restaurant menus, and recipes. In addition, resources such as video clips, films, television shows, documentaries, news segments, and music serve as authentic media sources to incorporate into instruction. Original works or documents, including art pieces, literature, poetry, maps, or historical records, are also valuable authentic resources for providing students with a real-world learning experience.

Locating and Implementing

Authentic classroom materials and resources are integral in creating a classroom environment that fosters engaging, relevant, and positive learning experiences. Teachers must work to develop an understanding of the diversities among their students and use this knowledge to locate and implement authentic classroom materials into daily instruction. In doing so, teachers create a positive learning environment that accepts and respects differences through incorporating **relevant** and **familiar** materials that make students from all backgrounds feel valued and included in instruction. When students can see aspects of their culture reflected in authentic learning materials, they can make **personal connections** between what they are learning and their own lives. This makes learning become more valuable, engaging, and relevant, thereby promoting success in learning.

Incorporating Diversity Education into the Classroom

Incorporating diversity into the classroom maximizes student opportunities for academic success through creating a welcoming, empowering, and inclusive atmosphere. Teachers can implement multiple strategies to incorporate **diversity education** into the curriculum both as its own unit and woven into content instruction once they develop an understanding of the diversities among their own students. Through **building relationships** with students, teachers can use their knowledge of students' lives to incorporate aspects of their backgrounds into the curriculum by creating specific **cultural lessons** on food, music, language, art, and history. Additionally, **cultural comparison** studies are an effective method of teaching students the value of diversity and highlighting the fact that people from different backgrounds often have more similarities than differences. Teachers can further implement diversity education by encouraging students to participate in learning through having them share elements of their culture and background with the class through activities such as show and tell or hosting family nights. Furthermore, integrating **cooperative learning** activities into instruction allows and encourages students from different backgrounds to work together and gain an understanding of the perspectives and backgrounds of others.

Incorporating Diversity in the Curriculum

Incorporating diversity into the curriculum is vital for teaching the value and importance of differences and for contributing to a respectful and accepting environment. Additionally, it is imperative that diversity education extend from the curriculum to the entire classroom environment to maximize student growth and opportunity to reach potential. When students learn in an atmosphere that celebrates diversity and identifies strengths in differences, they feel a sense of belonging and confidence that encourages them to engage in learning, thus maximizing the potential for academic success. Teachers can effectively integrate diversity into the classroom environment through making authentic cultural materials such as texts, music, and art readily accessible for students. Additionally, providing several opportunities for students to collaborate and socialize in a natural setting allows them to gain an understanding and respect for their peers' backgrounds. By encouraging students to share aspects of their own lives and backgrounds with the class through cultural activities, teachers facilitate a diverse climate that celebrates differences.

Culturally Responsive Teaching

Culturally responsive teaching is an instructional approach in which the teacher practices awareness, inclusivity, and sensitivity regarding the social and cultural diversities that are present within the classroom. With this awareness in mind, the culturally responsive teacher designs curriculum, instruction, activities, and assessments that are inclusive and reflective of students' social and cultural backgrounds and experiences. When planning instruction and learning experiences, teachers can demonstrate awareness of social and cultural norms through consciously educating themselves on the beliefs, values, and norms of their students. This is achieved through connecting with students and building positive relationships to learn about their individual backgrounds and locate authentic learning materials that are reflective of their experiences. Through communicating with students' parents, family members, and members of the community, teachers can practice and build awareness of the diverse social and cultural norms of their students to gain an understanding of how to design culturally responsive instruction. By educating themselves on the social and cultural norms of their students, teachers can effectively ensure that students' diversities are reflected in all areas of instruction in a culturally sensitive manner to create an empowering learning environment that engages all students.

Practices for Culturally Responsive Teaching	
1	Create an inclusive classroom environment.
2	Recognize personal biases and work to eliminate them.
3	Self-educate on the community and students' social and cultural backgrounds.
4	Use curriculum that reflects students' diversities using authentic materials.
5	Frequently communicate with students' families.
6	Build positive interpersonal relationships with students.
7	Be involved in the community.

Supporting Students with Varied Learning Needs

Planning and Adapting Lessons to Address Students' Needs

Varied Backgrounds

Effectively planning lessons and adapting instruction to address students' varied backgrounds requires teachers to gain an understanding of individual students and educate themselves on **customs, norms**, and **values** of the cultures in their classrooms. This allows teachers to effectively plan **culturally responsive** lessons with **authentic materials** to make learning valuable, interesting, and relevant and to allow students to feel included. Understanding students' backgrounds means teachers recognize variances in their knowledge and experiences on different topics and can effectively plan engaging and inclusive lessons that build upon it. Teachers must assess students' knowledge on material prior to creating lessons to effectively plan instruction that adapts to the needs of students' varied backgrounds and reflects students' experiences. Teachers must plan lesson materials such as texts, art, music, and language that accurately and sensitively reflect students' diverse backgrounds. Cooperative learning strategies should be incorporated to facilitate communication among students with varying backgrounds, as doing so helps them build knowledge from others' experiences and teaches them to respect and value differences among their peers. Teachers must plan instruction that communicates high academic expectations for all students and adapt instruction as necessary by implementing supports to create equity and address the needs of varying backgrounds.

Review Video: Adapting and Modifying Lessons or Activities
Visit mometrix.com/academy and enter code: 834946

Differences in Individual Students' Skills

Teachers must use their knowledge of differences in students' skills to plan multifaceted, adaptable lessons that highlight students' strengths while providing instructional supports where needed based on individual skill level. To effectively plan, teachers must incorporate multiple strategies and mediums for instruction, activities, and assessments to allow students of all skill levels equitable and enriching access to content material. This includes allowing multiple opportunities for **student choice** in learning and demonstration of understanding through strategies that allow students to approach content in multiple ways, such as choice boards, learning centers, project menus, and digital resources. In doing so, teachers effectively plan instruction that allows students to grasp new material and demonstrate learning in a way that best suits their skill level. Additionally, teachers must plan to incorporate **scaffolds** into their lessons and plan to adapt instruction as needed through continuous **formative assessments** to provide additional support for students of lower skill levels while adding opportunities for enrichment and acceleration for gifted students. Supports can also be effectively planned into lessons through providing several opportunities for small-group activities in which students of various skill levels can work together, provide peer tutoring, and build upon one another's knowledge.

Differences in Students' Individual Interests

In order to plan engaging instruction that fosters success in learning, teachers must plan lessons and adapt instruction to address differences in students' individual interests. To accomplish this, teachers first need to work to build relationships with students and develop an understanding of their unique interests to effectively tailor instruction that taps into these interests. Through **differentiated instruction** and the incorporation of **student-choice** opportunities for learning and assessment, teachers can effectively plan **student-centered** lessons that teach content in multiple ways that appeal to varying interests. Additionally, interest centers in the classroom foster engagement in learning, are easily adaptable, and can be planned into daily instruction. By frequently conducting **formative assessments**, teachers can gauge student interest in activities and adjust as necessary. This ultimately promotes self-direction, motivation, and curiosity in learning through providing students the opportunity to build content knowledge based on their individual interests.

Differences in Students' Individual Learning Needs

Differences in backgrounds, abilities, skills, and interests results in a wide spectrum of student learning needs that must be addressed when planning effective and adaptable instruction. Teachers must recognize the individual learning needs of students to plan lessons that are accommodating, equitable, and promote success in learning. Through **student-centered** and **differentiated** instruction, teachers can effectively provide multiple avenues for content instruction, learning, and assessment based on individual need. Planning for **student-choice** and **self-directed learning** allows teachers to successfully address all learning styles and needs. Additionally, teachers must incorporate scaffolds into their lessons to adapt instruction. This can be done through incorporating such supports as graphic organizers, outlines, charts, and visuals, as well as planning for small, mixed-ability group instruction based on learning needs to provide scaffolding. Teachers should plan to check frequently for understanding during instruction in order to adapt activities and adjust instruction to meet individual learning needs.

ELL Students

English language learners (ELLs) need support in both understanding content material and building their English proficiency levels. To effectively plan and adapt instruction to accommodate them and facilitate success in learning, it is important that teachers demonstrate respect for the student's native language while encouraging the acquisition of English language skills. Teachers should plan for some content instruction to be in the student's native language to begin to build knowledge. To effectively assist ELLs in building vocabulary on specific content areas, lessons should be planned around **themed units**. Additionally, planning multiple cooperative learning and peer-tutoring activities allows ELLs to practice and develop their English skills in a natural setting and provides support for understanding new instructional concepts. Teachers must plan to scaffold content material, texts, and writing assignments to align with students' proficiency levels through adding supports like graphic organizers, labels, and charts. Incorporating **linguistic aids**, such as verbal cues, gestures, pictures, and digital resources, allows teachers to effectively adapt instruction as necessary to support understanding and develop English language skills.

Students with Disabilities

Students with disabilities may require **instructional or physical supports** in order to have an equitable learning experience that facilitates their academic success. Teachers must be cognizant of any student disabilities and work to effectively plan instruction in a subtle, sensitive, and inclusive manner. Students with learning disabilities may require the planning of supports such as preferential seating, extra time for work and assessments, graphic organizers, and shorter or chunked assignments. These students may need to be paired with others who can provide scaffolding and peer-tutoring or may require individualized instruction or small, focused groups. Students with physical disabilities may require supports such as modified classroom environments to address their physical needs, audiovisual supplements, enlarged font, or braille texts. Teachers must work to incorporate these supports into their lesson planning to ensure that all students are included and empowered to learn while allowing for flexibility in their lesson plans to allow for necessary adaptations.

Cultural and Socioeconomic Differences

Addressing Differences in an Inclusive and Equitable Classroom Environment

In a **culturally responsive** classroom, the teacher recognizes and is sensitive to the importance of planning instruction that addresses cultural and socioeconomic differences among students for creating an **inclusive** and **equitable** learning environment. The teacher responds to differences in norms, values, interests, and lifestyles through designing relevant instruction that builds on students' experiences and facilitates personal connections that foster engagement in learning. This is important in conveying to students the value of their diverse experiences and highlighting their strengths in a manner that empowers them to achieve academic success while providing support where needed. It is important that the teacher incorporate supports in instructional planning to address academic, social, behavioral, and emotional needs of students from different cultural and socioeconomic backgrounds to provide all students an equitable opportunity for success in learning while maintaining high academic expectations.

Possible Impacts on Academic Achievement

If not properly addressed, cultural and socioeconomic differences among students pose potentially negative impacts on academic achievement. It is vital that teachers recognize and accommodate these differences to instill the proper supports for engagement and success in learning. Students from different cultural or socioeconomic backgrounds may feel excluded from curriculum and instruction, which may result in lowered self-concept, self-esteem, and disengagement toward learning. Thus, teachers must practice **culturally responsive teaching** to create instruction in which all students feel valued and included. Students from different cultural or socioeconomic backgrounds may lack the support or resources for education at home due to various cultural and social challenges, and students from low socioeconomic backgrounds may face health, behavioral, or emotional challenges that impact their development and ability to learn. It is important that the teacher recognize these challenges and subtly address them in the classroom to establish an inclusive, equitable, and empowering environment that fosters engagement in learning. Some strategies for addressing these differences include providing community classroom materials, extra time for tutoring and assistance outside of classroom hours, individualized instruction, or opportunities to use the internet at school for students who lack access at home.

Significance of Varied Student Learning Needs and Preferences

Implications on Instruction

Variances in students' learning needs and preferences implies that instruction must be **differentiated**, flexible, and allow for adaptations as necessary to accommodate students' individual needs, abilities, and interests. Furthermore, it means that teachers must work to build relationships with their students to develop an understanding of their different needs and preferences. This allows teachers to design instruction that emphasizes individual strengths while challenging students academically based on their abilities and providing instructional supports where necessary to ensure student success. To accomplish this, teachers must plan and deliver instructional material in multiple ways to address differences in learning needs and preferences as well as allow for student choice in learning, processing, and demonstrating understanding of content.

Review Video: Differentiated Instruction
Visit mometrix.com/academy and enter code: 100342

Possible Variances That May Be Encountered

Teachers will inevitably encounter an array of learning needs and preferences among their students. As students have varying **learning styles**, including visual, auditory, or kinesthetic, their methods for acquiring, processing, and retaining information will differ along with their **preferred modalities** for doing so. Some students may prefer written assignments in which they work independently, while others may prefer activities that involve active movement within a group. Similarly, some students require more individualized attention, while others may function better in a small group or whole-class setting. Students will also come to the classroom with differing **academic abilities** and will require varying levels of assistance, support, and guidance to facilitate their success in learning. In addition, students may have specific learning, physical, social, or emotional **disabilities** and will need varying degrees of support and accommodations to learn effectively.

Importance of Tailoring Curriculum, Instruction, and Assessments

Through tailoring curriculum, instruction, and assessments according to student learning needs and preferences, teachers create a **student-centered** learning environment. This motivates and empowers students to take ownership of their learning and allows every student an equal opportunity to achieve academic success. By creating a flexible curriculum and presenting instruction through multiple methods, teachers ensure that the learning needs and preferences of all students are met by facilitating a dynamic and engaging learning environment in which students can learn in the way that best suits their needs. Furthermore, in adapting assessments based upon students' learning needs and preferences by allowing **student choice**, teachers maximize student understanding of content material, allowing them to demonstrate learning according to their interests and abilities.

Teaching English Language Learners

English Language Learners

Characteristics and Needs of Language Proficiency Levels

The term ***English language learner*** **(ELL)** refers to students acquiring English as a second language and consists of beginner, intermediate, and advanced levels of English language proficiency. Each proficiency level is determined by specific characteristics and requires differing linguistic supports across listening, speaking, reading, and writing domains. **Beginning** ELLs have little or no ability to understand the English language across domains and rely heavily on linguistic aids such as visual representations, gestures, verbal cues, and environmental print. These students communicate through memorized high-frequency words or phrases and often require individualized instruction. **Intermediate** ELLs have acquired some foundational knowledge on the English language and can communicate with increasing complexity. They are generally able to understand, speak, read, and write in short, simple sentences and follow clear, routine directions. These students are able to seek clarification for misunderstandings but continue to require linguistic supports such as repetition, slowed speech, visual representations, and body language. **Advanced** ELL students are generally able to understand and utilize the English language with minimal error and often do not require extensive linguistic support outside of occasional repetition or clarification. Their proficiency is comparable to that of their native English-speaking peers. Language proficiency lies on a fluid spectrum and does not allow for perfect classification of different skill levels. Certain scales also include more or fewer descriptors for the different levels.

Acquiring Listening and Speaking Skills

The acquisition of **listening** and **speaking** skills are interrelated and often are the first two domains in which English language proficiency is developed. As ELLs hear and observe teachers modeling proper speech and active listening, they begin acquiring listening skills. Additionally, listening to and observing classmates is integral for the development of listening and speaking skills. By watching and imitating their peers, ELLs build understanding of the nuances of the English language in different settings. When words and phrases heard are linked to a particular action or event, the ELL derives meaning and can utilize the newly acquired vocabulary, thus developing listening and speaking skills simultaneously. The development of listening and speaking skills is enhanced in a **language-rich environment** in which students are provided multiple opportunities to practice and develop their skills in a natural setting; therefore, the teacher must include opportunities for ELLs to speak, actively listen, and work collaboratively. Language-rich environments can be created by incorporating materials such as songs, games, stories, and digital media, which allow ELLs to attach meaning to new vocabulary to build proficiency.

Acquiring Reading and Writing Skills

The acquisition of listening and speaking skills in English provides the foundation for developing **reading** and **writing** skills. Reading and writing abilities develop in relation to one another, as when students begin acquiring reading skills, they learn to attach meaning to vocabulary and texts that enable them to express themselves in writing. The development of reading skills begins with understanding simple, high-frequency vocabulary and simple sentence structures as a foundation, building upon this knowledge with increasingly complex vocabulary and sentence structures. Similarly, writing ability increases in complexity from basic labels, lists, and copying and develops into expression though simple sentences on familiar topics and complex writing abilities that employ higher-order thinking on abstract concepts. Reading and writing skill development is enhanced through consistent practice in a **print-** and **literacy-rich** environment. Students should be provided with multiple opportunities for reading and expressing themselves through writing throughout instruction. Reading materials with varying levels of complexity should be readily available for students, and literacy development must be incorporated into all subject areas to build vocabulary and comprehension.

Review Video: Stages of Reading Development
Visit mometrix.com/academy and enter code: 121184

Review Video: Grammar Skills and Reading Comprehension
Visit mometrix.com/academy and enter code: 411287

Print- and Literacy-Rich Learning Environment

A print- and literacy-rich learning environment is beneficial for providing an **immersive** experience that promotes the development of students' reading, writing, speaking, and listening skills. Such an environment typically incorporates a variety of learning resources and strategies to encourage literacy. The walls are often decorated with a variety of print materials, such as posters, captions, word walls with high-frequency or thematic vocabulary words, signs, labels, bulletin boards, and anchor charts. Students are provided with authentic printed and digital literacy materials, such as newspapers, magazines, shopping advertisements, video clips, songs, and documentaries to increase relevancy and personal connections. A print and literacy-rich classroom also includes a class library that offers texts of varying genres, formats, and levels of complexity. Learning activities provide multiple opportunities to develop literacy skills in a natural setting, such as opportunities for collaborative learning, self-selected reading, and free-write sessions.

Review Video: Print Awareness and Alphabet Knowledge
Visit mometrix.com/academy and enter code: 541069

Components of Language

All languages include syntax, semantics, morphology, phonology, and pragmatics.

- **Syntax** refers to the structure and arrangement of words within a sentence, which controls the functions of grammar.
- **Semantics** refers to how language conveys meaning.
- **Morphology** refers to how words are constructed of smaller parts, such as root words, prefixes, and suffixes.
- **Phonology** refers to how words are pronounced.
- **Pragmatics** refers to the practical, social applications of language and its use in the real world, including non-verbal communication.

These components heavily overlap with one another. For instance, morphology is heavily involved in constructing the meaning of a word, which largely falls under the category of semantics, and without a logical ordering of the words in a sentence (syntax), the sentence could mean something completely different or be altogether incoherent. Each of these systems needs to be well-established for communication in English or any other language. Some of these components, such as morphology, can be particularly targeted to support content-based instruction. For instance, a teacher might work on prefixes and root words that commonly occur in science, such as bio-, geo-, tele-, -logy, -scope, and -graphy.

English Language Proficiency for Listening and Speaking

Descriptors for English Language Proficiency for Each Ability Level

Development of English language proficiency is marked by descriptors for each ability level in listening and speaking. **Beginner** ELLs are highly limited or unable to understand or speak English in any setting. They have difficulty understanding and using simple vocabulary even with the help of linguistic aids and rely on single words for basic communication. Grammatically, they are unable to construct full sentences. **Intermediate** ELLs understand and speak using high-frequency English vocabulary on familiar topics and settings. They speak and understand short sentences and demonstrate a basic understanding of English grammatical patterns for constructing simple sentences but need linguistic aids for unfamiliar vocabulary. Additionally, they make several errors when communicating but can ask in English for clarification and are usually understood by those familiar with working with ELLs. **Advanced** ELLs can speak and understand grade-appropriate English with linguistic supports. They understand and participate in longer conversations about familiar and unfamiliar topics but may rely on linguistic aids, repetition, or clarification. These students still make some errors in communication but are often understood by people unfamiliar with working with ELLs. **Advanced high** ELLs require minimal linguistic support and can understand and speak English at a similar level to native English-speaking peers. Language proficiency lies on a fluid spectrum and does not allow for perfect classification of different skill levels. Certain scales also include more or fewer descriptors for the different levels. Some scales also include low-intermediate and proficient or natural/fluent as descriptive levels.

Teaching Students at Different Proficiency Levels

Teaching students with different proficiency levels for listening and speaking English implies that students will require varying degrees of linguistic support to develop their skills and provide them with an equitable learning environment. Specifically, students with lower proficiency levels in these areas will rely more on linguistic accommodations than students with more developed abilities. Teachers must be knowledgeable of the descriptors for each proficiency level to implement the proper supports and instructional strategies to address individual learning needs for developing listening and speaking skills in English. Instructional strategies should aim to promote the acquisition of skills through building background knowledge and providing context in multiple ways. This includes modeling proper speaking and listening skills and accompanying instruction with verbal cues, slower speech, repetition, gestures, and visual aids to improve student comprehension and build vocabulary. Additionally, incorporating several cooperative learning opportunities provides scaffolding and opportunities to practice and build upon listening and speaking abilities. Content instruction can be supported with the implementation of digital resources that promote the acquisition and development of listening and speaking skills and can be tailored to students' individual abilities.

Review Video: ESL/ESOL/Second Language Learning
Visit mometrix.com/academy and enter code: 795047

English Language Proficiency for Reading and Writing

Descriptors for English Language Proficiency at Each Ability Level

English language proficiency for ELLs is determined by descriptors for each ability level in reading and writing. **Beginning** ELLs possess little or no ability to read, understand, or write in English. Comprehension is restricted to single, familiar vocabulary words, and writing is limited to lists, labels, and vocabulary accompanied by pictures. These students rely heavily on linguistic supports for understanding, and their writing is unclear to those unfamiliar with working with ELLs. **Intermediate** ELLs can read, understand, and write short sentences and simple language structures on familiar material with the help of linguistic aids. They engage in writing assignments, but their writing contains errors and is unclear to those unfamiliar with working with ELLs. **Advanced** ELLs read, understand, and write using more expansive vocabulary and sentence structures with the help of linguistic accommodations. They may have difficulty with unfamiliar vocabulary but can read and write at a faster pace with increased accuracy. These students demonstrate more complex writing abilities, and their writing is usually understood by those unfamiliar with working with ELLs. **Advanced high** ELLs can read, understand, and write using grade-appropriate English with minimal linguistic support at a level similar to native English-speaking peers. Language proficiency lies on a fluid spectrum and does not allow for perfect classification of different skill levels. Certain scales also include more or fewer descriptors for the different levels. Some scales also include low-intermediate and proficient or natural/fluent as descriptive levels.

Teaching Students at Different Proficiency Levels

Teaching students with different proficiency levels for reading and writing English means linguistic accommodations in the classroom will need to be scaffolded to address the needs and abilities of individual students and promote the development of skills in these areas. Students with lower proficiency levels in reading and writing will require more linguistic aids than students with more developed abilities. Thus, the teacher must have a deep understanding both of individual student needs and of descriptors for proficiency at each level to effectively support students in their acquisition of reading and writing skills. Instructional strategies should foster the acquisition of these skills through providing several ways to allow students to build background knowledge and context to increase understanding. This includes creating a language-rich classroom environment that emphasizes the development of literacy skills in the form of environmental print, word walls and charts for new vocabulary and high-frequency words, labels, and visual aids. Reading materials on subject content should be available at each reading level. Additionally, the use of graphic organizers and outlines increases comprehension and writing ability through breaking information into smaller portions to provide scaffolding.

Creating Equitable Learning Environments for ELLs Using Linguistic Supports

To create an equitable learning environment, ELL students must be provided with linguistic supports that are applicable across content areas in order to ensure they are provided with an equal opportunity for success in learning. Teachers can implement varying supports appropriate to students' levels of English language proficiency that are beneficial in facilitating both English language and content-specific learning. Such supports include incorporating verbal cues, gestures, and visual representations into instruction to provide context and build background knowledge. The use of environmental print, word walls, and labels are also effective in supporting English language skills while simultaneously providing context for facilitating learning in the content area. Teachers should model speaking and listening skills and practice slow speech or repetition when necessary to ensure understanding. Scaffolding instruction and activities across content areas through supports such as graphic organizers, outlines, and cooperative learning opportunities serve to assist ELL students in building English language proficiency skills across content areas at a pace appropriate for their ability levels. By implementing the proper supports, teachers can effectively foster English language learning in all subject areas while ensuring that students simultaneously learn content-specific material.

Instructional Strategies for English Language Learning in All Subject Areas

Language acquisition occurs across content areas for ELL students, as each subject is composed of different vocabulary, grammatical patterns, and methods of expressing ideas. Thus, it is important that teachers provide these students with learning strategies that are applicable in all subject areas in order to effectively support English language acquisition and content-specific learning. Through a metacognitive approach, teachers can facilitate ELL students in thinking about how they learn, reflecting on their strengths and weaknesses, and applying useful learning strategies from one content area to another to develop their English language skills in all subjects. This strategy enhances learning through teaching students how to apply learning strategies from one instructional context to another when developing language skills. By activating students' prior knowledge when introducing new material in a given subject area, teachers promote English language learning through providing context and encouraging students to consider what they may already know about a new concept. Methods such as pre-teaching, anticipatory guides, graphic organizers, and brainstorming allow ELL students to make connections that build their language abilities across content areas.

Adapting Instruction for Varying Levels of English Language Proficiency

When encountering ELL students with varying English language skills, it is imperative to adapt instruction to accommodate these differences and ensure that all students receive appropriate linguistic support. Instruction must be communicated, sequenced, and scaffolded to support learners with different English proficiency abilities. The teacher must communicate instruction clearly while allowing time for repetition or slowed speech as necessary. In addition, teachers must supplement instruction with linguistic supports, such as verbal cues, gestures, and visual representations, as needed to provide assistance and context appropriate to individual ability levels. Instruction must also be sequenced logically and clearly communicate the expectations and steps of learning experiences. This is achieved by indicating an explicit beginning, middle, and end to activities through transition words and actions appropriate to students' levels of English proficiency. Teachers must scaffold instruction, activities, and assessments to meet individual students' language learning needs. Supports such as word walls, graphic organizers, charts, labels, and pairing students with others who can provide assistance are effective means of scaffolding learning to accommodate varying ability. By communicating, sequencing, and scaffolding instruction in a way that is tailored to ELL students' individual language needs, teachers effectively foster an equitable environment that promotes success in learning.

Promoting Higher-Order Thinking

Stimulating Reflection, Critical Thinking, and Inquiry Among Young Children

Opportunities for Play, Manipulating Materials, and Testing Ideas and Hypotheses

In providing age-appropriate learning experiences, teachers effectively stimulate critical thinking, inquiry, and reflection. For young children, opportunities for play, manipulating learning materials, and testing ideas and hypotheses are integral components of development, as children at this stage learn through interacting with their environment. These learning experiences stimulate inquiry and critical thinking through providing children with the space to explore, imagine, create, and form new ideas by directly and concretely engaging with their surroundings. In forming and testing new ideas, critical thinking abilities are further developed, as young children are encouraged to utilize problem-solving skills to craft new solutions. These methods of learning also serve to stimulate reflection in that they foster the ability to understand, rationalize, and organize how the world around them functions. When young children have the opportunity to explore, inquire, and test new ideas, they are able to reflect on their learning through processing and integrating new information to build understanding and experience.

Structured, Hands-On Problem-Solving Activities, Exploration, and Risk-Taking

Opportunities for structured, hands-on problem solving, exploration, and risk-taking enhance the learning experience through stimulating inquiry, critical thinking, and reflection. Physically exploring and interacting with learning materials actively engages students in the learning process, thus fostering curiosity and inquiry. This encourages students to take risks, test their ideas, and examine how materials work. When students are actively engaged through these learning methods, critical thinking is stimulated, as students must consider, analyze, and evaluate information to make informed choices for problem solving as they work to reach their desired outcomes. Through hands-on learning experiences, student understanding is deepened in a way that fosters connections and stimulates reflection. These methods allow students to see and analyze the results of their own inquiry and problem solving, thus allowing them to evaluate and reflect upon their learning for further exploration and improvement.

Promoting Positive Contributions, Communication, and Respectful Exchange of Ideas

Positive contributions, communication, and respectful exchanging of ideas facilitate a welcoming learning community that stimulates inquiry, critical thinking, and reflection. In such a learning environment, students feel a sense of security, inclusiveness, and trust that empowers them to engage in curiosity and inquiry through asking questions, exploring, and taking risks. When students can positively contribute to the learning experience through communicating their viewpoints with the trust that they will be respected, critical thinking is enhanced. Critical thinking encourages students to consider multiple viewpoints and challenges their own frames of reference. In addition, positive and respectful communication and exchanging of ideas stimulates inquiry and critical thinking through establishing a space in which students feel safe to share their experiences. This allows for students to constructively contribute to cooperative learning activities in which they can build critical thinking skills by feeling empowered to take risks and learning from others' perspectives, skills, and approaches to problem solving. When students feel comfortable discussing their learning in a respectful and positive environment, it allows for deeper reflection and understanding that enhances the learning experience.

ACTIVITIES THAT ENCOURAGE THE DEVELOPMENT OF HIGHER-ORDER THINKING SKILLS

The learning experience is enhanced and student understanding is strengthened when instruction focuses on the use and development of higher-order thinking skills. When instructional activities encourage students to **apply**, **analyze**, and **synthesize** information rather than simply know it, they develop the critical thinking and problem-solving skills necessary for academic and real-world success. By using **Bloom's taxonomy** when determining learning outcomes and creating instruction, teachers can effectively incorporate activities that foster students' refinement of higher-order thinking abilities. Activities that encourage exploration of diverse perspectives broaden students' worldviews and teach them to consider different approaches to problem-solving by exposing them to new viewpoints. Cooperative learning experiences further allow students to explore others' approaches to problem solving, build upon one another's experiences, and synthesize different perspectives to create new solutions. Cooperative and other active learning experiences that allow for problem-solving, open-ended questioning, and inquiry promote the development of higher-order thinking skills through encouraging students to explore and analyze information, test hypotheses, make connections, and synthesize information to formulate their own conclusions. Activities that develop students' research skills promote higher-order thinking through encouraging students to make inferences, consider and analyze other's perspectives, synthesize information to create new conclusions, and elaborate on their findings.

TEACHING AND MODELING ORGANIZATIONAL AND TIME-MANAGEMENT SKILLS

Helping Students Develop *AND* Build Upon Real-World Life Skills

Teaching and modeling time management and organizational skills to students is vital in instilling positive habits that serve as the foundation for academic success and the development of important life skills. As students progress through their academic careers and into the real world, these skills will allow them to succeed in setting and achieving measurable goals in an organized, timely fashion and successfully managing increasing responsibilities, commitments, and schedules. Furthermore, mastering these skills fosters efficient learning through teaching students to effectively plan, organize, and maximize their time and prioritize the completion of tasks. **Modeling** these skills is necessary for students to observe how to effectively manage and organize their time to be successful. The development of these skills is integral in creating empowered, confident lifelong learners who are successful in real-world situations and in effectively preparing them for future academic achievement and success in the professional realm.

IMPORTANCE AND METHODS OF ADAPTING FOR DIFFERENT AGE GROUPS

Organizational and time management skills are developed over time, so it is integral to introduce these concepts to students in their early school years at an age-appropriate level. In teaching, modeling, and monitoring these skills, teachers provide a strong foundation that students can develop with increasing independence throughout their academic careers. By adapting organizational and time management techniques to address different age groups' needs, teachers ensure that students internalize, implement, and develop these habits. For younger children, these skills can be taught and modeled through creating specific places for classroom materials, keeping like items together, and establishing smooth transitions between activities based on a schedule. Teachers can then monitor to ensure that students successfully follow these procedures. As students mature, their academic and extracurricular schedules become increasingly complex, and it is important that teachers continue to build organizational and time management skills while adapting to students' age levels through allowing increasing independence. Through teaching, modeling, and monitoring organizational tools, such as a daily agenda, and teaching effective strategies for systematically locating and organizing information, students develop and learn to independently implement tools that will allow for success as they transition through their academic careers and into adulthood.

TEACHING AND MODELING STUDY SKILLS FOR ACADEMIC AND PROFESSIONAL SUCCESS

Establishing strong study skills from an early age is integral for acquiring the tools necessary for academic and professional success. By teaching, modeling, and monitoring age-appropriate study techniques in the early school years, teachers provide students with foundational skills to develop and build upon as they progress through their academic careers and into the real world. Teachers can begin instilling effective study habits by teaching and modeling the use of graphic organizers and outlines to organize and process information with increasing levels of difficulty and independence based on age level. As students mature and academics become progressively challenging, effectively teaching, modeling, and monitoring note taking, summarizing, and test taking strategies with increasing levels of independence teaches students to organize and prepare new information. When study skills are taught and modeled at an age-appropriate level through adapting the amount of monitoring to address the needs of different age groups, teachers equip students with the tools necessary and the ability to develop these skills for lifelong learning and success.

Importance of Appropriately Structured Research Projects

The research process instills valuable organizational, time management, and study skills that contribute to academic preparedness and success. When teachers effectively structure and monitor the research process, they teach students strategies that can be implemented for success in real-world situations. Teachers should begin by instructing students on the steps in research. This includes identifying a problem, issue, or argument for research, how to gather pertinent information related to the topic, and strategies for organizing, prioritizing, processing, and synthesizing supporting evidence. These steps teach students important organizational skills that will allow them to successfully think critically and problem solve in real-world situations. Throughout the project, teachers should establish checkpoints to monitor student progress and foster independence through encouraging the use of time management tools. In doing so, teachers foster the development of important real-world life skills by instilling in students the ability to effectively and efficiently structure and prioritize their time for the completion of tasks, thus preparing them for future success.

The Research Process

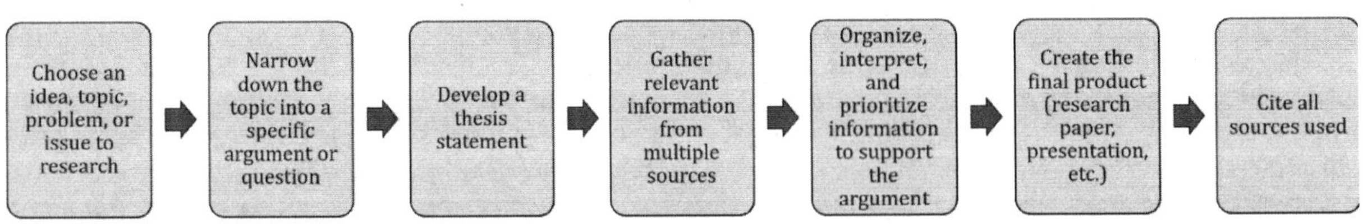

Teacher Attitudes and Behaviors on Student Achievement and Self-Concept

Teachers' behavior significantly impacts the learning experience, as their actions are highly influential to students. Often unconsciously, teachers exhibit attitudes and behaviors that impact students' self-concept, self-esteem, and consequently, academic achievement. If a teacher indicates negative sentiments toward students, their self-perception and belief in their abilities may be hindered, thus negatively impacting their academic performance. To minimize negative factors, promote students' growth mindset, and enhance learning, teachers must engage positively with all students in communication, instruction, and assessment. They must be cognizant of their own bias toward students and eliminate all negative notions to ensure that exchanges with students are equally positive. Teachers must display positive modeling and be conscientious of interactions both with individual students and the class as a whole. Additionally, teachers must ensure that they hold equally high academic and behavioral expectations for students and make certain that each student receives equal attention, praise, and discipline. Teachers must be aware of how they group students and do so in a way that does not insinuate bias, negative connotation, or difference in expectations. Instruction and assessments must also be free of bias and include necessary supports for individual student needs to provide equal opportunities for success in learning.

Equity in Education

Equality vs. Equity

Equality refers to providing everyone with the same resources when working toward a goal, regardless of the unique needs or situation of the individual. **Equity** means considering an individual's needs and circumstances to provide the proper supports that allow the individual a fair opportunity to achieve a common goal. In the classroom, creating an equitable environment requires the consideration of students' individual learning styles, needs, and personal situations and using this knowledge to instill necessary supports to help each student achieve the same objectives relative to their peers. Equity in the classroom is especially important for closing the achievement gap, particularly in low socioeconomic areas, because many of these students come from disadvantaged situations and need additional help to gain a fair opportunity for academic success.

Review Video: Equality vs Equity
Visit mometrix.com/academy and enter code: 685648

Supports Utilized to Provide an Equitable Learning Environment

The nature of academic, physical, and behavioral supports depends largely on the needs of the individual student; however, some common supports are effective in addressing an array of needs to facilitate an equitable learning environment. Students with **learning disabilities** may benefit from academic supports such as preferential seating near the front of the room and minimized distractions to enhance focus. Modified test questions or alternate assignments, graphic organizers, scaffolded texts, extra copies of class notes, and individualized instruction are also valuable in enhancing focus, preventing students from becoming overwhelmed, and ensuring learning activities are aligned with students' capabilities. Students with **physical disabilities** may require wheelchair access, a sign language interpreter or scribe, braille text, enlarged fonts, or the use of technology devices to aid in reading and writing. Common **behavioral supports** in the classroom include opportunities for frequent breaks or movement as needed, a daily check-in with a caseworker or other dedicated staff member, or a behavior chart to allow students to self-monitor.

Establishing High Academic Expectations

In any classroom, establishing high academic standards is imperative for motivating and empowering students to succeed. By communicating high expectations clearly and frequently, the teacher demonstrates belief that each student can overcome obstacles and excel academically, thus inspiring student engagement, curiosity for learning, and an overall positive and productive learning environment. To create an environment of high academic standards, the teachers' expectations must be apparent in instruction. The teacher must provide lessons and activities that are rigorous but not so challenging that students are unable to complete them without assistance, as this would disempower and disengage students from learning. The teacher must set achievable learning goals based on knowledge of student abilities and encourage self-reflection. Additionally, the teacher must utilize knowledge of students' individual needs to instill necessary supports to help students in achieving tasks and create an equitable environment for learning. This will ultimately empower students to overcome obstacles and motivate them for academic success.

Chapter Quiz

Ready to see how well you retained what you just read? Scan the QR code to go directly to the chapter quiz interface for this study guide. If you're using a computer, simply visit the online resources page at **mometrix.com/resources719/texespprte370** and click the Chapter Quizzes link.

The Learning Environment

Learning Environments in Early Childhood

Guidelines for Indoor and Outdoor Space Use

Indoor and outdoor early childhood learning environments should be safe, clean, and attractive. They should include at least 35 square feet indoors and 75 square feet outdoors of usable play space per child. Staff must have access to prepare spaces before children's arrival. Gyms or other larger indoor spaces can substitute if outdoor spaces are smaller. The youngest children should be given separate outdoor times/places. Outdoor scheduling should ensure enough room and prevent altercations/competition among different age groups. Teachers can assess if enough space exists by observing children's interactions and engagement in activities. Children's products and other visuals should be displayed at child's-eye level. Spaces should be arranged to allow individual, small-group, and large-group activity. Space organization should create clear pathways enabling children to move easily among activities without overly disturbing others, and should promote positive social interactions and behaviors; activities in each area should not distract children in other areas.

Arrangement of Learning Environments

Arranging Indoor Learning Environments According to Curricular Activities

EC experts indicate that rooms should be organized to enable various activities, but not necessarily to limit activities to certain areas. For example, mathematical and scientific preschool activities may occur in multiple parts of a classroom, though the room should still be laid out to facilitate their occurrence. Sufficient space for infants to crawl and toddlers to toddle is necessary, as are both hard and carpeted floors. Bolted-down/heavy, sturdy furniture is needed for infants and toddlers to use for pulling up, balancing, and cruising. Art and cooking activities should be positioned near sinks/water sources for cleanup. Designating separate areas for activities like block-building, book-reading, musical activities, and dramatic play facilitates engaging in each of these. To allow ongoing project work and other age-appropriate activities, school-aged children should have separate areas. Materials should be appropriate for each age group and varied. Books, recordings, art supplies, and equipment and materials for sensory stimulation, manipulation, construction, active play, and dramatic play, all arranged for easy, independent child access and rotated for variety, are needed.

Arranging Learning Environments to Children's Personal, Privacy, and Sensory Needs

In any early childhood learning environment, the indoor space should include easily identifiable places where children and adults can store their personal belongings. Since early childhood involves children in groups for long time periods, they should be given indoor and outdoor areas allowing solitude and privacy while still easily permitting adult supervision. Playhouses and tunnels can be used outdoors, while small interior rooms and partitions can be used indoors. Environments should include softness in various forms like grass outdoors; carpet, pillows, and soft chairs indoors; adult laps to sit in and be cuddled; and soft play materials like clay, Play-Doh, finger paints, water, and sand. While noise is predictable, even desirable in early childhood environments, undue noise causing fatigue and stress should be controlled by noise-absorbing elements like rugs, carpets, drapes, acoustic ceilings, and other building materials. Outdoor play areas supplied by a school or community should be separated from roadways and other hazards by fencing and/or natural barriers. Awnings can substitute for shade, and inclines/ramps for hills, when these are not naturally available. Surfaces and equipment should be varied.

Schedules, Routines, and Activities for Young Children

Ideal Schedule for Young Children

An ideal schedule for young children reflects their developmental characteristics and capabilities to maximize their learning. A **predictable** routine is necessary for young children to feel secure in their learning environment, so each day should follow a similar schedule while allowing room for **flexibility** if an activity takes longer than expected. Each day should begin with a clear routine, such as unpacking, a warm-up activity, and a class meeting to allow students to share thoughts, ask questions, and allow the teacher to discuss what will occur that day. This establishes a positive tone for the day while focusing the attention on learning. Similarly, the end of the day should have a specific routine, such as cleaning up materials and packing up for dismissal. Young children learn best by physically interacting with and exploring their environments. As such, each day should include large blocks of time for **active movement** throughout the day in the form of play, projects, and learning centers. Periods of **rest** must follow such activities, as this enables young children to process and internalize what they learned. **Direct instruction** should occur before active movement periods and last approximately 15-20 minutes to sustain engagement and attention toward learning.

Example Daily Schedule for the Early Childhood Education Classroom	
8:00-8:30	Welcome, unpack, morning work
8:30-8:45	Circle time, review class calendar
8:45-9:30	Literacy/language arts
9:30-10:15	Learning stations
10:15-11:00	Math
11:00-11:30	Music/dance/movement
11:30-12:15	Lunch
12:15-1:00	Recess/unstructured play
1:00-1:20	Rest/quiet time
1:20-2:00	Science
2:00-2:45	Creative arts
2:45-3:15	Daily reflection, pack up, dismissal

Some examples of restful and active movement activities for young children are discussed below:

- **Restful:** Incorporating restful activities into the early childhood classroom are beneficial in helping young children process and retain new concepts and providing them the opportunity to unwind after active movement activities. Examples of such activities include nap time, class meditation, self-reflection activities, independent art projects, or self-selected reading time. Teachers can also read aloud to students or play an audiobook during these periods.
- **Active:** Providing young children with multiple opportunities for active movement throughout the day is beneficial in promoting the development of gross motor skills, connections to learning, and the ability to function in a group setting. Active movement opportunities should include whole-class, small group, and independent activities. Examples include class dances, songs, games, nature walks, or total participation activities such as gallery walks or four corners. Physical education activities, such as jump rope, tag, sports, or using playground equipment are also beneficial. Young children should also be provided with ample time for both structured and unstructured play throughout the day.

Balancing Restful and Active Movement Activities

A schedule that balances **rest** and **active movement** is necessary for positive cognitive, physical, emotional, and social development in young children. Connecting learning to active movement strengthens students' understanding of new concepts, as it allows them to physically explore and interact with their environment, experiment with new ideas, and gain new experiences for healthy **cognitive development**. In addition, incorporating active movement encourages the use of **gross motor skills** and provides students with the space to physically express themselves in an appropriate setting, thus promoting physical and emotional development. Active movement also encourages the development of positive **interpersonal skills** as young children interact and explore with one another. Restful periods are equally as important to the development of young children. Incorporating rest after a period of active movement further strengthens young children's connection to learning by providing them the opportunity to reflect, process, and internalize new information.

Providing Large Blocks of Time for Play, Projects, and Learning Centers

Providing young children with ample time for play, projects, and learning centers throughout the school day is integral to fostering their development across domains. Young children learn most effectively through active movement as they physically interact with their environment, and incorporating large blocks of time for such activities allows them to do so. Significant time dedicated to active play, projects, and learning centers on a variety of topics allows young children to explore and experiment with the world around them, test new ideas, draw conclusions, and acquire new knowledge. This supports healthy **physical** and **cognitive development**, as it provides young children the opportunity to engage in learning across subject areas while connecting it to active movement for strengthened understanding. In addition, allowing large blocks of time for these activities is necessary for **social** and **emotional development**, as it provides young children the space to interact with one another and develop important skills such as cooperation, sharing, conflict resolution, and emotional self-regulation. Dedicating large blocks of time to play, projects, and learning centers establishes a student-led, hands-on learning environment that is reflective of the developmental characteristics and needs of young children.

Characteristics of Young Children in Relation to Interactions with Others

Designing group activities that align with the ability of young children to collaborate while supporting social development requires a realistic understanding of their capacity to do so. This entails understanding the **developmental characteristics** of young children at varying stages, including how the nature of their interactions with others evolves. Young children learn by exploring and interacting with their environments, so they need ample opportunities for play and active movement to do so; however, the teacher must recognize that the way young children play and collaborate develops over time. Young children typically exhibit little interest in actively playing with others until approximately age four. Until then, they progress through stages of solitary play, observing their peers, playing independently alongside others, and, eventually, loosely interacting (sometimes with the same toys) while still primarily engaging in independent play. During these stages, it is important that teachers foster **collaboration** by providing multiple opportunities for play as well as learning materials that encourage **cooperation** and **sharing**. The teacher must, however, maintain the understanding that these children have yet to develop the capacity to intentionally work with others. Once this ability is developed, the teacher can integrate coordinated group activities that encourage collaboration toward a common goal.

Considerations When Designing Group Activities for Young Children

For young children, thoughtfully designed group activities are integral in promoting development across domains. These opportunities facilitate social and emotional development by encouraging collaboration and positive communication. They also facilitate physical and cognitive growth by allowing children to play, explore, and interact with others in the learning environment. It is important that teachers carefully consider the particulars of group activities when planning to ensure maximized learning and development. Teachers must consider the **developmental characteristics** of their students' age groups, including their capacity to collaborate with others. This enables the teacher to plan group activities that align with students' abilities while promoting collaboration and development. All **learning materials** must be carefully selected to encourage collaboration, sharing, and the development of positive social skills at a developmentally appropriate level. The teacher must also consider **desired learning outcomes** and the nature of the learning taking place to determine whether group activities should be structured or unstructured. Unstructured play is valuable in allowing students to develop their social and emotional skills in a natural setting, whereas structured, teacher-led group activities allow for more focused learning. Desired outcomes also determine the size of groups for the activity to best promote collaboration and learning.

Activities that Reflect and Develop Young Children's Ability to Collaborate

Young children benefit from a variety of **whole-class** and **small-group** activities designed to reflect and develop their collaborative skills. When the teacher incorporates group activities to encourage cooperation, sharing, and positive interactions, young children gain important social and emotional skills necessary for development across domains. Whole-group activities such as **circle time** provide young children with the opportunity to interact with others, express ideas, and ask questions in a developmentally appropriate setting. This activity develops important collaborative skills, such as taking turns, active listening, and respectful communication. Other **whole-group activities**, such as reading aloud, group songs, dances, games, or class nature walks, are effective in teaching young children how to productively contribute to and function in a group setting. **Small-group activities** can be incorporated throughout all aspects of structured and unstructured learning to develop young children's collaborative skills. Learning centers, such as a science area, pretend play area, or building block center, provide materials that encourage collaboration while allowing students to interact with others according to their abilities in a student-led setting. Problem-solving activities, such as puzzles, games, age-appropriate science experiments, or scavenger hunts, are effective in teaching young children how to work together toward a common goal.

Managing Group Activities to Promote Collaborative Skills and Accountability

Well-planned group activities are beneficial in developing students' collaborative skills and sense of individual accountability. Such group activities are well-organized, effectively managed, and intentionally structured with a **clear goal** or problem that must be solved while allowing room for creativity to enhance the collaborative process. When designing these activities, the teacher must incorporate enough **significant components** to ensure all students within the group can productively contribute. If the assignment is too simple, students can easily complete it on their own, whereas a multifaceted activity instills a sense of interdependence within the group that fosters the development of collaborative skills. To promote individual accountability, **meaningful roles** and responsibilities should be assigned to each group member because when students feel others are relying on their contributions to complete a task, they develop a sense of ownership that motivates active participation. To further develop collaborative skills and individual accountability, students should be graded both as a **whole group** and **individually**. This encourages group cooperation while ensuring that students' individual contributions are recognized. Including **self-assessments** at the end of group activities is beneficial in allowing students to reflect on the quality of their contributions to the group and ways they could improve their collaborative skills.

Thoughtful consideration of how to best organize and manage collaborative activities helps establish an environment that supports students in learning to work together productively and assume responsible roles within a group. When planning group activities, the teacher must consider the **desired learning outcomes** and the **nature of the task** to determine whether there are enough significant components that would benefit from collaboration. **Group size** must also be considered to most effectively foster collaboration and individual accountability when assuming responsible roles. Groups with too few students may be inadequate for addressing all the components of a complex task, whereas grouping too many students together limits productive collaboration and makes it difficult for each member to assume a significant, responsible role. The teacher must be selective regarding which students are grouped together to best facilitate productive collaboration. This includes determining which students will work well together as well as grouping students that may need support with those who can provide scaffolding. It is also important to consider how **responsibilities** will be divided to ensure each member is given a significant role that allows him or her to contribute productively to the group. How students' contributions will be monitored and **assessed** should also be considered.

The Learning Environment

Establishing a Positive, Productive Classroom Environment

Unique Characteristics and Needs of Students at Varying Developmental Levels

Students at each developmental level possess unique characteristics and needs that must be met in the classroom to ensure productivity and a positive classroom environment. For successful learning, the teacher must recognize the nuances of varying developmental levels to properly understand their students' abilities and design instruction accordingly. When the teacher is attuned to the distinct characteristics and needs of their students, they can align **curriculum**, **instructional strategies**, **activities**, and **assessments** in a way that is accessible and comprehensible to all students. This understanding enables the teacher to deliver instruction at a **pace** appropriate to students' developmental stage while ensuring they are challenged across domains based upon their ability for continuous whole-child development. In addition, knowledge of the general characteristics and needs of developmental stages enables the teacher to effectively identify and accommodate individual variances that occur within these stages for **student-centered** learning. When instruction is tailored to address the needs of varying developmental stages and individual differences, students feel supported in their learning. This ultimately fosters increased self-esteem, student engagement, and positive attitudes toward learning that contribute to an overall productive and successful classroom environment.

Addressing Developmental Characteristics and Needs of Younger Students

A positive and productive classroom environment for younger children requires the teacher to understand the intricacies of this developmental stage and implement strategies accordingly to promote success in learning. Younger students learn by **exploring** and **interacting** with the world around them and must be provided with multiple opportunities to do so. **Play** is integral to young students' development across domains; therefore, both planned and free play should be incorporated throughout instruction. Play enables students to explore their environments and make connections that strengthen their learning while promoting the development of problem-solving and higher-order thinking skills. In addition, allowing frequent opportunities for play facilitates the acquisition of important social and emotional skills, such as cooperation, conflict resolution, and sharing. Likewise, incorporating frequent **movement** throughout lessons allows young students to explore their physical spaces and actively engage in learning for deeper understanding. Additionally, **cooperative learning** strategies encourage the development of necessary social and emotional skills and are important in teaching young children how to effectively work with others to solve a problem. When the teacher implements strategies appropriate to younger students' developmental levels, it enhances motivation, active engagement, and promotes positive attitudes toward learning for a productive classroom environment.

Collaborative Opportunities in of Middle-Level Students

Middle-level students experience significant developmental changes as they approach adolescence and have unique characteristics and needs that must be met to ensure a positive and productive learning environment. **Collaborative opportunities** are beneficial in supporting the development of cognitive, social, and emotional skills of middle-level students and should be implemented frequently. This strategy enables these students to work productively with others and promotes the development of positive **interpersonal** and **communication** skills. This is especially important in middle-level education, as students at this developmental stage begin forming their identities, attitudes toward learning, and influential peer relationships. Middle-level students build **self-confidence** through collaborative learning, as it enables them to develop positive leadership skills. Additionally, collaborative opportunities expose students to the varying backgrounds and perspectives of their classmates, thus fostering appreciation for individual differences and contributing to a positive classroom climate. Collaborative learning is also beneficial for **cognitive development**, as it allows students to build upon one another's background knowledge for enhanced learning and encourages critical and higher-order thinking while working together to solve a problem. Providing middle-level students with collaborative opportunities increases overall engagement for a positive and productive classroom environment and develops necessary skills for successful transition into adolescence.

Promoting Respect for the Community and People in It Among Older Students

As older students prepare for adulthood, it is important that they develop a respect for their community and the people in it. Implementing strategies to facilitate this is vital in equipping older students with **real-world skills** necessary to become productive contributors to society. By self-educating and modeling respect for the community and its people, the teacher can influence students to adopt the same sentiment. Establishing a positive community within the classroom through activities like class meetings, discussions, and cultural activities promotes respect for others that extends to real-world situations. Strategies that demonstrate connection to the community strengthen students' overall respect and responsibility for it. This can be achieved by incorporating **authentic materials**, including news stories, art, music, and relevant speakers, to develop students' understanding and insight regarding the characteristics and needs of the community. Encouraging students to bring items from home to share fosters appreciation for their community by exposing them to the backgrounds and perspectives within it. **Community service** projects such as fundraisers, food drives, and service field trips further promote students' respect for their community while demonstrating the real-world applications of their learning. This ultimately makes learning meaningful and contributes to a positive, productive learning environment.

Positive Classroom Climate

Classroom climate refers to the overall atmosphere that the teacher establishes and is powerful in determining the nature of the learning experience. Students are most successful in their learning when the climate is positive, encouraging, and focused on creating a collaborative, supportive community. A positive classroom climate is **welcoming**, **inclusive**, and **respectful** of all individuals. Instruction is delivered in an engaging, comprehensible way in a structured, orderly, and safe environment. The atmosphere is **visually appealing**, stimulating, not overwhelming, and arranged in a way that maximizes learning. **Collaboration** and **supportive interactions** are encouraged throughout the learning process to enhance engagement and develop positive social and emotional skills. Such an environment builds students' self-esteem and confidence by ensuring they feel safe and empowered to participate and work with others in the learning process. In addition, it encourages positive attitudes toward learning that are necessary for active student engagement and productivity. When the classroom climate is positive, students are more self-motivated, thus strengthening their learning and promoting academic achievement.

Collaboration and Supportive Interactions

Collaboration and **supportive interactions** are key components of a positive classroom climate and should be integrated throughout instruction to promote active engagement and success in learning for all students. To achieve this, the teacher must establish a classroom community focused on respect, inclusiveness, and open dialogue. This ensures students feel safe and empowered to express themselves and interact constructively. By teaching and **modeling** active listening skills, the teacher can demonstrate and influence respectful communication in the classroom. **Team-building activities**, including class meetings, games, and discussions, are valuable strategies for creating a community that encourages productive collaboration and supportive interactions. In addition, establishing **clear expectations** for positive communication and involving students in their creation instills a sense of personal responsibility to adhere to them when working with others. Once expectations are understood, students must be provided with multiple and varied **collaborative learning** opportunities to continuously practice developing positive interpersonal skills. As students participate in learning, the teacher must be sure to consistently praise cooperation and positive interactions to reinforce the standards of communication. When teachers promote collaboration and supportive interactions, they create a positive classroom climate that increases students' productivity and self-motivation to actively participate in learning for maximized achievement.

Respect for Diversity and Individual Differences

An emphasis on respect for **diversity** and **individual differences** in the classroom is necessary to establish a positive, productive learning atmosphere. Teaching and modeling this sentiment to students instills the notion that everyone has unique and valuable experiences, perspectives, and characteristics to contribute to the classroom community. Emphasizing respect for all individuals ensures students feel validated and secure in their own identities while teaching them to appreciate diversities among their classmates. Such an environment promotes collaboration and supportive interactions, as it is built on a foundation of welcoming, inclusiveness, and acceptance that empowers students to confidently interact with peers as they engage in learning. When students feel respected, it increases their self-esteem and positive self-concept. Students who feel confident in the classroom are more likely to develop positive attitudes toward learning. This ultimately fosters a positive classroom climate in which students are motivated to actively engage in instruction and achieve academic success.

Impact of Interactions on Classroom Climate

Teacher-Student Interactions

Interactions between teachers and their students play a significant role in determining overall classroom climate and the quality of the learning experience. The way in which the teacher interacts with students influences their **social**, **emotional**, and **cognitive development** as well as sets the tone for how students interact with each other. This ultimately shapes students' **self-esteem** and contributes to their level of engagement, attitude toward learning, and academic achievement; therefore, it is important that the teacher ensure all interactions with students on a whole-class and individual level are positive, unbiased, encouraging, and respectful of each individual. Working to build relationships with students demonstrates a genuine interest in their lives that contributes to a positive, productive classroom climate in which students feel welcomed, accepted, and empowered to actively engage in learning. Positive interactions between the teacher and students support a healthy sense of self-esteem as well as positive social and emotional skills that contribute to cognitive development. Students with greater self-esteem are more likely to develop positive attitudes toward learning that foster increased self-motivation to actively participate in learning, thus contributing to enhanced academic achievement.

Students' Interactions with One Another

The classroom climate is dependent on the nature of **students' interactions** with one another. These interactions largely determine the quality of student learning as well as development across domains. Positive communication facilitates the development of healthy **social** and emotional skills that serve to enhance cognitive development. Students with strong social and **emotional skills** are often more motivated to actively participate in learning and are more productive in collaborative situations, as they can build upon one another's knowledge; therefore, the teacher must implement a variety of strategies to ensure interactions among students are positive, respectful, and supportive to establish a classroom climate focused on productive learning. **Community building** exercises establish a climate built on positive and supportive communication while demonstrating the benefits of productive cooperation in achieving a goal. Teaching and **modeling** positive communication skills sets the tone and expectations for how students will interact with one another. Students should be given **frequent opportunities** to interact both during and outside of instructional time to promote the development of necessary interpersonal skills for healthy social development. In addition, **strategic student groupings** during collaborative work and consistent monitoring help ensure maximized productivity and that the standards for communication are reinforced.

Communicating an Enthusiasm for Learning

Establishing Environments Promoting Positive Attitudes Toward Learning

The nature of the classroom environment is reliant on the **efforts**, **behaviors**, and **attitudes** of the teacher. The teacher is responsible for setting the tone of the classroom, which determines the overall climate and has significant impacts on the quality and effectiveness of the learning experience. The classroom environment influences students' engagement, positive communication, and attitudes toward learning, which contribute to their overall academic achievement. Successful teaching and learning require the teacher to intentionally take measures to establish a welcoming, accepting, and encouraging classroom environment that promotes excitement and positive attitudes toward learning. Teachers must model genuine respect for their students and enthusiasm for learning, as well as present instruction in a way that is engaging, comprehensible, and responsive to students' needs and interests. The physical classroom must be arranged in a way that is visually appealing, safe, and facilitative of productive learning. It is also important that the teacher establish and consistently reinforce structured routines, procedures, and behavioral expectations to contribute to an overall positive climate and ensure students feel secure and willing to participate in learning. When the classroom environment is exciting, positive, and engaging, it encourages positive attitudes toward learning that increase motivation to succeed.

Influence on Students' Motivation, Productivity, and Academic Achievement

Modeling is perhaps one of the most powerful strategies in influencing students' attitudes, behaviors, and actions in the classroom. As students spend a great deal of time with their teachers, the level of enthusiasm for learning demonstrated by the teacher inevitably influences their own excitement in the classroom; therefore, the teacher must conscientiously model enthusiasm for teaching and learning to positively influence students' internal motivation for productivity, learning, and achievement. Students are highly perceptive, and as such, if the teacher appears unmotivated in his or her practice or disinterested in the content, students will likely adopt the same sentiment and become disengaged or apathetic toward learning. The enthusiasm modeled by the teacher must be **authentic** to elicit the same genuine interest in learning from students. When teachers demonstrate sincere excitement about the content they are teaching, it prompts curiosity for learning among students that enhances their motivation and attitudes toward learning. In addition, modeling enthusiasm for teaching and learning enhances the relationship between the teacher and students, thus contributing to a positive classroom climate that makes students excited to learn. When students have a positive attitude toward learning, they are more motivated to productively engage in learning and achieve academic success.

Methods and Impact on Classroom Climate and Student Engagement

Communicating sincere enthusiasm for teaching and learning is essential in establishing a positive, productive classroom climate focused on student engagement and achievement. Students' interest and excitement for learning are directly reflective of the sentiments exhibited by the teacher. As such, it is important that teachers intentionally and consistently communicate excitement for their practice and content. To achieve this, teachers must ensure that their **behaviors, actions, language, tone of voice**, and **interactions** with students are positive in nature. By working to build positive **interpersonal relationships** with students and demonstrating genuine interest in their lives, experiences, interests, and needs, teachers can effectively communicate enthusiasm for their practice that motivates students to engage in learning. This is further reflected in the physical **arrangement of the classroom**. A classroom that is visually appealing, stimulating, and reflective of students' interests and achievements illustrates the teacher's enthusiasm and promotes a positive classroom climate in which students are excited and motivated to engage in learning.

Conveying High Expectations for All Students

Significance in Promoting Productivity, Active Engagement, and Success in Learning

Communicating **high academic** and **behavioral expectations** is necessary for establishing a classroom climate focused on productivity, active engagement, and achievement. Students are heavily influenced by the teacher's expectations for them; therefore, when high learning standards are set, students will more likely strive to achieve them. High expectations increase the **relevancy** of learning by focusing instruction and providing a clear purpose that motivates students to participate. In addition, by conveying high expectations, teachers demonstrate a **belief in their students' abilities** to overcome personal challenges and achieve success. This notion promotes a **growth mindset** among students, which is the belief that intelligence is not inherent but rather something that can be attained and consistently improved upon. This enhances students' self-esteem and confidence, which promotes positive attitudes toward learning that foster active engagement, productivity, and success. Communicating high expectations while providing necessary supports motivates students to challenge themselves academically and gives them a sense of self-responsibility over their learning that encourages them to work to their highest potential. This ultimately creates a positive classroom climate in which students feel supported and empowered to productively engage in learning and achieve success.

Strategies and Impact on Classroom Climate and Student Achievement

Communicating **high academic** and **behavioral expectations** is most effective when done so through a variety of means. This ensures that students are aware of the teacher's expectations of them and consistently reinforces high standards to establish a positive classroom climate focused on student motivation, productivity, and achievement. Expectations must always be **clear** and **visible** in the classroom, and the teacher must frequently remind students by restating them throughout instruction. Establishing learning goals and objectives that are challenging yet attainable based on students' abilities effectively communicates high expectations and the teacher's belief that students can achieve them. This is further iterated when students encounter challenges and rather than lowering expectations, the teacher maintains the same high standards while providing necessary supports for achievement. Teachers can also communicate high expectations by ensuring they provide students with timely, clear, and constructive **feedback** on their progress and ways in which they can improve to meet them. Frequent **communication with families** is beneficial in reinforcing academic and behavioral expectations at home to ensure student awareness and maximize their effectiveness in the classroom.

Literacy-Rich Environment

A **literacy-rich** classroom focuses on the development of all literacy components by immersing students in reading, writing, speaking, and listening skills across subject areas. While all students benefit from such an environment, it is especially important for **ELL students** and students with **developmental disabilities** in acquiring the literacy and language skills necessary for success. In a literacy-rich environment, the teacher provides multiple opportunities to engage in teacher-led and student-selected reading, writing, speaking, and listening activities in all areas of instruction. Students may be asked to solve word problems in math, write a report on a famous artist in art, or keep an observation log in science to encourage literacy development across content areas. Students are provided with multiple print and digital literacy materials on a variety of topics with varying levels of complexity to accommodate individual developmental levels while encouraging reading, vocabulary acquisition, and listening skills. Additionally, the teacher surrounds students with **print-rich** materials, including posters, word walls, labels, and bulletin boards on a variety of topics to further promote literacy development. A literacy-rich environment continuously promotes and emphasizes the importance of literacy skills in all areas of life that serve as a necessary foundation for academic and real-world success.

Review Video: Importance of Promoting Literacy in the Home
Visit mometrix.com/academy and enter code: 862347

Review Video: Literacy-Rich Content-Area Classrooms
Visit mometrix.com/academy and enter code: 571455

Safe, Nurturing, and Inclusive Classroom Environment

A safe, nurturing, and inclusive classroom environment focuses on meeting students' emotional needs for healthy development in this domain. The overall climate in such an environment is welcoming and emphasizes **respect**, **acceptance**, and **positive communication** among the teacher and students. The classroom is brightly decorated and reflective of students' diversities, interests, and achievements to promote a sense of security and inclusivity that motivates active participation in learning. Instructional activities are also reflective of students' differences, learning styles, and interests, with necessary supports instilled to accommodate individual learning needs. This establishes an **equitable environment** that ensures all students feel respected, nurtured, and supported both academically and emotionally. Such an environment is **structured** and orderly with clear expectations, procedures, and routines to foster a sense of security as students engage in learning. Collaboration and supportive interactions among students are encouraged to create a positive, productive classroom community in which students feel confident to express themselves and participate in learning. A classroom environment that is safe, nurturing, and inclusive develops students' sense of self-concept that contributes to positive communication, relationships, and attitudes necessary for emotional development.

Developing Students' Emotional Intelligence

Emotional intelligence refers to the ability to recognize and regulate one's own emotions as well as identify and empathetically respond to the emotions of others. Developing this skill through a variety of strategies is integral to successful development across other domains. By **modeling** such skills as empathy and active listening, the teacher can influence students' abilities to identify and properly respond to their own and other's emotions. Teaching **coping strategies**, including journaling, breathing, or counting techniques, promotes students' self-regulation to manage emotions when faced with a conflict or challenge. Teaching emotional intelligence can also be integrated throughout instruction, such as prompting students to describe the feelings of a character in a book or discuss emotions evoked from a painting. Students with strong emotional intelligence are likely to develop positive interpersonal relationships for healthy social development. This contributes to improved cognitive development in that when students collaborate productively, they build upon one another's knowledge. Emotionally intelligent students are also likely to have positive attitudes toward learning, as they have the capacity to self-regulate when faced with obstacles and properly engage in instruction for enhanced cognitive development.

Meeting Students' Emotional Needs, Individual Rights, and Dignity

Successful learning and **whole-child** development are reliant on the degree to which students' emotional needs, individual rights, and dignity are met and respected in the classroom. This establishes the tone of the overall classroom climate that determines students' sense of safety, nurturing, and inclusion when interacting with others and engaging in learning. By taking measures to prioritize students' emotional needs and create a respectful, accepting classroom community, the teacher establishes a positive learning atmosphere that promotes cognitive, social, and emotional growth for whole-child development. When students feel emotionally supported and respected in their identities, they develop a healthy sense of self-esteem that positively influences their attitude toward learning and motivation to participate. This ultimately impacts **cognitive development**, as students that actively and confidently engage in learning are more likely to be academically successful. These students are also more effectively able to develop important interpersonal communication skills necessary for healthy **social development**, as students who feel secure and accepted are more likely to be supportive of others. By meeting students' emotional needs and respecting their individual rights and dignities, the teacher effectively prepares students with the skills necessary for academic and real-world success.

Classroom Routines and Procedures

Influence on Classroom Climate, Productivity, Student Behavior, and Learning

A well-managed classroom focused on productivity, positive behavior, and success in learning relies on the effectiveness and consistency of **routines** and **procedures** instilled for daily activities. By implementing these at the beginning of the school year and continuously reinforcing them throughout, the teacher establishes an orderly, efficient classroom that facilitates students' ability to productively engage in learning. Classroom management, student behavior, and productivity are enhanced by structured routines and procedures, as students who understand expectations are more inclined to follow them. Such structure provides students with a sense of predictability and security in their environment that contributes to their willingness to participate in learning. Routines and procedures simplify daily tasks and allow for smooth transitions between activities. This minimizes opportunities for student distraction or disruption, thus promoting positive behavior, increasing instructional time, and enhancing students' ability to focus on learning in an orderly, productive classroom climate.

Review Video: Classroom Management - Rhythms of Teaching
Visit mometrix.com/academy and enter code: 809399

Considerations Regarding Age-Appropriateness to Ensure Effectiveness

Classroom procedures and routines must reflect the characteristics and capabilities of the **age group** of the students. It is important that teachers understand and apply their knowledge of students' **developmental levels** across domains when considering which routines and procedures to establish in their classrooms. In doing so, teachers ensure that expectations are age-appropriate, realistic, and effective in creating an orderly, productive environment. Procedures and routines must always be clear, succinct, and limited in number to avoid overwhelming students; however, in communicating them, the teacher must use comprehensible language relative to students' age-groups. The nature of learning must be considered when determining age-appropriate routines and procedures. For young children, procedures for cleaning up toys after playtime is appropriate, whereas procedures for turning in homework and taking assessments applies to older students. The degree to which students are expected to perform routines and procedures independently must also be considered and reflective of their capabilities. Young children may need a great deal of assistance, whereas older students can perform certain tasks independently. Consequences for not following expectations must be appropriate to students' age groups. Losing free play time may be appropriate for young children, whereas parent communication may be effective for older students.

Examples of Age-Appropriate Routines and Procedures

Young children: Young children can reasonably be expected to perform **basic daily routines** independently, although they likely will need frequent reminders. Daily procedures may include having young children hang up their coats, put away lunchboxes, and unpack their backpacks at the beginning of the day as they prepare to begin morning work. Similarly, young children can be expected to independently follow end-of-day procedures and routines, such as packing up their backpacks, cleaning up learning materials, and lining up at the door for dismissal. Young children should be able to follow simple behavioral procedures as well, such as keeping hands to themselves, responding to attention signals from the teacher, and cleaning up learning materials before transitioning between activities. Young children also benefit from being assigned classroom "jobs," such as line leader, paper collector, or teacher assistant, as these routines instill a sense of accountability and self-responsibility.

Middle-level: Middle-level students can be expected to follow a variety of routines and procedures with **increasing levels of independence**. These students can reasonably be expected to enter the classroom on time and prepare necessary learning materials. In addition, middle-level students can be held responsible for independently turning in homework according to the procedures for doing so and beginning their morning work. Middle-level students should be able to follow procedures for accessing learning materials, transitioning to cooperative learning activities, cleaning up their own materials before moving to a new activity, and non-instructional tasks, such as sharpening pencils, using the restroom, or throwing away trash with minimal reminders from the teacher.

High school: Routines and procedures in the high school classroom should **reflect** students' levels of **maturity and increasing capabilities for independence** as they approach adulthood. These students can reasonably be expected to independently come to class on time, prepared, and follow procedures for turning in homework and beginning morning work. In addition, high school students can be expected to follow procedures for direct instruction, cooperative learning activities, and independently transitioning between activities. High school students can be held to a greater degree of accountability regarding grading procedures, tardiness and attendance, and procedures for turning in late assignments.

Facilitating an Organized, Productive Environment that Maximizes Student Learning

Clear routines and procedures for daily classroom activities are necessary to create an organized, productive environment that maximizes student learning. In order to be effective, routines and procedures must be reflective of the teacher's **instructional** and **classroom management** style, explicitly stated, and consistently reinforced. This ensures expectations are relevant, realistic, and that students are continuously aware of them as they engage in learning. Procedures for entering and exiting the classroom as well as how students will begin and end their day, establish a structured, **predictable** routine that enhances focus on instruction.

Smooth **transition procedures** maintain order and enhance efficiency when moving between activities, as they eliminate idle time, minimize student distraction, and allow for increased time dedicated to productive teaching and learning. Such transition procedures include how and when to access and clean up materials, move from independent to collaborative group work, or move between learning stations. The teacher must also consider procedures for performing non-instructional activities, such as sharpening pencils or going to the restroom, as these further avoid disruptions to instructional time. Procedures and routines establish organization and efficiency in the classroom by simplifying tasks to allow for increased productive instructional time and enhanced student learning.

While the specifics of routines may vary depending upon the teacher's classroom management style and students' learning needs, many common procedures and routines share similar guidelines.

- **Entering the classroom/morning routine:** A procedure for the beginning of class ensures that students enter the room in an orderly manner with a clear understanding of what is expected of them. This routine should include entering the room quietly, unpacking necessary items for class, turning in homework, and working on an opening activity while the teacher takes attendance.
- **Leaving the classroom/packing up routine:** A procedure for packing up and leaving the classroom at the end of class or the school day ensures that students have all of their necessary materials, leave the room clean and organized, and exit in an orderly manner. Such a routine may include cleaning up learning materials, putting away assignments or papers, straightening desks, throwing away trash, packing up backpacks, and lining up by the door prior to dismissal. Students may be assigned specific jobs for cleaning up and organizing the room.
- **Turning in work:** Procedures for turning in classwork and homework allow for smoother transitions between activities and limit interruptions to instruction. This should occur at a specific time during the class period and can include designating a "turn in" box in the classroom for students to hand in assignments, or having students pass their papers to the front in a specific order. A student may be designated to collect papers at the end of an activity as well.
- **Using the restroom:** Restroom procedures limit student distraction and interruptions to instruction. Restroom breaks should generally not occur during direct instruction, and students should be permitted to go one at a time to avoid misbehavior. Students should be given a restroom pass, sign out before leaving the room, and sign back in upon returning to ensure that the teacher is always aware of students' whereabouts. Specific hand signals in which students can silently request permission to use the restroom are beneficial in further minimizing disruptions.
- **Transitions between activities:** Procedures for transitions allow for an orderly learning environment in that they indicate to students when and how to move between activities in the classroom. These procedures should include an attention signal and a clear explanation of the steps for transitioning, such as cleaning up materials from the previous activity, and a signal to indicate when students are permitted to move. Students should be expected to transition between activities quickly, quietly, and without disruption.
- **Non-instructional tasks:** Procedures for non-instructional tasks limit interruptions to instructional time for more focused learning. Activities such as getting a tissue, sharpening pencils, and throwing away trash should occur during specific times when the teacher is not directly instructing and should be done quietly and without disruption.
- **Managing student behavior:** Clear procedures for misbehavior establish a predictable, orderly learning environment. These procedures should be explicit, consistent, and follow a logical sequence. They may include a verbal warning, seating change, loss of privileges, or communication with home.
- **Accessing and using materials, supplies, and technology:** Procedures for these activities are beneficial in limiting disruption, maintaining organization, and avoiding interruptions to instruction. Such procedures indicate when and how to access and use materials, supplies, and technology in a respectful and orderly manner. The teacher should clearly communicate expectations for access and use as well as utilize a specific signal to indicate when students are permitted to move. These procedures should also include methods for proper cleanup at the end of the activity.

- **Finishing work early:** A procedure for finishing work early minimizes idle time and limits student disruption. Students who finish early may be permitted to work on other assignments or read quietly, or the teacher can dedicate an area of the room for extra practice and review activities for students to work on if they finish early. The teacher may also permit early finishers to assist other students in applicable learning situations.
- **Emergency drills:** Procedures for emergency drills ensure that students know how to complete them in a safe, orderly manner. When the drill begins, students should immediately stop what they are doing, leave all materials on their desks, and line up by the door in an organized fashion. Students should exit the room with the teacher and move quickly and quietly through the hallways to the designated drill location. For emergency drills that occur inside the classroom, students should move quickly and quietly to a previously designated location within the room and remain there until the drill is over.
- **Attention signal:** A dedicated signal to capture students' attention indicates that they need to stop what they are doing, focus, and listen quietly to the teacher for further information or instructions. This signal could be in the form of a hand signal, call and response, phrase, or sound and should be used consistently.
- **Direct instruction:** A procedure for direct instruction is beneficial in maintaining students' focus on learning. This should include steps for active listening, including sitting up straight, facing the teacher, maintaining eye contact, and refraining from distracting neighboring classmates. Students should have clear steps regarding how to ask questions, such as raising their hands or utilizing color-coded cards to indicate levels of understanding, and how to take notes, when applicable.
- **Independent work:** An independent work procedure limits distractions and promotes students' ability to focus. This should include communicating expectations for quiet time during this period, including refraining from talking to neighboring peers, working at and remaining in assigned seats, and engaging in the proper procedure if a student finishes early. A student can indicate a need for assistance by raising a hand or utilizing a dedicated signal to request help, such as color-coded cards.
- **Collaborative work:** A procedure for collaborative work indicates to students how to move from independent to group activities. This includes moving to a group setting without disruption, maintaining a normal volume, communicating respectfully, and cleaning up materials when finished before moving back to assigned seats in an orderly manner.

Non-Instructional Duties and Instructional Activities Maximizing Efficiency

Many non-instructional duties, such as taking attendance, grading papers, and facilitating communication, can be coordinated with instructional activities when effective **routines** and **procedures** are instilled to accomplish them. This enhances overall efficiency in the classroom, as time is not lost on completing administrative tasks, allowing more time dedicated to instruction. Taking attendance, for example, can be incorporated into students' morning work routines, as they can mark their own presence as part of the procedure for entering the classroom and beginning the day. Grading and communication with colleagues or families can take place during independent work, assessments, or recreational time. The teacher can also observe, monitor, and assess students' progress as they engage in learning. Student **self-correction** in lieu of formal grading can be beneficial in allowing students to reflect on their performance, seek areas for improvement, and strengthen their understanding while integrating grading as an instructional activity. In addition, a variety of **digital resources** are available that allow for immediate student feedback and communication with families throughout instruction. In utilizing such resources, the teacher can efficiently coordinate administrative duties with instructional activities to maximize time for student learning.

Effective Time Management

Practicing effective time management is beneficial in establishing an efficient, orderly classroom environment focused on productivity and maximizing student learning. By instilling specific **procedures** for managing daily routines such as transitioning, accessing materials and supplies, and using technology, the teacher can ensure that these tasks are completed in a timely manner while minimizing time lost on non-instructional activities and student distraction. This allows more time to be focused on instruction and student learning. To achieve this, procedures for such tasks must be **explicit** and consistently reinforced. Prior to transitioning between activities, accessing materials, or using technology, the teacher must provide a clear, detailed explanation of each step of the procedure as well as expectations for how students will complete it. Modeling the procedure is beneficial in providing a visual example to ensure student understanding. In order to be effective, each procedure must include a specific **signal** to indicate when students can begin, and the teacher must consistently monitor to ensure students are completing the task correctly. When students have a clear understanding on how to accomplish daily activities, they can do so quickly, effectively, and without disruption. This increases overall efficiency in the classroom and maximizes time dedicated to student learning.

Using Technology to Perform Administrative Tasks

Technology resources are widely available to assist teachers in accomplishing a variety of administrative tasks and are highly beneficial in establishing a **well-managed**, **organized**, and **productive** learning environment. Tasks such as taking attendance, maintaining gradebooks, or facilitating communication can be completed more efficiently through the use of technology. This allows for more time dedicated to productive teaching and learning as well as smoother transitions between activities, as time is not lost on completing such duties. Increased efficiency in completing administrative duties is beneficial in sustaining students' attention, engagement, and productivity in learning, as it minimizes idle time that could lead to distraction or disruption. In addition, utilizing technology to perform administrative duties enhances overall organization, as all tasks performed digitally can be stored in a single area on the device used for easy access and recall of information. Through email, digital apps, or class websites, the teacher can efficiently communicate with colleagues and students' families to update them regarding important events, assignments, and individual progress. This creates a sense of connectedness between the teacher and community that contributes to a positive, productive classroom climate.

Volunteers and Paraprofessionals

Enhancing and Enriching Instruction

Paraprofessionals and **volunteers** are highly valuable in enhancing and enriching the overall learning experience, as their efforts contribute to an organized, positive, and productive classroom environment. These aides collaborate with the teacher throughout planning and instruction to implement best practices in meeting students' learning needs. Paraprofessionals and volunteers can lead small groups of students as they engage in instruction for a more focused, **student-centered** learning experience. They can also provide additional support to struggling students while the teacher engages in whole-class instruction. Specifically, paraprofessionals are typically licensed in the educational field and are qualified to provide **individual accommodations** to students with individual learning needs to create an inclusive learning environment. In addition, working with paraprofessionals and volunteers is beneficial in creating an efficient, organized classroom that enhances student learning, as they can assist with **non-instructional duties** that allow for smooth transitions during instruction, such as preparing learning materials, handing back papers, or grading assignments. **Classroom management** is also enhanced when paraprofessionals and volunteers are present, as they can assist in reinforcing expectations and monitoring behavior to ensure all students are positively and productively engaging in learning.

Monitoring Their Performance in the Classroom

Paraprofessionals and volunteers are invaluable resources for creating a positive, productive classroom environment; however, to ensure the contributions of these aides are consistently beneficial in meeting students' needs and maximizing learning, it is important to continuously monitor their performance in the classroom. Paraprofessionals and volunteers are typically interviewed by administration prior to entering the classroom to determine whether their qualifications are aligned with meeting students' needs to enhance instruction. The administration is also often responsible for monitoring their performance throughout the school year. Specifically, paraprofessionals are licensed in the field of education and are often formally evaluated against specific **performance measurement tools**. **Observations** by administration can either be scheduled or conducted as an informal "walk-through" to assess how the paraprofessional or volunteer interacts with the teacher and students and his or her effectiveness in contributing to a productive learning environment. Teachers can also monitor the performance of volunteers and paraprofessionals in their classrooms. By analyzing **students' progress** when working with these aides and eliciting **feedback** from students, teachers can determine their effectiveness in enhancing the learning experience. Frequently communicating with paraprofessionals and volunteers provides valuable insight regarding whether they contribute to a positive classroom climate focused on student learning.

Classroom Organization

Physical Characteristics of a Safe and Productive Learning Environment

A classroom environment that is **safe** and facilitates **productivity** in learning is essential to fostering student motivation, engagement, and achievement. The physical space must be **clean, well-organized**, and **orderly**. All equipment, furniture, and materials must be in usable condition, well-maintained, and free of damage. This ensures that students are safe when engaging with the learning environment and provides an appealing space that encourages participation. Furniture and equipment must be arranged in a way that facilitates safety and ease of movement as students transition between activities. Likewise, all furniture, materials, and equipment must be appropriate to the students' **age group** in terms of level of difficulty, height, and size to enable students to properly interact with them for productive learning. Students must have access to a **variety** of learning materials to promote interest and engagement for productive learning, including areas for individual and collaborative learning. The classroom should be decorated in a way that is welcoming, stimulating without being overwhelming, and reflective of students' diversities and interests. When the physical environment is inviting, safe, and tailored to students' developmental levels, it creates a positive classroom climate in which students are motivated to productively engage in learning.

Significance of Effective Classroom Arrangement

A thoughtfully arranged classroom has significant and positive impacts on the nature of the learning atmosphere. Effective classroom arrangement creates an inviting learning environment in which students are motivated to engage in learning actively and productively. The manner in which the teacher organizes furniture, equipment, and learning materials influences students' **focus**, **access** to resources, and **behavior.** It also influences the teacher's ability to effectively implement **classroom management** strategies. An organized, orderly classroom in which necessary resources are easily accessible enables students to properly focus on instruction, thus promoting active engagement and productivity in learning. This reinforces positive behavior, as students are less likely to be disruptive when their learning environment is free of unnecessary distractions. The classroom arrangement determines the flow and ease of movement and should be strategically planned to facilitate productive learning while enabling the teacher to easily monitor and assist all students for effective classroom management. Effective arrangement allows the teacher to control the level of student movement and prevent potential distractions while ensuring students can easily transition from one learning activity to the next to promote efficiency, active engagement, and productivity.

Establishing Safe, Productive, and Successful Learning Environments

Establishing a safe, productive, and successful learning environment requires the teacher to thoughtfully consider several factors when determining the most effective classroom arrangement for meeting desired learning outcomes and students' needs. Students' **age group, size**, and **developmental levels** influence which arrangement best facilitates safety and productivity in learning. For example, younger students learn through interaction with their environment and therefore need ample space for movement and play to support their development. A more structured arrangement that enables direct instruction while also facilitating hands-on, collaborative learning meets the needs of middle-level and older students. In addition, students' **individual needs** must be considered when determining classroom arrangement in order to ensure equitable access to instruction and learning materials. The teacher must also consider the **size** and **layout** of the classroom, including the location of learning resources such as the projector screen, computers, and chalkboard. With this in mind, teachers must determine the **style** of teaching and learning taking place, how they want students to move, what information must be visible, as well as which materials must be accessible to create a safe, productive learning environment that meets students' needs in achieving learning outcomes.

Considerations for Desk Arrangement

There are numerous possibilities for desk arrangements in the classroom, each with advantages and limitations that must be considered and addressed. **Desired learning outcomes**, as well as the style of teaching and learning, influence which arrangement is most effective. Arrangements that facilitate individual focus, limited distraction, and clear teacher-student visibility are suited to **direct instruction;** however, these arrangements often limit collaborative learning. To address this, the teacher can designate an area in the classroom for group work, utilize common areas such as the library, or move students' desks for collaborative activities. Variations of group arrangements facilitate **collaborative learning**, as students can easily face one another and work together; however, grouped seating may cause student distraction during individual work and limit teacher-student visibility. It is therefore important that the teacher establish clear expectations and frequently monitor students' progress to ensure they remain on task. The **classroom size** must be considered, as the space may not allow for certain desk arrangements and still facilitate ease of movement, visibility, and student learning. **Individual learning needs** must also be considered when determining seating arrangements. Some students require specific accommodations, such as preferential seating, an individual learning space for limited distractions, or a physical accommodation.

Various types of seating arrangements are described below:

- **Stadium Seating**—Desks in this classroom are situated in lines at a slight angle with the students facing directly toward the teacher. This seating method is useful for lectures and individual work, as the teacher can easily monitor whether each student is on task. This arrangement is generally unsuited for group work, as students are not able to easily face one another and may limit the teacher's ease of movement between students to provide individual assistance.
- **Cluster Seating**—Desks in this classroom are arranged in groups of 3-5 throughout the classroom. This method is beneficial for supporting collaborative work and pairing students that need support with others who can provide scaffolding; however, this arrangement may be distracting during individual work and limit teacher-student visibility.
- **Rows and Columns**—Desks are individually spaced apart with the students facing directly toward the teacher and front of the room. This arrangement is useful for presentations, direct instruction, and individual work, as it limits distractions from other students. The teacher can easily see whether individual students are on task; however, this arrangement is not facilitative of group work, as students cannot easily face each other. This arrangement also limits the teacher's ability to move between students to provide assistance.
- **Horseshoe**—Desks in this classroom are arranged in a large "U" shape with students facing the teacher at the front of the room. This arrangement is useful for individual instruction, as it ensures teacher-student visibility and equal view of the chalkboard and projector screen during direct instruction. This method also facilitates whole-class discussions; however, this arrangement inhibits students' abilities to work collaboratively in groups and, depending on classroom size, may limit ease of teacher and student movement.
- **Miniature Horseshoes**—Desks in this classroom are arranged in 2-5 miniature horseshoes with students facing the front of the room. This arrangement is beneficial for both individual and collaborative work. The teacher can clearly monitor whether students are on task and can move between groups to provide individual assistance, and students can easily face one another for group activities; however, this method may lend itself to student distraction during individual work, and the physical size of the classroom may limit the possibility for this arrangement.

- **Pairs**—Desks in this classroom are arranged two-by-two in rows with students facing the front of the classroom. This arrangement is useful for partner work and pairing students who need support with others that provide scaffolding while limiting distractions during individual work. This method is not suitable for group work or whole-class activities, as students cannot easily face each other, and movement may be limited.
- **Combination**—This classroom incorporates a variety of desk arrangements, including individual seats, pairs, groups, and the horseshoe arrangements. This method is useful for accommodating varying learning styles and needs, as it can facilitate individual and collaborative work; however, this arrangement utilizes a great deal of space and may impede ease of movement and visibility for the teacher and students.
- **Flexible**—This classroom provides students with a variety of options for seating choices throughout the classroom, such as bean bag chairs, exercise balls, or floor seating. This option is beneficial for supporting students' individual learning needs, as they can choose to sit where they learn best. Flexible seating also supports collaborative learning and contributes to a welcoming, positive classroom climate; however, unstructured seating may lend itself to student distraction and limit student-teacher visibility during direct instruction.
- **Runway**—Desks in this classroom are arranged in rows on either side of the room with students facing the center, leaving the middle space clear for the teacher. This is useful for direct instruction, as students can easily see the teacher and class presentations, and the teacher can monitor whether each student is on task. This method also facilitates whole-class discussions. This arrangement is generally not suited for collaborative work, as students cannot easily face those seated near them, and it may limit the teacher's ability to provide individual assistance.
- **Conference**—All desks in this classroom are arranged in a large, two-by-two rectangle situated in the middle of the room with students facing one another. This arrangement is beneficial for collaborative work, whole-class activities, and class discussions, as students can easily face one another. The teacher can generally provide individual assistance and can easily monitor whether students are on task; however, the physical size of the classroom may not facilitate this arrangement. In addition, this method may lead to student distraction during individual work.

Classroom Seating Arrangements

Stadium Seating	Cluster Seating
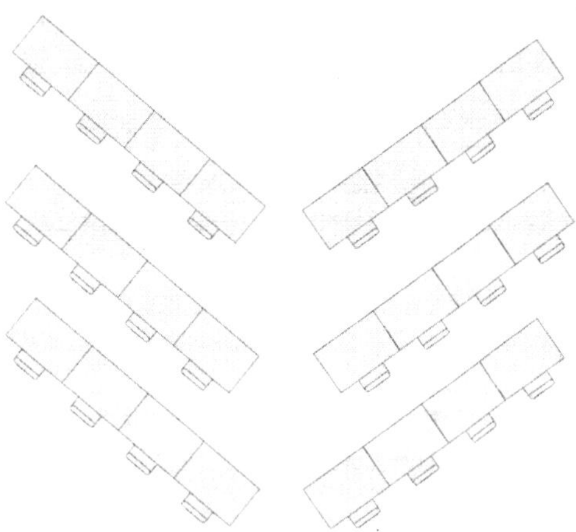	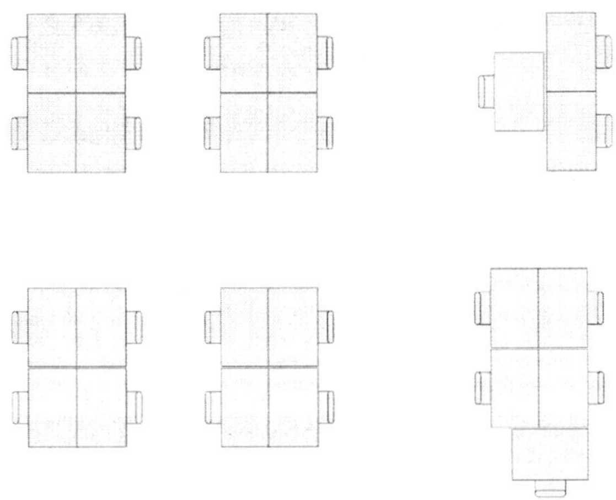

Rows and Columns

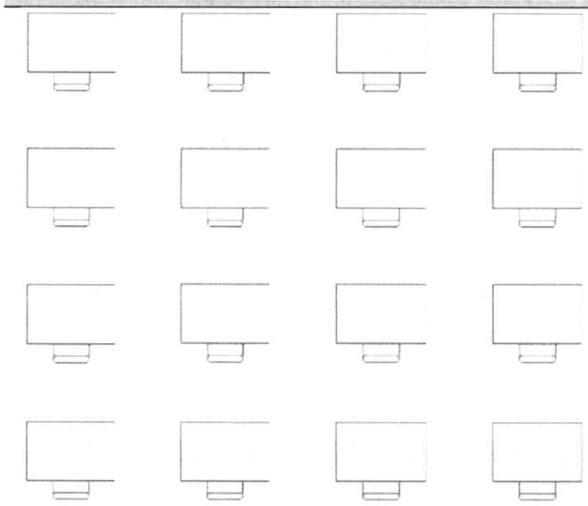

Horseshoe

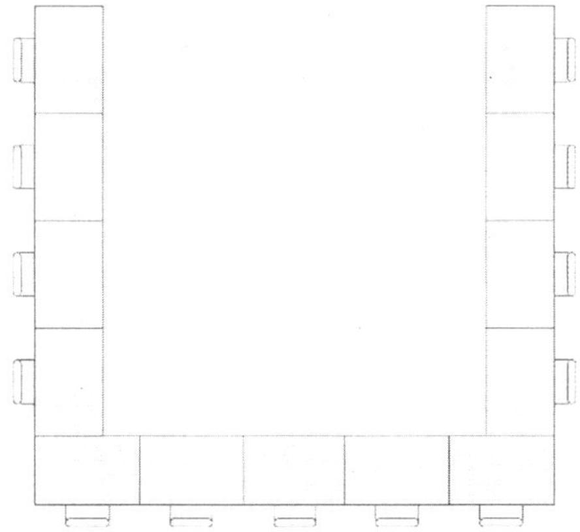

Miniature Horseshoes

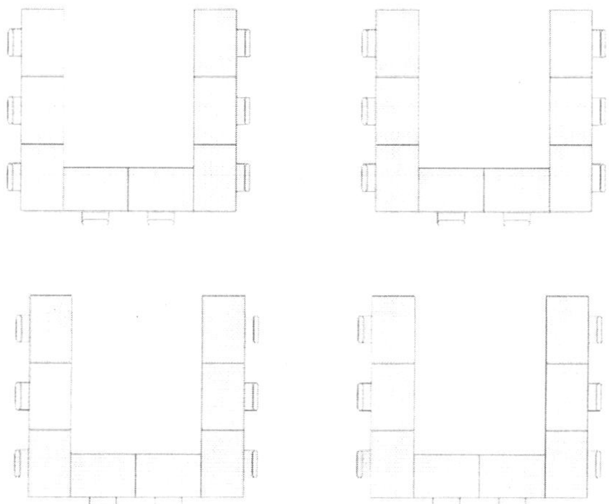

Pairs

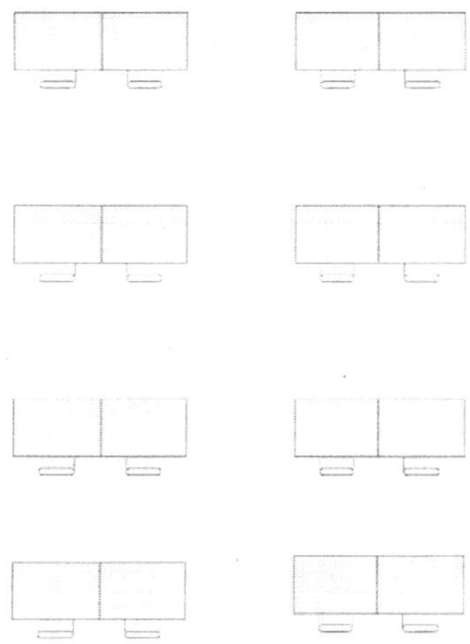

Combination

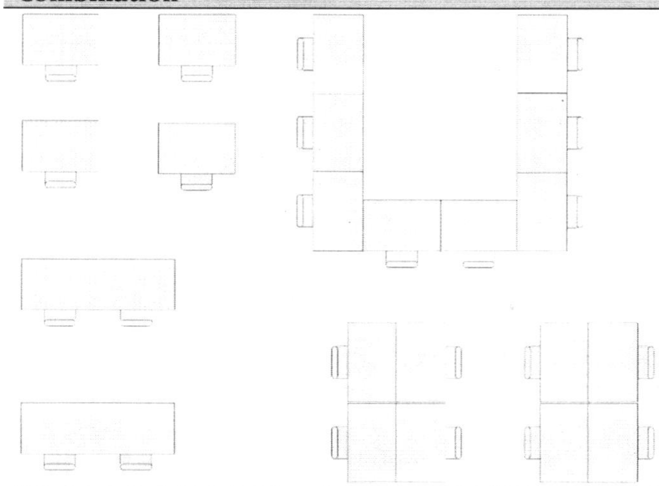

Flexible

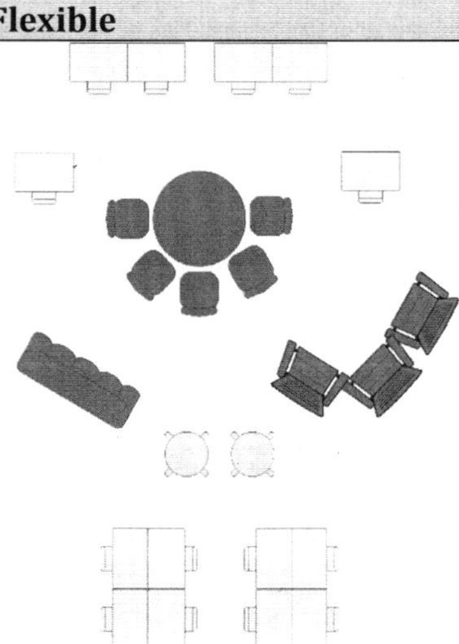

Runway	Conference
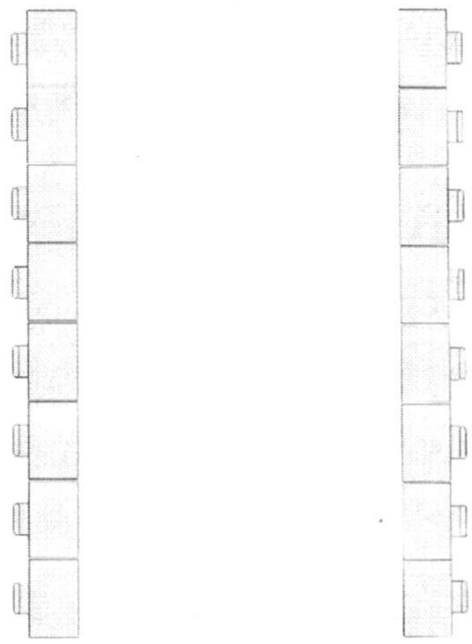	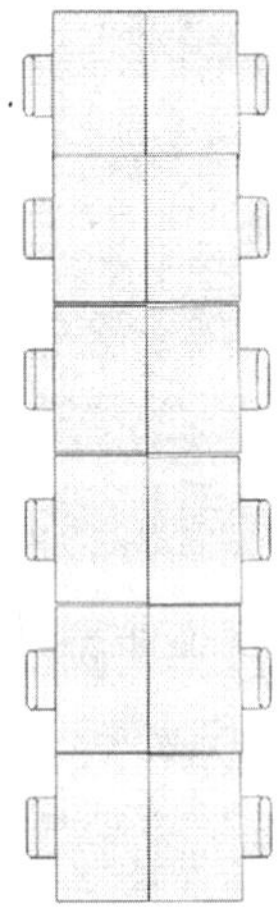

Classroom Organization Ensuring Accessibility and Facilitating Learning

Strategic classroom organization is necessary to ensure physical accessibility for all students and facilitate learning across instructional contexts. Students' **height, size**, and **special needs** must be considered and addressed when determining physical classroom arrangement. All furniture, equipment, and necessary materials must be equally accessible and facilitate ease of movement for all students as they participate in learning activities. Some students may require individualized **physical accommodations** to support their learning, such as preferential seating, special furniture arrangements to enable physical accessibility, or access to technology. By instilling these supports into the organization of the classroom, the teacher establishes an equitable environment that supports learning across instructional contexts. The classroom must be arranged to ensure all students have **visibility** and access to the teacher, pertinent instructional information, and resources, including the projector screen, chalk board, and computers. The physical environment must be aligned to and facilitative of the style of instruction taking place while supporting students' individual needs in achieving learning goals. When teachers ensure that the classroom environment is physically accessible to all students, they empower students to engage in learning across instructional contexts successfully.

Behavior Management Theory

Managing and Monitoring Student Behavior

Behaviorism and Conditioning

The theoretical school of **behaviorism** was established by John B. Watson and further developed by Ivan Pavlov and B.F. Skinner. Behaviorism emphasizes the role of environmental and experiential learning in the behavior of animals and humans. Simply put, if a person experiences a desirable result from a particular behavior, that person is more likely to perform the behavior in pursuit of the result. Likewise, undesirable results cause a person to avoid performing an associated behavior. This process of **reinforcing** or rewarding good behaviors and **punishing** unwanted behaviors is known as conditioning. Behaviorists use the terms *positive* and *negative* to refer to the mode of conditioning. The term ***positive*** refers to an added stimulus, such as giving a child a treat as positive reinforcement or giving added homework as positive punishment. ***Negative*** refers to removing a stimulus, such as taking recess away as a negative punishment or taking away extra classwork as negative reinforcement for students performing their homework independently. In the classroom, the teacher has the opportunity to help students learn to meet specific behavioral expectations. The tools of behaviorism may be carefully employed in the classrooms through positive and negative punishments and rewards. Classroom rules and expectations should be made clear as soon as possible and reinforced through verbal praise, prizes, or special privileges. Likewise, negative behaviors should be discouraged through verbal warnings, loss of privileges, and communication with the family or administrators when necessary.

Choice Theory

Choice theory, developed by **William Glasser**, states that behavior is chosen, either consciously or unconsciously, to meet the **five basic needs** of survival, love and belonging, power, freedom, and fun. Rather than implement positive and negative reinforcements to drive behavior, the teacher must aim to teach students self-responsibility for their actions. This includes encouraging students to reflect and consider the reasons for their actions and attempt to rectify any misbehavior. This method relies on the notion that if students understand how their desire to meet certain needs impacts their actions, they are more likely to engage in positive behavior. In the classroom, the teacher focuses on meeting students' **five basic needs** to encourage positive behavior by creating a classroom climate that emphasizes **communication, relationship building**, and **self-reflection**. This includes establishing positive relationships with students, holding class discussions, and teaching conflict resolution skills to create a safe, welcoming learning environment. Instructional activities are tailored to individual needs, and students have a great deal of choice in their own learning with the intention of promoting positive behavior by meeting their needs for power and freedom.

Assertive Discipline Theory

The **Assertive Discipline theory** was developed by **Lee** and **Marlene Canter**. This theory states that the teacher is in charge of **instruction, the classroom**, and **students' behavior**. The expectation is that the teacher establishes clear behavioral standards that protect their right to teach and students' right to learn without distraction or disruption. Negative consequences for unwanted behavior are instilled to deter students from deviating from behavioral expectations. This theory argues that if teachers are viewed as firm and consistent, students will have a greater respect for them and ultimately engage in positive behavior. In the classroom, the teacher is in control of **establishing** and **consistently reinforcing** standards for student behavior. This establishes a sense of predictability, as students are clear on what is expected of them as they engage in learning. Students are expected to comply with the teacher's expectations, and a system of **negative consequences** are in place to discourage unwanted behavior. Positive behavior is rewarded to further reinforce desired behavior. The teacher in this classroom believes that creating such an environment enhances students' ability to focus on learning without disruption.

Student-Directed Learning Theory

The **student-directed learning theory**, or the idea of the **democratic classroom**, was founded by **Alfie Kohn** and emphasizes the importance of **student choice** and **classroom community** in influencing behavior. This includes having students contribute to the development of behavioral expectations, as this helps students understand their purpose while instilling a sense of ownership and accountability. Instructional activities are tailored to accommodate students' individual interests and natural curiosity while emphasizing cooperation to foster an engaging learning environment that promotes positive behavior. This theory focuses on eliciting students' intrinsic motivation to engage in positive behavior rather than relying on positive and negative reinforcements. In the classroom, students primarily direct their own learning based upon their **natural curiosity** while the teacher acts as a **facilitator**. Students contribute to the development of behavioral expectations that are instilled to promote respect and focus on learning. **Active engagement**, **cooperation**, and **collaborative learning** are emphasized over direct instruction. Students may be engaging in differing activities simultaneously as the teacher moves around the classroom to monitor progress and assist as necessary.

Social Learning Theory and Behavior Management

The **social learning theory**, developed by **Albert Bandura**, asserts that one's **environment** and the **people** within it heavily influence behavior. As humans are social creatures, they learn a great deal by **observing** and **imitating** one another. This theory is also rooted in the importance of **self-efficacy** in achieving desired behavior, as students must be motivated and confident that they can effectively imitate what they observe. In the classroom, the teacher establishes behavioral expectations and focuses on **modeling** positive behaviors, attitudes, and interactions with the intention of encouraging students to do the same. The teacher recognizes and praises positive behavior from students to elicit the same behavior from others. The teacher also emphasizes a growth mindset in the classroom to promote students' sense of self-efficacy.

Behavior Standards and Expectations for Students at Developmental Levels

Behavioral standards that emphasize respect for oneself, others, and property are necessary in creating a safe, positive, and productive learning environment for students of all ages; however, as students at varying developmental levels differ in their capabilities across domains, behavioral expectations must be **realistic**, **applicable**, and reflect an **awareness** of these **differences** while encouraging growth. Young children, for example, are learning to interact with others and function in a group setting. Behavioral expectations must be attuned to this understanding while promoting the development of positive interpersonal skills. Young children also require ample opportunities for active movement and cannot reasonably be expected to sit still for long periods of time. Middle-level students are at a unique transitional period in their development and often exhibit characteristics of both young children and adolescents. Behavioral standards for these students must recognize the significant social, emotional, cognitive, and physical changes occurring at this stage by emphasizing self-control, emotional regulation, and positive interactions. As older students prepare for adulthood, they can generally be expected to conduct themselves with a degree of maturity and responsibility in a variety of settings. Appropriate behavioral standards for these students emphasize self-responsibility, respectful interactions, and independently completing necessary tasks.

Effective Management of Student Behavior

Management and Significance in Positive, Productive, and Organized Environments

Promoting **appropriate behavior** and **ethical work habits** while taking specific measures to **manage student behavior** creates a safe, organized, and productive classroom. Such an environment is beneficial for students' motivation, engagement, and ability to focus on learning. This is achieved by communicating and consistently reinforcing **high** yet **realistic behavioral expectations** for all students. This, when combined with **relationship building** strategies, establishes a positive rapport between the teacher and students that encourages appropriate behavior and ethical work habits. Students are more inclined to adhere to expectations for behavior and work habits when their relationship with the teacher is founded on mutual understanding and respect. In addition, students who feel they are a part of developing academic and behavioral expectations feel a greater sense of **ownership** and responsibility to follow them, and, therefore, it is beneficial to include students in this process. Encouraging students to **self-monitor** their behavior and utilize conflict resolution strategies furthers this sense of accountability, as it prompts students to positively manage their own actions and work habits. Misbehavior must be addressed appropriately and in a timely manner, and consequences must follow a logical sequence, such as a verbal warning, followed by loss of privileges or communication with family.

Review Video: Student Behavior Management Approaches
Visit mometrix.com/academy and enter code: 843846

Review Video: Promoting Appropriate Behavior
Visit mometrix.com/academy and enter code: 321015

Strategies

Proactively implementing effective behavior management strategies is beneficial to establishing and maintaining a positive, productive learning environment. The **physical environment** should be arranged in such a way that facilitates ease of movement while limiting the amount of free space that could encourage student disruption. Planning for **smooth transitions** from one activity to the next further discourages behavioral disruptions. Desks should be arranged so that students can easily view the teacher, projector, chalkboard, or other information pertinent to learning. Expectations for behavior, procedures, and routines, including consequences, should be predictable, consistent, succinct, and visible at all times. Allowing students to participate in the development of classroom procedures and routines is valuable in providing students with a sense of personal accountability that increases the likelihood that they will follow them. Students also often respond well to incentives for modeling appropriate behavior, such as a **PBIS reward system**, verbal praise, or a positive phone call home. Nonverbal strategies are valuable in subtly managing student behavior throughout instruction, such as hand gestures, proximity, or eye contact. Misbehavior should be addressed discreetly and privately so as to avoid embarrassing the student or encouraging further disruption.

Importance of Consistency

Standards for behavior must be enforced consistently in order to establish a well-managed classroom in which students can focus on learning. This includes communicating **clear expectations**, holding all students equally accountable with specific **positive and negative consequences**, and **following through** on implementing them. In doing so, the teacher ensures that students are always aware of the behavior expected from them and what will happen if they do not adhere to the standards. When students are clear regarding behavioral expectations and assured that they will be enforced, they are more inclined to demonstrate appropriate conduct. This creates a predictable, secure environment that promotes student motivation, engagement, and focused productivity in learning. Consistently enforcing behavior standards gives the teacher a sense of credibility among students, and, therefore, students are more likely to respect and adhere to these expectations. In addition, holding all students to the same high behavioral standards contributes to a positive classroom climate in which all students feel they are treated fairly.

Safety and Regulations

SDS

An **SDS**, or **Safety Data Sheet** (formerly MSDS), explains the properties of a specific substance, and provides a means of cataloging substances according to their effects and risks. It is an integral component of **workplace safety** as it provides information necessary to the safe handling and storage of the substance. SDS information has sixteen sections: Identification, Hazard identification, Composition/information on ingredients, First-aid measures, Fire-fighting measures, Accidental release measures, Handling and storage, Exposure controls/ personal protection, Physical and chemical properties, Stability and reactivity, Toxicological information, Ecological information, Disposal considerations, Transport information, Regulatory information, and Other information. The SDS should be present wherever chemicals are being used or kept. SDS sheets are not necessarily intended for general consumers; rather, they are meant for those who work with chemicals in an occupational setting.

Standard Procedures

Standard procedures when working around materials and equipment related to technology include the following:

- Do not bring pets or nonessential personnel.
- Do not consume food or drink.
- Familiarize yourself with the proper operation of all equipment and materials by consulting user guides.
- Wear shoes, shirts, and all other appropriate attire.
- Tie back long hair and remove loose clothing (ties, scarves, dangling jewelry, etc.) so that they do not contact equipment or materials.
- Refrain from dropping equipment.
- Observe appropriate precautions when working around electrical equipment.
- Ensure that all equipment and instrumentation is calibrated correctly.
- Ensure that that power is off before making circuit connections.
- Power untested circuits with adjustable power sources at their lowest levels.
- Be professional in your conduct.

Emergency Fire Procedures

The following procedures should be undertaken in the event of fire:

- Sound the fire alarm if you will be unable to extinguish the fire on your own or a serious emergency has occurred, such as the release of toxic gas.
- Use a nearby fire extinguisher to extinguish the fire. If possible, extinguish the fire using CO2 units rather than dry chemical units. CO2 units often pose less risk to equipment.
- Carry a fire extinguisher with you when going to an area in which a fire might be present.
- When a person's clothing is on fire, roll them on the floor or wrap them in a coat or blanket.
- Immediately leave a building in which a fire alarm has been sounded.

Electrocution

Electrocution refers to severe injury or death caused by direct exposure to an electric current. The following procedures should be undertaken in the event that someone is being electrocuted:

- Never touch someone who is being electrocuted.
- Turn off the power supply if possible. This can be done at the work bench or at a breaker panel.
- If the power cannot be turned off, use a piece of non-conducting material (such as lumber) to separate the person from the energized conductor.
- Ensure that the person is breathing and check for pulse. Administer CPR if necessary; only qualified individuals should administer CPR.
- Seek medical assistance.

Whenever equipment is damaged, report it to the appropriate personnel for repair. Damaged equipment can be very hazardous. A blown fuse or circuit breaker indicates a faulty circuit; therefore, identify and correct the faulty circuit before resetting the breaker or replacing the fuse.

OSHA

OSHA, or **Occupational Safety and Health Administration**, is a federal regulatory agency that enforces workplace safety and health standards to prevent work-related injuries, illnesses, and fatalities. OSHA applies to most workplaces and requires the following workplace safeguards:

- **Guards** must be placed on all moving parts where contact is possible.
- **Permissible exposure limits**, or **PEL**, prevent chemical or dust concentrations from exceeding certain limits.
- **Personal protective equipment**, or **PPE**, require use of respirators, gloves, coveralls, goggles, face shields, and/or other protective equipment when working in certain industrial environments.
- **Lockout/tagout** requires that energy sources be secured in an off condition when maintenance or repairs are being performed.
- **Confined space** requires air sampling and use of a buddy system while working in enclosed areas, such as tanks, pits, manholes, etc.
- **Hazard communication** requires that workers are informed of workplace chemical hazards.
- **Process safety management** lessens risk of large industrial accidents.
- **Blood borne pathogens**, or **BBP**, protections prevent workers from being exposed to blood borne pathogens, such as HIV.
- **Excavations and trenches** must follow certain procedures and use certain safety equipment if they are more than five feet down.
- **Asbestos exposure** limit occupational exposure to asbestos.

Review Video: Intro to OSHA
Visit mometrix.com/academy and enter code: 913559

Career and Technical Education Course Approval and Re-Approval Process

According to the Carl D. Perkins Career and Technical Education Improvement Act of 2006, **career and technical education (CTE)** programs in all states must emulate the New York CTE program. In Washington, the CTE program has the following goals:

- Maintain rigorous academic standards.
- Provide the skills necessary to fill any deficiencies or gaps in Washington's economy.
- Ensure that all state education reform requirements are aligned.
- Create and design good career and technical education programs by building and facilitating relationships with local CTE advisory councils.

The approval/re-approval process for CTE courses can be performed online. Approval request deadlines vary by state or region. Approval and re-approval for specific courses follow a schedule that can be found at the same site.

Safety and Health Standards

The **Safety Guide for Career and Technical Education** contains the most recent instructions and checklists for vocational education curricula. This lengthy document is published by OSPI, and can be found online. It contains a comprehensive list of safety practices and requirements that students and teachers should observe in CTE courses. These practices and requirements include the following:

- Proper floor cleanliness and maintenance
- Proper maintenance, storage, and handling of power tools, shop machinery, and equipment
- Required shop equipment
- Safety rules and standards displayed in plain sight
- Proper material handling and storage

- Storage, labeling, and handling of electrical devices and equipment
- Disposal of hazardous waste
- Non-asbestos fire blankets
- Proper safety equipment, such as eyewear and face shields
- Eye wash stations
- Proper ventilation
- Safety Signs
- Ambient noise level limits

Career and Technical Education Curriculum Advisory Committee

The career and technical education (CTE) advisory committee is responsible for **determining and recommending a curriculum** that will best prepare students for passing state assessments and earning a Certificate of Academic Achievement, or CAA. The specific duties of the CTE advisory committee include the following:

- Establishing criteria, processes, and tools that state and district boards will use to identify and evaluate appropriate CTE equivalency courses. These courses should gain equivalent academic credit in the core subject areas of math, science, social studies, English, health/fitness, and art.
- Using these criteria, processes, and tools to determine if existing CTE courses fulfill the equivalency requirements.

Tech Prep Articulation

Tech Prep is a high school program that provides students with technical training, applied academics, and assistance in finding workplace internship and guidance. Tech Prep offers a number of advantages to high school students:

- Provides **college credit**, ultimately saving both time and money. Tech Prep enables high school graduates to bypass entry level courses and enroll in higher level classes. The manner in which college credit and standing are awarded is based on an articulation agreement between the high school and the college program. In most cases, this agreement awards college credit using tests, certification by a high school teacher, or college course completion.
- Prepares high school students for the **rigors of college courses**.
- Prepares high school students for a **career in technical professions**, such as engineering, science, health care, computers, etc. Upon leaving college, Tech Prep students often receive better wages and benefits than students who did not take Tech Prep courses.

Membership in Professional Career and Technical Organizations

There are many different **professional career and technical organizations**. When deciding which organization to join, the best choice will vary depending on the specific CTE field and personal preference. However, most organizations offer similar benefits, such as the following:

- **Networking and professional development** opportunities through expos, seminars, and webinars. Members have the opportunity to meet and speak with CTE educators, business partners, institutional representatives, and policy makers.
- Helpful **classroom tools**, best practices, and analysis.
- **Partnerships** with and access to industry experts.
- A **news periodical** that keeps members up-to-date on the newest developments in the field.
- **Awards programs** that offer national recognition.
- **Online courses** that may improve career advancement prospects.
- **Job banks**.
- **Connection** to other education worldwide.

Primary Business Management Functions

Business management usually includes the following functions:

- **Planning** involves creating plans for action based on forecasts over certain periods of time, such as weeks, months, and years.
- **Organizing** requires the optimization of resource usage so that plans will be successful and can be carried out in the most efficient ways possible.
- **Staffing** recruits and assigns personnel to the appropriate jobs. This function involves job analysis.
- **Directing** identifies the specific tasks necessary for plan completion and gets workers to carry them out.
- **Monitoring** checks the progress of the project team against the plan, and it determines whether it is on schedule.
- **Motivating** is fundamental and a very important aspect of business management. Workers must be motivated to carry out their specific tasks and contribute to other functions.

Work Schedule

A **work schedule** breaks a project down into its most basic work activities. These activities are known as terminal elements and cannot be further divided into smaller tasks. The work schedule will include estimates for the resources, cost, and duration of each activity, and then arrange them by their dependencies and order of completion. To create a work schedule, the project manager must have a **work breakdown structure**, which includes an effort estimate and the resource availability for each task. There is software that can perform much of the work necessary to create a work schedule; however, even when using these applications, the manager must have an understanding of certain key concepts and tools, such as dependencies, resource allocation, earned value, critical paths, and Gantt charts. A **Gantt chart** is a bar chart that shows each terminal element, its duration, and other summary information.

Workflow Tracking

A **workflow** is an abstraction of work that is performed by a single person or group of people. It depicts a sequence of steps that, upon completion, produces a certain outcome or product. Any workflow must have input, such as information or materials. This input then undergoes a change or transformation in accordance with certain rules. Finally, a workflow will produce an output, which consists of new information or a new product. When monitoring workflow, management may track a document as it passes through each step within the sequence. Workflow plays an important role in issue tracking, the purpose of which is identifying and resolving customer problems. A problem is input into the customer call support center (via a customer complaint), tracked as it passes through all the steps, and is then resolved.

Safety Assessments

A **safety assessment** is a method of quantifying and understanding the hazards and risks associated with certain products and materials, such as hazardous chemicals. Safety assessments incorporate multiple scientific disciplines, and they typically involve professional risk assessors hired by the company. Chemical companies, consumer product companies, government agencies, insurance agencies, consulting firms, medical device manufacturers, and many others make use of risk assessors. Most safety or risk assessments involve three steps:

- Identify the hazard (i.e. the consequences of exposure).
- Perform a dose-response analysis to determine the dosage necessary to produce a certain response.
- Perform exposure quantification in order to determine the dosage that the population is likely to receive.

The information gained during safety assessments should be incorporated into demonstrations, training, tests, and record keeping.

Chapter Quiz

Ready to see how well you retained what you just read? Scan the QR code to go directly to the chapter quiz interface for this study guide. If you're using a computer, simply visit the online resources page at **mometrix.com/resources719/texespprte370** and click the Chapter Quizzes link.

Professional Practices and Responsibilities

Legal and Ethical Use of Resources

Legal and Ethical Requirements for Using Resources and Technologies

The legal and ethical requirements regarding the use of educational resources and technologies serve as an important frame of reference for teachers when selecting learning materials. Understanding these guidelines is beneficial in effectively determining which resources and technologies are **safe**, **secure**, **appropriate**, and **legal** for classroom use. This helps to protect the data and privacy of both teachers and students when interacting with instructional materials. In addition, this ensures that teachers and students are aware of what constitutes acceptable use of technology resources to protect their safety when engaging online. It is also important to be cognizant of legal and ethical standards in relation to the **reproduction** and **redistribution** of learning materials and technologies. Doing so ensures teachers understand how to properly adhere to copyright laws so as not to infringe upon the original creator's ability to profit from their work.

Copyright Act

When selecting educational resources and technologies to implement in the classroom, it is important that teachers consider the guidelines of the **Copyright Act**. The Copyright Act protects creators by prohibiting the unauthorized use, reproduction, or redistribution of their original works. This extends to digital resources as well, including photographs, video clips, website articles, or online learning materials. While the **Fair Use Doctrine** permits teachers to utilize copyrighted materials for educational purposes, they must be mindful of its restrictions and take the proper precautions to avoid **copyright infringement**. When using copyrighted resources or technologies, teachers can obtain permission directly from the creator, purchase the materials or licenses for use themselves, or ask their school, district, or students to purchase them. In addition, when using, reproducing, or distributing lesson materials, teachers should always cite the appropriate source in order to give credit to the original creator.

Fair Use Doctrine

Under the **Fair Use Doctrine**, teachers are permitted to utilize, reproduce, and redistribute copyrighted materials for educational purposes; however, this doctrine includes limitations that teachers must adhere to when selecting educational resources and technologies to implement in the classroom. The **purpose** of utilizing copyrighted materials must be strictly educational and intended to achieve specific objectives. Teachers must also consider the **nature** of all copyrighted resources and technologies to determine whether they meet the requirements of the Fair Use Doctrine. All copyrighted materials must be used for informational purposes and typically should be limited to published, nonfiction works. The **amount** of copyrighted material that is reproduced or redistributed must be limited to small excerpts rather than the entire work, and teachers must appropriately cite the original source. In addition, teachers must consider the effect of their use of copyrighted resources and technologies on the future **potential market**. Use of copyrighted materials must not interfere with the creator's ability to profit from his or her work.

Data Security

Teachers, staff, and students engage with numerous digital resources for a variety of administrative and educational purposes. As such, protecting **data security** when interacting with these materials is increasingly important in establishing a safe, secure learning environment. When selecting educational technologies, such as student information systems (SIS) or digital learning tools, it is imperative that teachers ensure they are aligned with legal and ethical standards regarding data security. All resources must adhere to the requirements outlined by the **Family Educational Rights and Privacy Act (FERPA)** regarding the disclosure of students' sensitive or personally identifiable information. Teachers must also observe their **districts' and schools' policies** regarding the implementation of educational technologies to ensure they are approved for use. In addition, many education technology companies collect students' data as they interact with digital resources with the intention of utilizing it to inform future educational decisions. It is therefore important that teachers consider the nature of the technologies that they implement to ensure that the data collected from students is used strictly for educational purposes. Taking measures to protect students' data when interacting with educational technology resources ensures their safety both within and outside of the classroom.

Privacy

Protecting students' privacy when interacting with educational resources and technologies is paramount to ensuring their safety both within and outside of the classroom. Prior to selecting learning materials, teachers must ensure that they follow all legal and ethical requirements regarding student privacy. This includes determining whether the resources and technologies in question follow the standards outlined by the **Family Educational Rights and Privacy Act (FERPA)** and the **Children's Online Privacy Protection Act (COPPA)**. In doing so, teachers ensure that students' sensitive and personally identifiable information, such as academic, behavioral, or medical records, are secure when interacting with instructional materials. This is necessary to protect students from encountering potentially harmful situations or individuals that could compromise their privacy and cause long-term negative impacts.

Acceptable Use Policies

Acceptable use policies to govern the use of educational technologies are integral to ensuring a safe, secure learning environment. These documents provide guidelines for **acceptable behavior** when interacting with digital resources under the school network, and they outline the **consequences** of violating the terms. Acceptable use policies also inform teachers, staff, students, and families of the measures in place to protect **data security** and **privacy** within the school, such as only allowing individuals with the proper credentials to access the network. Acceptable use policies are beneficial in discouraging users from engaging in inappropriate behavior by outlining standards for responsible use to ensure that sensitive information remains secure. This helps to prevent interaction with potentially harmful individuals or situations that could threaten the safety and privacy of students, teachers, staff, or families, as well as the security of the school network.

Legal and Ethical Obligations Surrounding Student Rights

Legal Requirements for Educators

Special Education Services

Establishing an inclusive, equitable learning environment for students with disabilities requires educators to adhere to strict legal guidelines regarding special education services. According to **IDEA (Individuals with Disabilities Education Act)**, educators must provide students with disabilities a **free and appropriate public education (FAPE)** in the **least restrictive environment (LRE)**. To do this effectively, educators are required to fully comply with students' **IEPs (Individual Education Plans)** at all times. This includes providing students requiring special education services with the necessary supports, accommodations, and modifications according to their IEPs throughout all stages of instruction. Educators must also document the academic and behavioral progress of these students in relation to the goals outlined in their IEPs to report to the designated case manager. In addition, the specifics of students' special education services must be kept confidential in order to protect their privacy. Adhering to these legal requirements promotes equity in the classroom by ensuring that the unique needs of students with disabilities are met, thus allowing them to effectively participate and engage in learning.

Review Video: Legal and Ethical Issues
Visit mometrix.com/academy and enter code: 934372

Review Video: IEPs
Visit mometrix.com/academy and enter code: 153484

Review Video: **Development of the Individuals with Disabilities Education Act**
Visit mometrix.com/academy and enter code: 100350

FERPA

Understanding and observing the legal requirements related to students' and families' rights is integral to maintaining their confidentiality and establishing a safe, secure learning environment. Educators are required to follow the guidelines of **FERPA (Family Educational Rights and Privacy Act)** regarding students' education records and personally identifiable information. According to FERPA, educators may not release students' education records or personally identifiable information except in authorized situations, such as when the student enrolls in another school or the information is requested by a financial aid institution to which the student has applied. In all other instances, the educator must have written permission to disclose this information. FERPA also provides students' parents or legal guardians the right to access their child's education records and request that the education records be amended. While educators may not disclose personally identifiable information, they are permitted to release directory information regarding the student, including their name, phone number, or student identification number; however, educators must provide an appropriate amount of time to allow for the refusal of such disclosure. It is also important to note that the rights guaranteed under FERPA become applicable only to students once they have turned 18 or begun postsecondary education.

Discipline Procedures and Student Code of Conduct

Adhering to legal requirements regarding student discipline procedures is necessary to ensure a safe, orderly, and unbiased learning environment. School districts are responsible for developing a **student code of conduct** to distribute among teachers, staff, students, and families. This document outlines expectations for student behavior as well as specific consequences for varying degrees of infractions that may occur on school grounds. Educators must strictly adhere to the guidelines stated in the student code of conduct when enacting disciplinary measures. This includes ensuring that consequences for student misbehavior align with the nature of the action and do not interfere with the student's right to a free public education. Disciplinary actions must be free of bias and must not endanger the student's physical, mental, or emotional health. In addition, the educator must document instances of student discipline and keep these records confidential to protect the student's right to privacy. Extended suspensions and expulsions must be reserved for instances in which all other disciplinary measures have been exhausted. In such cases, the student is entitled to a hearing at the board of education, and teachers must provide adequate instructional materials for the time that the student is out of the classroom.

Guidelines for acceptable student behavior on school property are outlined in a student code of conduct. Providing students with this reference helps to ensure that the school functions in a safe, orderly, and productive manner so as to create and maintain an environment focused on learning. This document typically addresses a number of topics related to **daily school procedures**, including student dress code standards, acceptable use policies for the internet and digital devices, attendance, grading policies, and academic integrity. Student codes of conduct also address **potential behavioral issues**, such as acceptable conduct while riding school buses, the use of illegal substances on school property, and harmful or disruptive behavior, including bullying, harassment, or fighting. The expectations iterated in student codes of conduct are typically accompanied by an ascending matrix of classroom, administrative, and district-level **consequences** that coincide with the severity and frequency of student infractions.

Establishing an Equitable Learning Environment for All Students

An **equitable environment** is one in which students receive the individual support necessary to facilitate their success in learning. Establishing such an environment requires educators to adhere to several legal guidelines to ensure all students are provided with fair access to learning opportunities. Educators must be sure that all students are included in the educational program, and may not discriminate based upon students' races, religions, genders, backgrounds, disabilities, or any other differentiating characteristics. All students must be provided with equal access to learning materials, resources, technologies, and supports. In addition, educators must fully comply with all accommodations outlined in students' **IEPs**, **504 plans**, and **Behavior Intervention Plans (BIP)**, and implement all required supports to provide them with equitable access to learning.

> **Review Video: 504 Plans and IEPs**
> Visit mometrix.com/academy and enter code: 881103

Child Abuse

One of the primary responsibilities of an educator is to ensure the safety of all students. In order to do so, it is important that educators understand and follow all legal requirements related to child abuse. Within the classroom, educators are responsible for establishing a safe, secure learning environment. All interactions with students must be appropriate and refrain from harming students' **physical**, **mental**, or **emotional health**. Educators must also recognize the signs of potential **child abuse** or **neglect** among their students. If any abuse or neglect is suspected, educators are legally required to report it immediately to the proper agency according to their state and local laws regardless of whether there is concrete evidence, as waiting to report it may place the student in continued danger. Reports of potential child abuse or neglect must be **confidential** so as to protect the students' privacy. Depending on the protocols established by individual school districts, educators may be required to notify their school's administration and resource officer of the report.

Significance of Understanding and Adhering to Legal Requirements

Understanding the legal requirements for educators ensures that teachers know what is expected of them to maintain professionalism and establish a safe, secure learning environment. This avoids misconception regarding the teacher's **roles** and **responsibilities** within the educational program so that teachers understand how to adhere to legal guidelines properly. When teachers are aware of the legal requirements they must follow, they are more effectively able to implement the appropriate protocols for addressing specific education-related situations. This includes instances related to establishing an equitable learning environment, providing special education services, interacting appropriately with students, colleagues, and families as well as protecting students' privacy. In addition, understanding the legal requirements for educators ensures that they are aware of their own professional rights and how to protect themselves in various education-related situations.

Ethical Guidelines

Confidentiality

Adhering to ethical guidelines in relation to confidentiality is an important part of demonstrating professionalism as well as protecting the privacy of students, their families, and others in the school building. Teachers are required to follow all standards outlined by **FERPA** regarding student and family privacy. This includes preserving the confidentiality of all **personally identifiable information** about students, such as grades, medical history, discipline records, or special education services, except in authorized situations. By following these guidelines, teachers ensure that they do not release any information that may compromise the safety of students or their families. In addition, when students and families feel their personal information is kept confidential, they are more likely to seek necessary supports from the educational program without the fear of being stigmatized. Similarly, teachers must follow ethical guidelines to protect the privacy of their colleagues. Any knowledge about a colleague's personal information must be kept confidential so as to establish positive, professional relationships founded on mutual trust. Doing so facilitates productive collaboration among colleagues to benefit student success in learning.

Interactions with Students and Others in the School Community

The daily interactions among students, teachers, staff, and administration largely determine the quality of the school environment. A positive, safe, and professional school community is one in which educators adhere to ethical guidelines regarding interactions with one another and students. Communication with colleagues must be respectful of one another's privacy and confidentiality. This includes avoiding gossip and ensuring that all discussions about colleagues are factual, neutral, and professional in nature. In addition, interactions with members of the school community must **avoid discrimination** of any sort. Similarly, all interactions with students must be inclusive, accepting, and respectful of differences. In addition, educators must maintain proper **boundaries** when communicating with students. This includes avoiding communication outside of the school setting except in authorized situations and ensuring that all interactions maintain professionalism. Any interactions with students must avoid compromising their **physical or mental health**, **safety**, or **ability to learn**. By adhering to these ethical guidelines, educators can ensure that all communication with students and members of the school community contribute to establishing and maintaining a safe, appropriate, and professional learning environment.

Teacher's Role as an Advocate

Advocating for Students

The teacher's role as an advocate is invaluable in ensuring students receive the necessary support to facilitate their achievement. As teachers spend most of the school day with students, they are equipped with an understanding of how to best meet the unique needs within their classrooms. Teachers will inevitably encounter situations in which advocacy for students is integral to providing equitable learning opportunities. Students with **physical**, **social**, **emotional**, or **learning disabilities** need teachers to advocate on their behalf to ensure special education services or accommodations are implemented. Teachers may also need to advocate for **underprivileged students** to ensure they have equitable access to the learning materials, resources, and technologies necessary for success. Additionally, students experiencing **bullying** may need teachers to ensure the appropriate measures are taken to resolve the issue and maintain a safe learning environment. Effective advocacy requires teachers to listen and communicate with students to determine their needs and seek the appropriate avenues for support. Teachers must also communicate with colleagues, administration, and families to collaborate in addressing students' needs. In some instances, teachers may need to contact the board of education or education advocacy organizations specific to students' needs to ensure they are provided with adequate support.

Advocating for the Educational Profession

Teachers offer valuable perspectives regarding ways to enhance the quality of the education profession. As such, it is important that teachers advocate for themselves in order to help ensure they have the **conditions**, **resources**, and **support systems** necessary to facilitate student success. This includes advocating for equitable allocation of funding, learning materials, technology resources, and professional development opportunities that would help teachers more effectively meet students' learning needs. Teachers can advocate for the profession in a variety of ways. **Communicating frequently** with students, families, and administration allows teachers to discuss their needs and ways to improve the education system. Attending **PTA meetings, public forums**, or **school board meetings** allows teachers to voice their concerns and offer potential solutions. Teachers can also contact **state legislators** to influence their decisions regarding education policies that would impact the quality of the profession. In addition, there are numerous **education advocacy organizations** that teachers can join to connect with one another and influence such decisions. Taking measures to advocate for the education profession is an important part of creating a positive, productive school climate focused on supporting student achievement.

Roles and Responsibilities within the Local Education System

Department Chairpersons

Department chairpersons are appointed to act as **leaders** within their subject areas. These individuals are responsible for a variety of instructional and administrative duties to ensure the **efficacy** of their academic department in supporting the goals and mission of the school. This includes contributing to curriculum development, communicating instructional expectations from administration to their colleagues, and ensuring that daily instruction within the department aligns with campus and district academic standards. Department chairpersons also serve as **resources** for their teams, including collaborating with them to design instructional activities and assessments, offering support, and facilitating positive communication with administration. When working with administration, department chairpersons discuss the progress of their departments in meeting academic goals, collaborate to develop strategies for assisting faculty in supporting student learning, and ensure their colleagues have the support, materials, and resources necessary for effective instruction. In addition, department chairpersons are often responsible for coordinating department activities and programs that promote student achievement and contribute to creating a positive school community.

School Principal

The primary role of the **principal** is establishing and maintaining a **school culture** that supports students, teachers, staff, and families in the educational program. This role comprises a multifaceted array of responsibilities that extend to nearly every aspect of the school. The principal is responsible for supervising the **daily operations** of the school to ensure a safe, orderly environment in which teachers, staff, and students are working in alignment with the school's mission. To achieve this, the principal must communicate expectations for a positive, productive school community, ensure academic and behavioral policies are followed by staff and students, and assign staff members specific duties to facilitate an organized, efficient learning environment. In addition, it is important that the principal support staff, students, and families by engaging in frequent, open communication, addressing concerns, and providing resources necessary to promote growth and achievement. The principal is also responsible for ensuring that the school's educational program is effective in supporting teachers, staff, and students in the achievement of academic standards. This includes overseeing curriculum, monitoring instructional practices, measuring the school's performance in relation to district academic standards, as well as communicating the progress and needs of the school to the board of education.

Board of Trustees

Each school within a district is overseen by a **board of trustees** responsible for making decisions to ensure that the educational program supports students' learning needs for academic achievement. The board of trustees is composed of a group of **elected individuals** who are typically members of the community in which they serve. As such, they have an understanding of the educational needs of the students within the community and can apply this knowledge to make effective decisions regarding the learning program. Members within a board of trustees are responsible for creating an educational program in alignment with students' needs as well as setting goals and developing strategies that support students in achieving them. This includes determining a **budget plan, allocating resources**, and making **administrative decisions** that benefit the school. In addition, board members are responsible for analyzing assessment data to make informed decisions regarding strategies to best support individual schools within the district and ensuring that measures are being implemented to effectively meet students' learning needs.

Curriculum Coordinators

Curriculum coordinators are responsible for the **development** and **implementation** of curriculum that is aligned with campus and district academic goals. These individuals work closely with teachers and administrators to analyze student progress in relation to the educational program, primarily through **assessment scores**, to determine the overall effectiveness of the curriculum in supporting students' achievement. Analyzing student progress enables curriculum coordinators to identify strengths and areas for improvement within the curriculum to make adjustments that best meet students' learning needs as they work to achieve learning targets. Ensuring that curriculum aligns with academic standards and students' learning needs facilitates more effective teaching and learning. Doing so provides teachers with a clear understanding of how to adequately prepare students for success, thus allowing them to design focused instruction and implement necessary supports to promote the achievement of campus and district academic standards.

School Technology Coordinators

Incorporating technology into the classroom is highly valuable in diversifying instructional strategies to promote student learning and engagement. School **technology coordinators** facilitate this integration to enhance teaching and learning, as they are responsible for the **organization, maintenance**, and **allocation** of available technology resources within the school building. This includes ensuring that all technology is functional, updated, properly stored, and accessible to teachers. These individuals are also responsible for **staying current** on developing digital resources that could be implemented to improve the learning experience as well as communicating with the board of education regarding **acquiring** technology resources for their schools. Doing so ensures that teachers have the materials necessary to best support students' learning. In addition, technology coordinators **educate** teachers and staff on the uses of technology resources as well as strategies to implement them in the classroom for more effective instruction.

Special Education Professionals

Special education professionals work with students of various disabilities, their teachers, and families to provide an equitable, inclusive environment that supports learning and development. These individuals are responsible for creating an educational plan that is tailored to support the unique needs of disabled students and ensuring that this plan is followed in all areas of the school. Special educators develop **individualized education programs** (IEPs) according to students' areas of need, develop academic and behavioral goals, as well as provide supports and modifications to accommodate students in achieving them. Special education professionals work with teachers to educate them on the proper implementation of individualized accommodations to ensure all students have the support necessary to successfully engage in learning. This includes collaborating with teachers to adapt and modify curriculum, instructional activities, and assessments to meet the individual needs of students with disabilities. In addition, special educators may work alongside classroom teachers in a team-teaching setting or provide individualized instruction as necessary. Students' academic and behavioral progress is monitored over time, and special educators communicate this information to families in order to collaborate in developing future goals and strategies to support achievement.

Roles and Responsibilities of Professionals Within the Education Program

The roles and responsibilities of various professionals within the educational program are described as follows:

- **Principal**—The principal is responsible for ensuring that the daily operations of the school function in a safe, orderly manner that aligns with the goals of the educational program. This includes delegating tasks to staff, enforcing academic and behavioral policies, ensuring instructional practices support student achievement, and communicating with students, staff, and families to establish a positive learning environment.
- **Vice principal**—The vice principal's role is to assist the principal in supervising the daily operations of the school to create a safe, orderly, and productive learning environment. The vice principal is responsible for working with teachers, staff, students, and families to support them in the educational program. This includes enforcing academic and behavioral policies, addressing concerns, facilitating communication, and ensuring instructional practices support student achievement of campus and district academic goals.

- **Board of trustees**—The board of trustees is responsible for developing an educational program that reflects the learning needs of students within the community. This includes developing educational goals, strategies to support students in achieving them, and ensuring that schools within the district are in alignment with the educational program. The board of trustees is also responsible for administrative decisions such as developing a budget plan and allocating resources to schools within the district according to students' needs.
- **Curriculum coordinator**—Curriculum coordinators are responsible for developing a curriculum that aligns with campus and district academic goals and ensuring it is implemented properly to support student achievement. This includes working with teachers and administrators to measure student progress within the curriculum and adjusting instructional strategies as necessary to support student success.
- **Assessment coordinator**—Assessment coordinators schedule, disperse, and collect standardized assessments and testing materials within the school building. They are responsible for educating teachers on proper assessment protocols to ensure that all practices align with district policies, collaborating with them to develop strategies that support student achievement, and ensuring all students are provided with necessary accommodations according to individual need.
- **Technology coordinator**—Technology coordinators facilitate the integration of digital resources into the curriculum. They are responsible for acquiring, organizing, maintaining, and allocating technology within the school. These individuals also work with teachers and staff to educate them on ways to utilize technology resources to enhance instruction.
- **Department chair**—Department chairpersons act as leaders among the teachers within their content areas. Their responsibilities include contributing to curriculum development, facilitating communication between administration and their colleagues, and ensuring instructional practices align with the educational program. They also collaborate with members of their team to develop instructional practices that best support student achievement of campus and district academic goals.
- **Teacher assistant**—The teacher assistant's role is to support the classroom teacher in both instructional and non-instructional duties. This includes assisting with the preparation, organization, and cleanup of lesson materials, working with small groups of students, managing student behavior, and ensuring the classroom functions in a safe, orderly manner.
- **Paraprofessional**—Paraprofessionals are licensed within the field of education and are responsible for assisting the teacher with daily classroom operations. This includes working with individual or small groups of students to provide instructional support, assisting with the preparation of lesson plans and materials, managing student behavior, and completing administrative duties.
- **Speech-language pathologist**—Speech-language pathologists are special education professionals who work with students who have varying degrees of language and communication difficulties. They are responsible for evaluating and diagnosing disabilities related to speech and language as well as developing individualized treatment programs. Speech-language pathologists then work with these students to remedy language and communication disabilities as well as collaborate with teachers, staff, and families regarding ways to support their progress.
- **ESL specialist**—ESL (English as a second language) specialists work with students for whom English is not their native language. They are responsible for evaluating students' levels of English language proficiency across the domains of reading, writing, speaking, and listening, determining necessary linguistic supports, and working with teachers to develop strategies that support English language acquisition. ESL specialists also work with individual or small groups of students to monitor progress and develop English language proficiency skills.
- **Guidance counselor**—The role of guidance counselors is to support students' social, emotional, academic, and behavioral needs. This includes providing counseling services, mediation, and, for upper grade level students, advice regarding course selection and career choices. These individuals communicate with teachers, staff, and families to develop and implement plans to support students' personal growth and academic achievement.

- **School nurse**—The school nurse is responsible for providing a range of healthcare to students and staff in the school building. This includes evaluating the physical, mental, and emotional health of students and staff as well as delivering general first-aid treatments. School nurses are also responsible for organizing and dispersing prescribed medications to students in accordance with their healthcare plan and educating teachers and staff regarding best practices for ensuring students' health and safety. School nurses may work with special education professionals to assess students' needs in the development of an individualized education program.
- **Building service worker**—Building service workers are responsible for the general maintenance of the school building and outside campus. This includes ensuring that all areas, equipment, and furniture are clean, functional, and safe for student and staff use. These individuals are also responsible for transporting heavy equipment and furniture throughout the school building.
- **Secretary**—The school secretary is responsible for assisting the principal, vice principal, and other office personnel in daily administrative duties. This individual assumes a variety of responsibilities to ensure the efficient function of daily operations within the school. Their responsibilities include communicating with students, families, and other office visitors, directing phone calls to the appropriate location, handling financial matters, and coordinating the school calendar.
- **Library/media specialist**—Library and media specialists coordinate the organization, maintenance, and allocation of all library and media resources within the school building. They are responsible for educating students regarding the proper use of library and media resources to locate information, including how to navigate the internet safely and appropriately for educational purposes. Library and media specialists also direct students toward reading material aligned with their literacy skills and provide teachers with learning materials to incorporate into instruction.
- **Instructional leadership team (ILT)**—An instructional leadership team is composed of individuals responsible for educating teachers regarding current and relevant instructional philosophies and practices to enhance student learning. These individuals collaborate with teachers to educate them regarding how to implement instructional strategies, activities, and assessments to effectively meet students' learning needs and support their achievement of campus and district academic goals.
- **School resource officer**—The role of the school resource officer is to maintain a safe, orderly environment for teachers, staff, and students. They are responsible for ensuring the physical security of the school, handling legal infractions within the school, and addressing conflicts among students. The school resource officer also works with administration and staff to develop emergency drill procedures.
- **Pupil personnel worker (PPW)**—Pupil personnel workers are responsible for addressing issues that hinder the academic achievement of at-risk students. These individuals communicate with teachers, administration, staff, and families to ensure these students are supported both within and outside of the school building. This includes addressing issues related to behavior, crisis intervention, attendance, and home lives. Pupil personnel workers direct families toward school and community support resources and collaborate with teachers to implement supports that facilitate success in learning.

Local, District, and State Educational Structure

Maintaining Accurate Student Records

Maintaining accurate **instructional** and **non-instructional** records is imperative for providing a comprehensive representation of students' academic and behavioral progress within the education program. Records pertaining to such matters as students' **academics**, **behavior**, **attendance**, **medical history**, and **special education services** must be well-organized and updated frequently in order to establish a safe, orderly environment that best supports their learning needs. Most school districts and campuses provide specific requirements regarding the procedures for maintaining accurate student records. This includes the frequency in which grades and attendance must be updated as well as the processes for documenting behavioral progress and information related to goals outlined in students' IEPs, BIPs, and 504 plans. Educators must strictly adhere to these policies at all times in order to gain accurate insight regarding students' progress in relation to reaching academic and behavioral goals. This allows educators to make informed instructional decisions, seek the proper supports, and adjust their practices as necessary to meet students' learning needs. In addition, maintaining accurate records is also beneficial for communicating productively with students' families to develop and implement plans to support their achievement.

Procedures for Administering State and District Mandated Assessments

State and district mandated assessments measure students' progress in relation to reaching academic benchmarks. Properly administering these assessments requires the consistent adherence to strict procedures to ensure confidentiality, equity, and accuracy. Only authorized test **proctors** may administer these tests. These individuals are responsible for preparing the testing room and testing materials prior to the assessment. For digital exams, they must ensure all students have the proper credentials. Proctors must follow all testing instructions, including the procedures for administering test materials and reading directions aloud exactly as they are written. All students with IEPs must receive the proper **accommodations** for an equitable testing environment. Students must receive the same allotted time to complete the assessment unless IEP accommodations permit extra time. The testing environment must be free of any materials unrelated to the exam, and the proctor must observe students throughout the test to ensure they follow the correct procedures. After the test, proctors must collect and organize all answer sheets and booklets. For digital assessments, proctors must ensure students log off properly. Testing materials must be packaged according to the instructions and stored in a secure area until they are sent to the testing agency for scoring.

Importance of Adhering to Procedures

State and district mandated assessments are intended to measure students' progress in relation to achieving academic benchmarks, and the results are used for a variety of purposes. Assessment results influence decisions regarding the allocation of funding and resources among schools, changes to curriculum, and adjustments to the education program to more effectively meet students' learning needs. These results are also used to identify and address achievement gaps among various populations to increase equity; therefore, strict adherence to all required procedures for administering state and district mandated assessments is imperative to produce an **objective** and **accurate** representation of student achievement. Doing so ensures the same degree of **uniformity** in regard to testing conditions, operations, and materials across schools as well as ensures all students are provided the necessary accommodations to ensure an **equitable** testing environment. Adhering to these procedures is also important in maintaining student **confidentiality** both during and after the assessment by preventing the sharing or reproduction of testing materials and ensuring students' completed exams are properly organized and stored in a secure area.

Seeking Information and Assistance

Understanding the State Education System Structure

State education systems are organized in a **tiered** structure, and each component is responsible for varying aspects of the education program. The **state department of education** is responsible for overseeing and establishing standards to regulate the operations of all school districts within the state. This includes allocating funds for individual districts, providing professional certifications, as well as developing comprehensive policies to govern curriculum, academic standards, and assessments at the district level. **School districts** are responsible for implementing the policies established by the state department of education. Each district is governed by a board of trustees elected by members of the community to oversee the operations of all public schools within the district. This includes hiring staff members, determining a budget plan for individual schools, and developing an education program aligned with state policies. **School campuses** within a district are tasked with maintaining the daily operations within the building. This includes addressing matters related to students, staff, and the community as well as ensuring instructional practices are aligned with the educational program created by the district. Recognizing the roles of the varying components within the education system is beneficial in understanding the proper avenues to take when seeking information or assistance.

Understanding the Professional Roles of Individuals Within the School Campus

The school campus is composed of a complex network of professional roles that work together to establish an efficient, orderly, and productive learning environment focused on student achievement. Each professional within the building is responsible for specific duties to maintain the daily operations of the school campus and meet students' learning needs. Understanding the nature and responsibilities of these varying roles, including how they work together in supporting the education program, is beneficial in effectively navigating the school campus when seeking information or assistance. This knowledge is important for determining which individual or department will be most helpful in addressing specific situations or providing support as well as the proper procedures for doing so.

Available Resources at the Campus, Local, and State Level

Understanding the structure of the education system is beneficial in determining the proper avenues for seeking information and assistance related to specific situations at the campus, local, and state levels. Professionals within the **school campus** serve as valuable support resources for a variety of matters, including those related to students, families, staff, and academics. For example, principals and administrators can provide information and assistance regarding the daily operations of the school building. Guidance counselors and other specialists are important resources for student and family matters, special education services, and support programs. Mentors, department chairs, and colleagues can provide support in relation to instructional practices. At the **district level**, members of the board of trustees can provide information and assistance regarding the education program, such as budget and resource allocation, assessments, curriculum development, and transportation. Additionally, varying departments within the local board of education are beneficial resources for information pertaining to human resource matters, professional development opportunities, and community support services. The **state department of education** is composed of several factions that provide a variety of services, including information and assistance regarding professional certification, continuing education, updates to education policies, and grants and funding for schools.

Professional Development

Available Resources and Support Systems

Effective educators continuously seek professional development opportunities to refine their teaching practice. There are multiple resources and support systems that teachers can utilize to develop their professional knowledge and skills. Within the school building, mentors are available to offer ideas, advice, and support in developing teaching practices and strategies to implement in the classroom for effective teaching and learning. The school's **instructional leadership team** (ILT) is also a valuable resource for educating teachers regarding current instructional practices to enhance student engagement and learning. Teachers can continue their professional education by enrolling in university courses or participating in state-initiated programs to stay informed on relevant pedagogical theories and practices. Service centers are also available that offer workshops, training, and conferences on a variety of topics related to education to support teachers' professional development. In addition, numerous digital support resources are available that allow teachers to enroll in courses, participate in informational webinars, and collaborate with other educators in professional learning communities to build and enhance their teaching practice.

Example Opportunities That Can Enhance Teaching Practice

Professional development opportunities are available to address a variety of needs for refining one's practice and developing pedagogical knowledge. Professional development trainings can serve to educate teachers on how to utilize and incorporate current technologies into the classroom as well as teach strategies for implementing relevant and engaging instructional techniques, materials, and resources into the classroom. These opportunities can also be beneficial in teaching educators how to demonstrate cultural competency and skills for productive collaboration with colleagues to enhance student learning. Teachers can also seek professional development opportunities to learn best practices for addressing a variety of student needs, such as intellectual, physical, social, or emotional disabilities, or linguistic needs of ELLs. Actively seeking and participating in professional development trainings helps to ensure teachers stay current on pedagogical theories that can serve as a framework for their instructional practice.

Effectively Utilizing Resources and Support Systems

The field of education is multifaceted and continuously evolving. As such, it is important that teachers of all experience levels engage in the vast array of **available resources** and **support systems** to develop and refine their professional skills. Doing so enhances students' learning, as teachers who actively seek professional development are more current on pedagogical theories and practices as well as instructional strategies, resources, and technologies to incorporate in the classroom. This allows teachers to design and implement more effective instruction, as it provides them with an increased range of knowledge and tools to enhance student engagement and understanding. In addition, as students' individual needs are diverse, participating in resources and support systems allows teachers to educate themselves on how to properly accommodate them to enhance the learning experience. Utilizing resources and support systems also enables teachers to learn from and collaborate with other educators in professional learning communities to continuously develop new skills, ideas, and instructional methods that enhance student learning.

Teacher Appraisals

Characteristics, Goals, and Procedures

Teacher appraisals are a method of evaluation intended to provide teachers with continuous feedback regarding their **performance** and areas in which they can improve their professional skills to enhance student learning. Feedback is provided periodically throughout the school year and derives from classroom **observations** typically conducted by the principal or grade-level administrator. Observations can either be **formally** scheduled and last the duration of a lesson or can be in the form of shorter, informal **walk-through** evaluations. In both instances, the observer watches and collects information as the teacher delivers instruction, directs learning activities, and interacts with students. The teacher's performance is then measured against **criteria** across several domains pertaining to planning, preparing, and delivering instruction. This score is used to provide the teacher with detailed feedback in post-observation meetings regarding their strengths and specific areas in which they can improve their practice to more effectively meet students' learning needs. Feedback is used to support the teacher in developing specific **professional goals** and strategies for improving their teaching skills.

Benefits of Appraisal Results in Improving Professional Skills

The results of teacher appraisals are beneficial in providing educators with **specific feedback** regarding areas in which they can improve their professional skills. Effective teachers understand the value of continuously **refining their practice** to enhance student learning and actively seek opportunities to do so; however, it may prove difficult for teachers to objectively assess their own efficacy in the classroom. Appraisal results communicate feedback from the outside perspective of the observer for a comprehensive evaluation of their performance, thus providing teachers with clarity regarding their strengths and areas for growth. This allows educators to effectively develop **professional goals** to improve their skills in targeted areas and **strategies** to achieve these goals successfully.

Working with Supervisors, Mentors, and Colleagues

Enhancing Professional Knowledge and Skills

When teachers collaborate with supervisors, mentors, and other colleagues, it facilitates a productive **professional learning community** that supports the continuous development of knowledge and skills related to education. Doing so provides teachers with the opportunity to work with educational professionals of varying backgrounds, experiences, and expertise. This exposes teachers to a wide range of **perspectives**, **approaches**, and **philosophies** that they can learn from to build and enhance their practice. In such a setting, teachers can interact with other professionals within the school community to share ideas, support one another, and collaborate productively in developing strategies to improve their efficacy in the classroom. Additionally, actively engaging with supervisors, mentors, and colleagues facilitates the open communication necessary for productive collaboration in effectively addressing issues to enhance the school community.

Addressing Issues and Building Professional Skills

Productive collaboration with supervisors, mentors, and colleagues is essential to addressing issues related to the educational program and continuously developing professional practices. There are multiple opportunities for such collaboration within the school community that accommodate varying purposes. By participating in **professional learning communities**, members of the educational program can collaborate and support one another in addressing concerns and building professional skills. In subject-area **department** or **team meetings**, educators can work together to share ideas, strategies, and resources related to their content areas for more effective instruction. Working with supervisors and mentors in **post-observation conferences** provides teachers with valuable feedback regarding their strengths and areas for improvement. Such collaboration is beneficial in creating specific goals and strategies for professional growth. Additionally, engaging in collaborative **professional development opportunities**, including workshops, conferences, programs, and courses, is beneficial in allowing educators to build upon one another's experiences, backgrounds, and expertise to enhance professional practices.

Professional Development Resources

The various professional development resources available to teachers and staff are discussed below:

- **Mentors/support systems**: Mentors and other dedicated support resources within the school system are intended to provide teachers with guidance to enhance their professional knowledge, skills, and expertise. These individuals are typically highly experienced and work with teachers to develop effective instructional strategies, classroom management techniques, and learning materials to improve their teaching skills.

- **Conferences**: Education conferences are multifaceted events in which teachers can learn about current developments in their field to improve their professional knowledge, pedagogical skills, and technical expertise. Conference events are composed of numerous professional development opportunities, including presentations on current pedagogical theories and practices, collaborative workshops, and training sessions regarding the implementation of new instructional strategies and technology resources. At these events, teachers can also network with one another to connect and share resources, ideas, and strategies that enhance their teaching practice.
- **Professional associations**: Education associations provide teachers with access to numerous professional development opportunities for improving knowledge, pedagogical skills, and technical expertise. These associations can be related to general education or be content specific, and they offer information regarding education conferences, workshops, training opportunities, and courses to enhance teaching practices. Professional education associations also allow teachers the opportunity to network with one another to build professional knowledge by sharing ideas, resources, and strategies to implement in the classroom.
- **Online resources**: Numerous online resources, including websites, blogs, webinar trainings, and discussion forums are available to support teachers in enhancing their professional knowledge, skills, and technical expertise on a variety of topics. Teachers can utilize these resources to learn current pedagogical theories and practices, instructional and classroom management strategies, and relevant technology resources to implement in the classroom for enhanced student learning. Online resources are also valuable for collaborating with other teachers in building professional knowledge and sharing ideas, learning materials, and resources that improve instructional practices.
- **Workshops**: Workshop training sessions provide teachers the opportunity to build professional knowledge, skills, and expertise by educating them on current instructional strategies, classroom management techniques, and digital resources in a hands-on setting. Workshops are typically dedicated to a specific pedagogical topic and allow teachers to collaborate with one another in learning how to implement it in their classroom.
- **Journals**: Education journals publish newly researched information regarding pedagogical theories and practices teachers can utilize to enhance their professional knowledge. These journals include scholarly articles and case studies regarding topics such as instructional strategies and practices, classroom management techniques, and the implementation of digital resources. Education journals allow teachers to stay current on pedagogical developments in order to continuously improve their teaching skills.
- **Coursework**: Engaging in coursework is beneficial in continuing formal professional education to enhance knowledge, pedagogical skills, and technical expertise. Doing so allows teachers to learn from other experienced educators regarding current educational theories, practices, instructional strategies, and technology resources. By participating in formal coursework, teachers can continuously build upon their teaching skills and stay current regarding developments in their field.

Reflection and Self-Assessment

Improving Teaching Performance and Achieving Professional Goals

Just as students are encouraged to reflect upon their academic performance, it is important that teachers **reflect** on and **self-assess** their own efficacy in the classroom. Doing so is integral for improving professional knowledge and skills to enhance student learning. Effective teachers continuously self-evaluate their performance to ensure they are providing engaging, relevant instruction that effectively meets students' learning needs for success. Frequently reflecting upon and assessing the effectiveness of their lesson plans, instructional strategies, assessments, and approaches to classroom management is beneficial in providing teachers with insight regarding their **professional strengths** as well as specific **areas for growth**. With this insight, teachers can identify the knowledge, skills, and strategies they need to improve upon to deliver more effective instruction. This ultimately allows teachers to set relevant professional goals to enhance their teaching practice and determine the steps they need to take in achieving them.

METHODS

Continuous reflection and self-assessment through a variety of methods is beneficial in providing teachers with insight into the effectiveness of their teaching practice. **Reflecting on lessons** after they are finished allows teachers to self-assess their instruction by identifying specific elements that were successful as well as components that can be improved in the future to enhance student learning. By eliciting **student feedback**, teachers can evaluate whether their instructional strategies, lesson activities, and assessments promote student engagement and understanding. Working with **mentors** and **colleagues** to discuss the effectiveness of lessons, instructional approaches, and classroom management techniques is also valuable in facilitating self-evaluation of teaching practices to seek areas for improvement. In addition, teachers are typically provided the opportunity to **respond to post-observation feedback** prior to attending an appraisal conference. This provides teachers with the opportunity to reflect on their overall performance and prepare to collaborate with the observer in developing professional goals.

Team Teaching and Professional Collaboration

TEAM TEACHING

Team teaching refers to the collaboration of two or more teachers, paraprofessionals, instructional aides, or special education workers in planning and delivering instruction and assessments. There are **several structures** to this approach to accommodate varying teaching styles and student needs. One teacher may provide direct instruction while another engages in lesson activities or monitors student progress. Similarly, one teacher may instruct while another observes and collects information to improve future planning. Students may be grouped with teachers according to their needs to provide differentiation, or teachers may participate simultaneously and equally in all aspects of the learning process. The intention of this approach is to create a **student-centered environment** focused on enhancing and deepening the learning experience. Team teaching is beneficial in allowing increased **individualized instruction** that more effectively meets students' learning needs. Additionally, when multiple teachers are present, students have access to varying **ideas** and **perspectives** that strengthen their understanding. Team teaching also benefits teachers, as it enables them to utilize one another's strengths for improved instruction. There are, however, limitations to this approach. Differences in **classroom management** styles, **teaching practices**, and **personalities**, when not addressed properly through respectful communication and flexibility, hinder the effectiveness of team teaching.

VERTICAL TEAMING

Communication and collaboration among teachers of varying grade levels is integral to effective instruction that supports students' learning and development. Through **vertical teaming**, content specific teachers **across grade levels** have the opportunity to work together in discussing and planning curriculum, instruction, assessments, and strategies that prepare students for achievement. Teachers of lower grade levels are often unsure of what students in upper grade levels are learning. As a result, these teachers may be uncertain of the skills and abilities their students need to be adequately prepared for success as they transition through grade levels. Likewise, teachers of upper grade levels are often unsure of what students have learned in previous grades, thus hindering their ability to adequately plan instruction and implement necessary learning supports. Vertical teaming facilitates the communication necessary for teachers across grade levels to collaborate in **establishing expectations for preparedness** at each grade level and developing a common curriculum path. This enhances teaching and learning, in that teachers are more effectively able to plan instruction that is aligned with learning targets and prepare students with the necessary knowledge, tools, and supports for continued academic success.

HORIZONTAL TEAMING

Horizontal teaming refers to the collaboration of **same grade level** teachers and staff that work with a common group of students. These teams may comprise teachers within a **single subject area** or **across disciplines** and may also include special education workers, grade-level administrators, paraprofessionals, and guidance counselors. Horizontal teaming is beneficial in facilitating the **coordinated planning** of curriculum, instruction, assessments, and discussion regarding students' progress in the educational program. In addition, this method of teaming provides teachers and staff the opportunity to work together in developing educational goals, addressing areas of need, and implementing strategies to support students' success in learning. Horizontal teaming is also beneficial in encouraging teachers and staff to cooperate with one another in alignment with the goals and mission of the school to create a positive learning community focused on promoting student achievement.

Benefits of Mentors in Enhancing Professional Knowledge and Skills

Mentors within the school community are typically experienced teachers who are available to offer support, guidance, and expertise to new teachers. As these individuals typically have a great deal of experience as educators, they are highly valuable resources in increasing professional knowledge and improving teaching skills. Mentors can provide **strategies, tools**, and **advice** for planning and delivering instruction, classroom management, and meeting students' learning needs to promote achievement. This includes suggesting ideas and resources for lesson activities and assessments as well as techniques for differentiating instruction, enhancing student engagement, and promoting positive behavior. In addition, mentors can offer insight on how to effectively **navigate the school community**, including how to interact appropriately with colleagues and superiors, complete administrative duties, and communicate effectively with students' families. Regularly working with mentors in the school building ensures that new teachers are supported in developing the knowledge and skills necessary to become effective educators.

Interaction with Professionals in the School Community

In order for an educational community to function effectively, professionals in the building must work together cohesively on a daily basis to support the school's mission and student learning. The nature of these interactions significantly determines the climate and culture of the school environment. Appropriate, professional interactions are important in facilitating the productive collaboration necessary to create a positive school community that promotes student success in learning. All interactions must therefore be **respectful**, **constructive**, and **sensitive** to the varying backgrounds, cultures, and beliefs among professionals in the school community. This includes using **appropriate language**, practicing **active listening**, and ensuring that discussions regarding colleagues, superiors, students, and other individuals in the building remain positive. When interacting in a team setting, it is important to maintain open dialogue and support one another's contributions to the educational program. All professionals in the school building must understand one another's roles and appreciate how these roles function together to support the educational program. Doing so ensures that collaboration is productive, purposeful, and aligned with enhancing students' learning experience.

Supportive and Cooperative Relationships with Professional Colleagues

Supports Learning and Achievement of Campus and District Goals

Effective collaboration among school staff and faculty members is reliant on establishing and maintaining supportive, cooperative professional relationships. Doing so facilitates a sense of **mutual respect** and **open communication** that allows colleagues to work together constructively in developing educational goals, plans to support students in achieving them, and strategies to address areas of need within the educational program. Mutual support and cooperation are also beneficial in fostering the **coordinated planning** of curriculum, learning activities, assessments, and accommodations to meet students' individual needs for academic achievement. Such professional relationships allow for more effective teaching and learning, as students are supported by a school community that works together cohesively to promote learning and the achievement of campus and district academic goals.

Strategies for Establishing and Maintaining Relationships

Building and maintaining professional relationships founded on mutual support and cooperation is integral in creating a positive, productive school community focused on student achievement. **Frequent communication** with colleagues in a variety of settings is an important factor in establishing and sustaining such professional relationships. Maintaining continuous and open communication allows professional colleagues in the school building to develop the respect for and understanding of one another necessary to establish a strong rapport. By participating together in **school activities**, **events**, and **programs**, teachers and staff members can build connections while contributing to enhancing the school community and climate. **Community building** strategies, such as participating in activities or games that require teamwork, are also valuable opportunities for developing supportive and cooperative professional relationships among colleagues. In addition, **collaborating** with one another in regard to curriculum, lesson planning, and promoting student achievement contributes significantly to developing positive professional relationships. There are multiple avenues for such collaboration, including participating in professional learning communities (PLC's), department meetings, vertical or horizontal teaming, or engaging in team teaching. Doing so provides teachers and staff the opportunity to communicate and develop mutual goals that support the educational program and student learning.

Review Video: Collaborating with Other Professionals
Visit mometrix.com/academy and enter code: 100351

Participating in the Local Educational Community

Impact of Volunteering on Positive Educational Community

Participating in school activities, events, and projects positively impacts the nature of the school community and culture. When teachers and staff members volunteer their time to contribute in such a way, it strengthens **connections** to the school community that foster positive attitudes toward it. By actively engaging in activities, events, and projects, teachers and staff have the opportunity to collaborate in making **positive contributions** to the school community. This facilitates the development of relationships among colleagues that enhance their ability to work cooperatively in creating a positive learning atmosphere that benefits students and the educational program. Students are more supported in such an environment and develop positive attitudes toward learning and strong relationships with their teachers that enhance the overall school **climate**. In addition, as students are influenced by the behaviors, actions, and attitudes modeled by adults in the building, contributing positively to the school community encourages them to do the same.

Participation Opportunities

Participating in school activities, events, and projects is valuable in integrating oneself into the school community while making positive contributions. Such participation can occur through a variety of avenues, both within and outside of the school campus. Teachers can assist in school fundraisers, food and clothing drives, or field trips. They can also serve as tutors and lead school clubs or other extracurricular activities. By attending school sporting events, recitals, concerts, and plays, teachers can participate in the school community while supporting students. Events such as open-house nights, parent-teacher nights, and public forum meetings are also valuable opportunities to participate in the school community in a way that positively contributes to students' learning.

Enhancing the Educational Community

As teachers work closely with students, colleagues, and administration, their contributions to the school and district are integral in enhancing the school community. Teachers provide valuable insight regarding the needs of the educational program and ways to improve the school environment. As such, their participation in the school and district is beneficial in helping to ensure the needs of staff and students are adequately met to create a positive educational community. In addition, active participation in the school and district facilitates the collaboration necessary for establishing relationships among colleagues that contribute to a positive school culture and climate. Teachers can contribute to building such an educational community in a variety of ways. By participating in **school activities**, **events**, and **projects**, teachers can work cooperatively to create a positive learning atmosphere. Teachers can also attend **school meetings** and serve on focused **committees** to solve problems and influence decisions that improve the nature of the school environment. At the district level, teachers can communicate with members of the board of education and participate in **public forums** to express ideas, discuss concerns, and offer input regarding ways to enhance the educational community.

Family Involvement and Collaboration

Effectively Working and Communicating with Families

Utilizing multiple means of communication when working with students' families ensures information is **accessible** to and **inclusive** of all involved family members. As students' home lives are dynamic, conveying information through several avenues allows families in various situations to participate in their child's education. This is invaluable in establishing and maintaining the positive relationships necessary between students' families and schools for effective teaching and learning. General classroom information, including concepts being taught, important dates, assignments, or suggestions for activities to do at home that reinforce learning in the classroom, can be communicated both digitally and in written form. Newsletters, calendars, or handouts can be both printed and included on a class website to ensure accessibility for all families. Updates regarding individual students can be communicated electronically, through writing, or in person. Email, digital communication apps, and the telephone allow for frequent communication to address students' progress, express concerns, or offer praise. Teachers and families can also communicate through handwritten notes, progress reports, or students' daily agendas. In-person communication, such as during a scheduled conference, is beneficial for discussing individual students' progress and goals related to the education program in depth as well as ways to support their success in learning.

Building Positive Relationships That Enhance Overall Learning

Students are more supported and learn more effectively when the relationships between their teachers and families are founded on **mutual respect**, **understanding**, and **cooperation**. Establishing this positive rapport requires the teacher to work and communicate frequently with students' families. Doing so creates an inviting learning atmosphere in which family members feel welcomed and included as **equal contributors** to the educational program. This sentiment empowers and encourages family members to take an active role in their children's education, thus strengthening students' support systems and enhancing the overall learning experience. In addition, family members who feel a strong connection to their children's school are more likely to model positive attitudes toward education and reinforce learning at home. When teachers and family members communicate frequently, they develop a mutual sense of trust for one another. This allows for **productive collaboration** and the exchange of valuable insight regarding how to best support students' learning needs both within and outside of the classroom.

Appropriate Collaboration and Communication with Families

To effectively collaborate and communicate with students' families, the teacher must carefully consider appropriate methods for doing so. Communication and collaboration must always be **positive**, **respectful,** and **inclusive** to all families to ensure they feel welcomed as equal participants in their children's education. As such, the teacher must be mindful and responsive to the fact that students come from a variety of backgrounds, family dynamics, and living situations. This includes demonstrating **cultural competency** when interacting with families from different backgrounds, providing multiple and varied opportunities for family involvement, and communicating through a variety of means. Doing so ensures that families of varying situations have access to pertinent information and feel equally included in the educational program. The teacher must also be mindful of the nature and purpose of communication in order to ensure that sensitive details about individual students are shared only with appropriate family members. General classroom information, such as important dates, events, or assignments, may be shared publicly among the classroom community, whereas things like individual student progress or behavior records must be reserved for private communication with the appropriate family members.

Involvement of Families, Parents, Guardians, and Legal Caregivers

Strategies to Encourage Engagement

As students' family dynamics are diverse, it is important that the teacher implement a variety of methods to engage parents, guardians, and legal caregivers into the educational program. Doing so creates an inviting atmosphere in which family members of all situations feel encouraged to participate in their children's education. Efforts to engage families must always be **positive, inclusive**, and **accommodating** to a variety of needs, schedules, and situations. This includes ensuring that all opportunities for involvement are culturally sensitive, meaningful, and accepting of all families. Utilizing a variety of **communication methods**, such as weekly newsletters, calendars, phone calls, and electronic communication, ensures that opportunities to engage in the educational program are accessible to all families. Providing **multiple** and **varied** opportunities for involvement, such as family nights, field trips, award ceremonies, or inviting families to participate in classroom activities, further encourages family engagement in the educational program. This enables families in various situations to become involved in their children's education in the way that best suits their needs and abilities.

Forms of Active Involvement

Active involvement in the educational program can take a variety of forms both within and outside of the classroom to accommodate differences in families' schedules, dynamics, and abilities. Providing multiple avenues for involvement engages families of various situations to actively participate in their children's education. Within the classroom, family members can **volunteer** their time to assist as teachers' aides, tutors, or chaperones. In addition, if a family member is skilled in an area related to instruction, the teacher can ask the family member to come in to speak or teach a lesson. Inviting family members to **visit the classroom** or participate in special class activities allows them to actively engage in the learning process and gain insight into the educational program. Outside of daily classroom activities, family members can be encouraged to participate by attending **family nights, school social events, fundraisers**, or **parent-teacher association meetings**. Active involvement in the educational program can also occur at home. By frequently communicating with teachers, assisting with projects or homework, and emphasizing the importance of learning at home, family members can be informed and actively involved in their children's education.

Importance in Children's Education

As students spend a great deal of time between school and home, the degree to which their family is involved in the educational program significantly influences the quality of the learning experience. When teachers take measures to engage families in their children's education, they establish a welcoming tone that facilitates relationships founded on mutual respect, understanding, and acceptance. These positive relationships are necessary for encouraging and empowering families to actively participate in the learning process. Such involvement contributes to establishing a **positive learning community** in which teachers and families can collaborate productively to enhance students' learning. When students' families are actively involved in their education, it strengthens the **support system** in both influential areas of their lives, thus establishing a sense of security that allows them to confidently engage in learning. Families that participate in the educational program are more likely to emphasize its value at home by extending and reinforcing learning outside of the classroom. This is highly beneficial in promoting positive attitudes toward learning, academic achievement, and social and emotional development.

Influence on Student Learning and Development

The degree of family involvement in the educational program significantly influences the quality of students' learning and development. Learning is more effective when parents, guardians, or legal caregivers are actively engaged in their child's education, as this promotes positive relationships between students' school and home lives that strengthen their **support system** and encourage the extension of learning beyond the classroom. Families that participate in the educational program are likely to emphasize and model its importance at home, thus influencing students to adopt the same positive attitudes toward learning. This facilitates **academic achievement**, **decreased absences** from school, and **positive learning habits**. In addition, when families are actively involved in the educational process, they are more effectively able to support students with resources at home that reinforce concepts learned in the classroom to strengthen connections and understanding. Students develop healthy **social and emotional skills** as well when their families are actively involved in the educational program. This facilitates positive self-esteem and interpersonal skills that contribute to academic success and fewer behavioral issues in the classroom.

Benefits for Parents, Families, Guardians, and Legal Caregivers

Families, parents, guardians, and legal caregivers that are actively involved in the educational program gain greater **insight**, **understanding**, and **resources** that enable them to support their children's learning more effectively both within and outside of the classroom. Active engagement in the educational program fosters a positive rapport founded on mutual respect and support among family members, teachers, and the school. This provides family members with a sense of **confidence** in the merits of the educational program while contributing to the sense that they are **equal participants** in the learning process. These family members are more informed regarding what is being taught in the classroom and beneficial resources to reinforce learning at home. This leaves family members feeling more **empowered** and willing to reinforce their students' learning. In addition, participating in the learning process provides family members with a greater understanding of the characteristics and capabilities of their children's developmental level, thus equipping them with the knowledge to effectively support learning and growth.

Benefits for Effective Teaching

The involvement of families, parents, guardians, and legal caregivers in the educational program is highly beneficial for effective teaching. Family members that actively participate in the learning process are likely to develop a greater sense of **understanding** and **appreciation** of the teacher's role within it. Such involvement also facilitates positive and frequent communication with families that fosters relationships founded on mutual respect and increases the teacher's **morale** and effectiveness in the classroom. Active engagement from family members also allows the teacher to gain a better understanding of how to support individual students' needs. Family members provide valuable insight regarding students' cultures, values, beliefs, educational goals, and learning needs to allow for more effective teaching. In addition, family members that are involved in their children's education are more likely to reinforce and extend learning at home, thus allowing for more effective teaching in the classroom.

Positive Rapport

A positive rapport between teachers and families enhances the quality of the learning experience. Establishing these positive relationships requires that teachers frequently take measures to engage families in the educational program in ways that are **meaningful**, **relevant**, and **responsive** to varying situations, backgrounds, and needs. In doing so, teachers communicate the sentiment that all families are welcomed, valued, and considered equal participants in the learning process. This serves to create an open, inviting learning atmosphere in which family involvement is encouraged, thus fostering the **participation** and **communication** necessary for developing a mutual positive rapport. Working to build positive relationships strengthens the connection between schools and families that facilitates productive **collaboration** to best support and enhance students' learning.

Interacting with Families of Various Backgrounds

Diversities That May Be Encountered

Appropriate interaction when working and communicating with students' families requires teachers to recognize the wide range of diversities in characteristics, backgrounds, and needs that they will inevitably encounter. With **culturally diverse** families, the teacher will likely experience variances in language, values, traditions, and customs, including differences in beliefs regarding best practices for raising and educating children. **Socioeconomic** differences may influence the degree to which families have the ability and access to resources to support their children in learning. In some instances, socioeconomic differences may also impact the level of education that family members have attained and potentially the value they place on the importance of education. The teacher must also be mindful of the diversities that exist among **family**

dynamics. Some families may have a single caregiver, whereas others may have many. Students may be only children, have several siblings, or come from a blended family. Differences in dynamics also include varying work schedules, lifestyle demands, and living situations that the teacher must consider when working and communicating with families. By acknowledging the diverse characteristics, backgrounds, and needs of students' families, the teacher can take measures to ensure appropriate and inclusive interactions that enhance the learning experience.

Appropriate and Productive Interactions

Recognizing the diverse nature of students' cultures, backgrounds, and experiences provides teachers with insight regarding how to interact with their families appropriately and productively. By self-educating to become **culturally competent** and building relationships with students, teachers develop an understanding of the unique characteristics, values, beliefs, and needs of each family. This enables teachers to tailor their communication with individual families in a way that is respectful, **culturally sensitive**, and responsive to their concerns and needs. Doing so ensures that all families feel welcomed and supported in the school environment, thus establishing positive relationships that encourage families to actively engage in the educational program and collaborate productively with teachers to enhance students' learning.

Possible Obstacles

As teachers work and interact with families of diverse backgrounds and experiences, they likely will encounter obstacles that must be addressed to facilitate effective communication. **Cultural differences** in values, beliefs, language, and nonverbal communication may cause misinterpretations between teachers and families that make it difficult to understand one another. It is, therefore, important that teachers educate themselves regarding students' backgrounds to learn how to communicate in a culturally sensitive manner. When language barriers are present, learning common words and phrases in the language or utilizing an interpreter is beneficial in facilitating communication. Family members may have experienced **negative interactions** with teachers in the past that affect their willingness to engage in communication. Taking measures to establish an inviting, accepting atmosphere that promotes open communication is beneficial in encouraging these families to become involved. **Lifestyle differences**, including varying work schedules, living situations, and family dynamics, may make it difficult to establish effective communication. In addition, **accessibility issues**, including lack of access to transportation, technology devices, or the internet, may hinder family members' abilities to maintain frequent communication. To address these issues, teachers must utilize several communication methods that accommodate families' varying needs and situations.

Considerations to Ensure Beneficial Interactions

The ultimate goal when working and communicating with families is to benefit students' learning and development. When teachers and families develop a positive rapport between one another, it fosters productive collaboration to support the students' educational and developmental goals. Doing so requires that teachers ensure all interactions with students' families are appropriate, respectful, and considerate. This includes demonstrating awareness of varying **backgrounds, characteristics**, and **needs** of each family and interacting in a way that is responsive and accepting of differences. Teachers must practice **cultural competency** when communicating with families, including recognizing differences in perspectives, values, beliefs, and nonverbal communication. Teachers must also consider families' unique situations, including differing **work schedules, living arrangements**, and **family dynamics** to ensure that all interactions are considerate of their time, accommodating to their needs, and supportive of their role in the educational program. When interacting with families, it is important that teachers practice active listening and respond appropriately, meaningfully, and constructively. This communicates to families that their opinions, goals, and concerns related to the educational program are respected, thus encouraging them to actively participate in supporting their children's progress and development.

Regular Communication with Families

Students' Progress and Important Classroom Information

Frequent communication regarding individual student progress and important classroom information is essential to actively engaging family members as equal contributors to the educational program. Doing so creates an inviting atmosphere focused on open and productive dialogue to enhance students' learning and development. Regular communication with families through a variety of methods establishes a strong connection between students' school and home lives that supports their achievement. When families are consistently updated and informed regarding their children's progress in the educational program, they can more effectively collaborate with the teacher to **proactively** address concerns and **implement necessary supports** for successful learning. Frequently communicating important classroom information, including curriculum, assignments, events, and opportunities for involvement, ensures that families are always informed regarding their children's educational program and ways in which they can actively participate. This equips family members with the knowledge and resources necessary to effectively support and reinforce learning both in the classroom and at home.

Review Video: Collaborating with Families
Visit mometrix.com/academy and enter code: 679996

Positive Rapport That Enhances Teaching and Learning

Regularly interacting and working with students' families facilitates the **continuous** and **open** line of communication necessary to establishing and sustaining a positive rapport. Building such positive relationships is integral to quality teaching and learning, as frequent communication allows families and teachers to develop a sense of mutual respect, trust, and understanding over time. By frequently communicating with families, teachers create a welcoming, inclusive learning environment in which family members feel encouraged and empowered to contribute as **equal participants** in their child's educational program. This facilitates productive collaboration between teachers and families that supports and enhances students' learning. Developing a positive rapport with family members is also valuable in providing teachers with insight regarding strategies to best support and accommodate students' learning styles, needs, and individual differences. When teachers and families have a positive relationship with one another, students feel more supported in their learning both within and outside of the classroom, thus promoting positive attitudes toward learning and academic achievement.

Listening and Responding to Families' Concerns

Actively **listening** and **responding** to students' families when interacting with them is an important part of building positive relationships that enhance teaching and learning. By listening attentively to families' concerns, ideas, and information regarding their child and the educational program, teachers gain a greater awareness of their unique backgrounds, characteristics, and experiences. With this understanding in mind, teachers can ensure that they respond to family members in a **sensitive**, **accepting**, and **empathetic** manner to promote the development of a mutual positive rapport. Doing so conveys the sentiment that family members are valued and respected as equal participants in the educational program, thus encouraging them to engage in positive communication to support their children's learning. Families can provide valuable insight regarding their children's learning styles, needs, and behaviors. When teachers listen and respond constructively to this information, they foster positive relationships with families by validating and including them in the learning process. In addition, listening and responding appropriately to students' families indicates acknowledgement and appreciation for their participation in the educational program that contributes to building positive relationships and encourages continued communication.

Conferences

Building Positive Relationships Between Schools and Families

Frequently conducting conferences with parents, guardians, and legal caregivers facilitates the consistent **in-person communication** necessary for building positive relationships founded on mutual understanding and respect. The conference setting provides a space in which teachers, school staff, and families can discuss the educational program and the student's individual progress as well as address concerns and collaborate in developing goals. By conducting conferences regularly, teachers, school staff, and families can maintain a continuous, **open dialogue** that provides insight regarding one another's perspectives, intentions, and roles in the educational program. This allows for increased understanding and appreciation for one another that contributes to building positive relationships. Families that attend conferences regularly feel more included in the educational program as equal contributors to their children's learning, thus encouraging them to establish positive strong connections with the school.

Support of Students' Success in Learning

Effective conferences between teachers and families are focused on open communication, productive collaboration, and strengthening the connection between students' home and school lives. When families and teachers work together in conferences to benefit the student, it strengthens their **support system** in both influential areas of their lives. This is beneficial in enhancing students' **academic achievement**, promoting **healthy development**, and encouraging **positive attitudes toward learning**. Conducting conferences frequently ensures that family members are consistently **informed** and **involved** as equal participants in their child's progress and the educational program. This equips families with the information, understanding, and resources to more effectively support their child's learning both within and outside of the classroom. In addition, effective conferences provide teachers with insight from families regarding students' learning needs, behaviors, and individual situations. With this knowledge in mind, teachers can work with families to develop a plan and implement strategies that best support students' learning and development.

Guidelines for Effectiveness

Family conferences are a valuable opportunity to discuss students' individual progress, collaborate to develop educational goals, and address concerns. To ensure conferences are productive, teachers must take measures to make families feel welcomed, respected, and included in the process. Conferences must be scheduled at a **convenient time** for all attending family members in order to accommodate varying needs and situations. It is also important that conferences take place in a comfortable, **inviting atmosphere**, as this establishes a positive tone and facilitates discussion. Teachers must arrive **on time** and **prepared** with specific information to discuss regarding the student, including positive remarks that highlight his or her strengths. This demonstrates that teachers know the student well and want him or her to succeed, thus making family members feel comfortable in discussing their child. Asking **open-ended questions**, encouraging families to talk, and practicing active listening is important in facilitating productive discussion as well as ensuring families feel heard and respected in their concerns. **Direct criticism** of the student must always be avoided; rather, teachers should focus on discussing ways that student can apply their strengths to improve in other areas.

Family Support Resources that Enhance Family Involvement

Families that are supported through school, community, and interagency resources are equipped to effectively support their child's learning and development. Often, families may be hesitant to become actively involved in their children's education because they lack the skills and understanding of how to do so. These support systems are beneficial in providing family members with the **tools, knowledge**, and **resources** that prepare them to effectively participate in the educational program and extend learning outside of the classroom. Such resources are valuable in educating families on the characteristics, needs, and abilities of their children's developmental level as well as strategies for developing and engaging in age-appropriate activities that support learning at home. This instills a sense of confidence within families regarding their ability to successfully support their children's learning that empowers and encourages them to become actively involved.

When families are supported through **school, community**, and **interagency** resources, they are able to more effectively become involved in the educational program. Numerous resources dedicated to educating families on ways they can support their children's learning are available to accommodate varying situations, needs, and abilities. Within the school, **teachers**, **guidance counselors**, and other **staff members** can provide valuable information regarding students' developmental characteristics, needs, and abilities as well as ways families can become involved to enhance learning within and outside of the classroom. **Support groups** hosted by the school enable families to share experiences and discuss ways to become involved in the learning process. Community support resources are often tailored to address the specific needs of families within the community. These resources offer **family education services**, such as classes, meetings, or programs, designed to provide families with the training, strategies, and knowledge necessary to become actively involved in their children's education. Several **national family support agencies** are also available to educate families on ways to become involved in their children's learning. Such agencies often have multiple locations as well as an array of digitally printed information, discussion forums, and training opportunities to enhance family involvement in learning.

History and Impact of Technology

Impact of Scientific and Technical Innovation

Scientific and technical innovation has played a major role in enhancing productivity, increasing society's wealth, and raising its standard of living. After a new innovation comes about, it must spread to other people and groups in order to be effective. This process is known as **diffusion**, and is illustrated using an **s-curve**, also known as a **diffusion curve**, which tracks an increase in revenue or productivity over time. An s-curve represents the product life of an innovation. During the early stages of product life, an innovation must establish its usefulness, and it experiences a very slow growth in terms of revenue and productivity. The middle stages of product life see rapid increases in growth, and the latter stages of product life involve gradual decline. Product improvements may extend the lifespan of an innovation, but it will inevitably fall off. Consequently, companies are always seeking new innovations to replace older ones.

Resource Management

Resource management seeks to allocate an organization's resources in the most efficient and economical ways possible—that is, the goal of resource management is the **optimization** of resource usage in a project. Resources include money, employees, inventory, production, and information technology, and they are allocated using a variety of processes and techniques. One such technique is **resource leveling**, which balances usage by eliminating inventory shortages and excesses. To avoid shortages and thereby reduce conflict, management should take care when scheduling multiple activities at the same time. If concurrent activities require more of one resource than is available or make use of the same person, they should be rescheduled. In many cases, management may be forced to delay an activity until the resource becomes available. If this activity is part of the critical path, the project may be delayed.

Stimulating Competitiveness and Creating New Goods and Services

Technological innovation provides a number of benefits to the marketplace. It can introduce new products, which are simply those with which customers have no prior experience. Technological innovation can also introduce an improved or more efficient means of production or commodity handling. In many cases, these new products or means of production will open up new markets and require the discovery of new sources of raw materials. This often stimulates the economy by creating additional competition and breaking up existing monopolies. Technological innovation is often the result of the pursuit of better quality, new market formation, new regulations, the need for replacement parts or services, decreased availability of materials, increased labor costs, or increased production costs, among other factors.

Major Scientific and Technological Innovations

The **automobile** was granted a patent in 1885. Karl Benz, who is widely regarded as the inventor of the gasoline-powered car, placed the first automobiles into production during the same year.

The **airplane** was developed in 1903 by Wilbur and Orville Wright. They used various principles of aerodynamics, such as drag and lift, to develop the first power and controlled flight.

The **integrated circuit** was developed in 1958 by Jack Kilby of Texas Instruments and Robert Noyce at Fairchild Semiconductor. It led to the development of the microchip by enabling semiconductor devices to perform the same functions as vacuum tubes. It revolutionized electronic equipment, leading to the development of personal computers, cellular phones, and various digital devices.

The **internet** came about with the first TCP/IP protocol, which was developed in 1983 by Robert E. Kahn and Vint Cerf.

Relationship Between Technology and Society and Culture

Technology and culture have a **synergistic relationship** which began with the simple tools developed during the dawn of man and continues today with modern technologies such as computers and other electronic devices. This relationship is **cyclical and codependent**, with each party exerting influence over the other. Funding for technological development comes from two primary sources in most modern cultures and societies: Private business and enterprise, or government programs. Once new technology is developed, it **influences** social attitudes and beliefs, which, in turn, influence the implementation of new technology. For instance, key values and beliefs that derive from this codependence between technology and culture are the notions that human productivity should work to achieve higher levels of efficiency and that technology drives social progress. According to these beliefs, humankind is improving as long as technology is improving.

Conservation and Sustainability

Conservation is the effort to reduce energy and material consumption by reducing usage and making more efficient use of existing resources. New technology can facilitate conservation in a variety of ways. Renewable energy sources (e.g., geothermal, hydroelectric energy, wind power), building techniques that take advantage of the local climate, and vehicles that consume less gas (such as hybrids) all help lower energy consumption. Real-time energy metering helps consumers to better understand the impact of their energy usage.

Sustainability determines the length of time over which an ecological system will endure. Sustainable systems are those that will remain healthy and productive for a long time. Technology is often a means of increasing energy efficiency and conserving natural resources so that the human environment can become more sustainable.

Biotechnology

Biotechnology is the technological application of biology. It uses living organisms and bioprocesses to create products or processes, and has numerous applications in the following fields:

- **Medicine** – includes drug production, gene therapy, gene testing, and pharmacogenomics (i.e. determining an individual's response to drugs based on inherited genetic traits).
- **Agriculture** – includes enhancing crop yield, increasing nutritional attributes of food, improving crop durability, producing new substances in crop plants, and reducing dependence on agrochemicals.
- **Biological engineering** – uses physics, chemistry, and mathematics to solve life science problems.
- **Bioremediation and biodegradation** – create organisms for purposes of removing environmental contamination.
- **Cloning** –two main types: reproductive, which brings a fully developed life into the world, and therapeutic, which involves using stem cells.
- **Human Genome Project** – seeks to discover all human genes and create a reference sequence for the human genome.

Biotechnology often makes use of mathematical biology, which models complex biological processes using various types of math: graph theory, calculus, probability theory, statistics, linear algebra, abstract algebra, combinatorics, algebraic geometry, topology, dynamical systems, differential equations, and coding theory.

Government Regulation and Facilitating Technological Development

Historically, the government has served a role not only in funding technological research but also in regulating its usage and side effects. One example of such regulation is the FDA, or Food and Drug administration. When selecting which types of research to fund, the government will choose those that offer the greatest benefit to mankind. However, the presence of different interest groups competing for resources can complicate the selection process. In reality, both the populace-at-large and special interests hold tremendous influence over governmental policy. The government also assumes a regulatory role in technological development, especially regarding the environment and the protection of ecological systems. The government is responsible for assigning liability to corporations whose products cause harm.

Material Disposals, and Environmental Emission Monitoring and Control

Materials disposal is carried out using a variety of technologies and techniques:

- **Incinerators** – subject solid waste to the process of combustion in order to convert it into residue and gas. This generates heat, gas, steam, and ash.
- **Landfills** – eliminate solid waste by burying it.
- **Recycling** – reprocesses discarded materials (e.g., aluminum cans, glass bottles, newspapers, cardboard boxes, paper) into their constituent materials and reuses them.
- **Sustainability methods** – include biological reprocessing (e.g., composting, anaerobic digestion) and energy recovery (which processes waste into fuel).

Environmental emission monitoring and control is performed by continuous emission monitoring systems, which use gas analyzers to test air samples for certain types of emissions (e.g., carbon dioxide, carbon monoxide, sulfur dioxide, mercury). Federal programs use these systems to ensure compliance with emission standards, such as the acid rain program and other EPA standards.

Medical and Agricultural Technology

Medical technology includes any device, procedure, pharmaceutical, or system whose purpose is improving health, preventing sickness, and diagnosing or treating disease. Medical technology covers a vast number of healthcare products, which often make use of mathematical principles and concepts. For instance, medical imaging machines (e.g., CAT, ultrasound) and pharmacology often make use of trigonometric functions for measurement problems. Mathematical tools such as dimensional analysis are often used to calculate the correct dosage for patients.

Agricultural technology encompasses a wide array of machinery, processes, and systems designed to enhance agricultural production. Agricultural technology also makes use of mathematical principles and concepts. For instance, dimensional analyses are often used to examine complex agricultural-social economic systems. Graph theory provides a means of modeling ecology, and quadratic equations are often used to solve economic problems related to agriculture.

Physics

The following concepts and principles of physics have been essential to the development of new technologies:

- **Bernoulli's principle** states that, when the speed of an inviscid flow increases, the pressure (or potential energy) of the flow will decrease. Consequently, faster moving air creates slower static pressure and higher dynamic pressure. Carburetors and pitot tubes work on Bernoulli's principle.

- **Aerodynamics** includes four forces relevant to flight: thrust, lift, drag, and weight. Thrust is a reaction force explained by Newton's Second and Third Laws. When mass is accelerated in one direction, it will generate an equal force in the opposite direction. Jet engines, propeller blades, and rockets generate thrust by pushing air in the direction opposite to flight. Lift is a force that is generated perpendicular to the oncoming air flow (using Bernoulli's Principle). Airplane wings are designed to take advantage of lift (climbing, descending, banking). Drag is a force that is generated parallel to the oncoming air flow, and opposes the motion of an object. Weight is applied by gravity. In order to achieve flight, all forces must be balanced.

Biology

Biology includes several fields with an especially strong focus on developing new technologies. One such field is **biological engineering**, which attempts to emulate biological systems and, thereby, develop new products or enhance existing biological systems. Biological engineering is responsible for the creation of renewable bioenergy, biocompatible materials, medical devices, diagnostic equipment, and similar technologies. A second field is **molecular biology**. It helped create the therapies and techniques used in gene therapy, which treats diseases by inserting, altering, and removing genes within a person's cells and tissue. Using techniques developed in molecular biology, gene therapy is capable of replacing mutated genes or even modifying and correcting mutated cells. A third field is **pathology**, which uses laboratory equipment to diagnose disease. Another field is **biotechnology**, which uses living organisms and bioprocesses to create products or processes.

Chemistry

An understanding of chemistry is necessary to convert raw materials (e.g., oil, air, water, minerals, metals) into usable and marketable materials such as solvents, soaps, pesticides, and cement. The chemical industry consists of numerous businesses that use chemical processes and reactions to create and refine products. Below is a partial list of such products:

- **Petrochemicals** include ethylene, propylene, benzene, and styrene.
- **Agrochemicals** include fertilizers, insecticides, and herbicides.
- **Polymers** include polyester, polyethylene, and Bakelite.
- **Fragrances/flavors** include vanillin and coumarin.
- **Inorganic industrial compounds** include ammonia, nitric acid, sodium hydroxide, and sulfuric acid.
- **Organic industrial compounds** include phenol, urea, and ethylene oxide.
- **Ceramics** include silica brick and frit.
- **Explosives** include ammonium nitrate, nitrocellulose, and nitroglycerin.
- **Oleochemicals** include lard and soybean oil.
- **Elastomers** includes polyisoprene, neoprene, and polyurethane.

Chapter Quiz

Ready to see how well you retained what you just read? Scan the QR code to go directly to the chapter quiz interface for this study guide. If you're using a computer, simply visit the online resources page at **mometrix.com/resources719/texespprte370** and click the Chapter Quizzes link.

TExES Practice Test

Want to take this practice test in an online interactive format?
Check out the online resources page, which includes interactive practice questions and much more: **mometrix.com/resources719/texespprte370**

1. How does assigning term papers, or other long-term assignments, help students to learn skills about real life?

a. It gets them accustomed to being under stress.
b. It does not; it only gives them an opportunity to cheat since they will not be working under teacher supervision.
c. It teaches the importance of time-management and planning for unexpected circumstances.
d. Such projects are rarely worth the effort, since more often than not, the parents end up doing most of the project.

2. If you decide to allow your students to check their own homework in class, which method of recording grades should not be used?

a. Collect the graded assignments and record them yourself.
b. Have the students call out the grades to you from their desks.
c. Walk around the room and visually check the grades yourself.
d. Have a teacher's aide record the grades.

3. Shortly after the first day of class, you decide to send out a mass email to the parents of all of your students. What is the most important information that you can share in such an email?

a. A specific list of the requirements that students must meet in order to make good grades in your class.
b. A list of websites that parents can use as a reference to help their children with the subject.
c. A detailed list of what you will be covering during each week of class.
d. A list of books that you expect all parents to read if they intend to be able to help their children.

Refer to the following for question 4:

> Your 9th grade biology class is about to take on its first animal dissection. You have already covered the procedure in detail during class, but you know that some of the students are still feeling nervous or even a little queasy.

4. What can you do to help make the dissection go more smoothly?

a. Remind them that medical students regularly dissect human cadavers, and that this is not really such a big deal
b. Set a timer for each section of the procedure, so the students stay on pace
c. Require each student to write out their own step-by-step explanation of what they plan to do
d. Have the students speak out loud as they work, describing what they are doing

5. For how long at a time should a teacher initially plan to hold open class discussions of subject matter at the middle school/junior high school level?

a. 3-5 minutes
b. 10-15 minutes
c. 30-45 minutes
d. For an entire class period

6. Which teacher characteristic will best help facilitate student cooperation in the classroom?

a. Rigid military-style discipline
b. Consistency in how rules are enforced
c. A playful, loving approach, even when rules are broken
d. Ignoring misbehavior so that the students will see that they can't get to you

7. A new student, Jethro, has been assigned to your class. Jethro comes from a much rougher neighborhood than most of the students in your class and is having a very hard time fitting in. He often seems angry, and he speaks insolently both to you and to his classmates. It always seems that he has something to prove, and anytime he knows an answer in class, he hurriedly blurts it out, as though he is competing with the other students. His behavior is steadily becoming worse, and some of the other students seem to be afraid of him. When you correct his behavior in class, he seems to be proud of himself and becomes even more insolent. Which of the following would be a good first step to get through to him?

a. Put him in a seat by himself in the corner of the room.
b. Point out to him in front of the class that his behavior is interfering with the entire class.
c. Send him to the vice principal's office each time he misbehaves.
d. Do not let him get away with anything, but make a point to always discipline him in private.

8. How should a teacher initially plan instruction to meet the needs of a highly diverse classroom?

a. On the first day of class, the teacher should ask each student to complete a survey to determine the students' cultural, ethnic, and racial background.
b. A good teacher should be intimately familiar with the major cultures within the local school district.
c. A teacher should plan lessons so that new material is introduced using a variety of different approaches.
d. Guest teachers from different ethnic backgrounds should occasionally be invited to teach so that all students will feel more comfortable.

9. Which of the following would be an unethical use of school property?

a. Mr. Jackson takes home a school-owned laptop because there is publishing software installed on it that will help him prepare handouts for class.
b. Mrs. Wallenstein goes to the school supply room and takes a box of colored chalk to use for drawing pie charts on the board for her math class.
c. Mr. Calhoun uses his classroom after school to sell Girl Scout cookies for his daughter.
d. Mr. Martinov asks the school secretary to requisition a laser pointer for his lectures.

10. When dealing with a class with widely varied levels of skill and knowledge, which of the following represents a harmful practice?

a. Giving extra attention to the lower performing students in class
b. Allowing the higher performing students to assist the lower performing students
c. Providing more individual tutoring time to higher performing students while letting lower performing students work independently
d. Providing specific feedback to lower performing students

11. Which of the following is a valid technique to use with non-native English speakers in your class if they are having trouble and your school has very limited ESL resources?

a. Ask the student's parents to hire a translator to sit with the child in class.
b. Use more visual aids and illustrative hand gestures while teaching.
c. Speak as rapidly as possible so that the student will get used to hearing English faster.
d. Repeat everything you say twice.

12. How can a teacher best ensure that a lesson will be coherent and logical?

a. Plan out the lesson in writing ahead of time.
b. Ask the class every day if they understand.
c. Make sure that your lesson never strays from the textbook.
d. Rely on the sample lesson plans from the teacher's guidebook.

13. When assigning large student projects, such as term papers or research projects, what is the most effective system for evaluation?

a. When the project is over, assign a single overall grade. This will teach the students what to expect in college.
b. Grade the projects on a curve
c. The projects should be evaluated as work progresses and according to multiple standards, including overall accuracy, timely completion of individual steps, quality of research, grammar and spelling, etc.
d. Projects should be graded on a simple pass/fail basis, since the overall experience is more important than the quality of the result.

Refer to the following for question 14:

Mrs. Sanchez is a new teacher of ninth-grade literature. She truly loves her subject, and the highlight of each class period is when she holds a 20-minute class discussion of the previous day's reading assignment. She is very enthusiastic about these discussions and encourages the students to form and express their own opinions. She often asks provocative questions and pushes the students to consider the motives of characters from different points of view. Many of the students enjoy this, but an observer notices some problems. Misbehavior by a few students is getting out of hand. And a couple of students seem to just zone out.

14. What common mistake is Mrs. Sanchez making that may be leading to these behavioral issues and lack of focus?

a. She is not being strict enough.
b. She is devoting too much time to discussions.
c. She is concentrating all her attention on the discussions.
d. Her enthusiasm makes her look weak to the students.

Refer to the following for question 15:

Mrs. Schubert is taking her biology class on a field trip to the local natural science museum. They have just finished a unit on world biomes, and the museum has exhibits on desert flora and fauna as well as wetland life.

15. What can she do to ensure that her students make the most of this opportunity?

a. Tell the students to pay attention during the tour.
b. Tell the students not to speak during the tour.
c. Ask the students to take notes, and tell them that the notes will be graded.
d. Give the students a pop quiz before going on the field trip.

16. Getting the classroom ready for the first day of school can be overwhelming for a new teacher. As the big day comes, one often must make some hard choices and leave a few things to be done later. Which of the following could wait a few more days if necessary?

a. Optimizing the arrangement of student desks
b. Decorating all bulletin boards and setting them up for display
c. Making sure that you have enough textbooks and that they are all in satisfactory condition
d. Verifying that equipment such as overhead projectors and computer workstations are functional and ready to use

17. During a class discussion, two students are in disagreement regarding the discussion topic and begin arguing about their perspectives in an increasingly heated exchange. What should the teacher do to ensure that the class can proceed in an organized fashion?

a. Immediately tell the class what the correct answer is and move on.
b. Encourage the students to continue presenting their cases in a controlled discourse while opening the floor for other perspectives.
c. Tell the students that whenever there is a disagreement in class, the student who is right will get extra credit.
d. Discourage the students from disagreeing with each other in class, and instead have them ask you when they have a question.

18. Suppose that you have taken over a 20th-century history class for a colleague who has come down with a prolonged illness and will be unable to finish out the term. The teacher has confided in you that she has HIV/AIDS, and has asked you not to tell anyone. The class is currently covering World War II, and you have a living relative who was a German soldier during the war. Some of your students are Jewish. One of the students in the class, Julie, happens to the principal's niece and she has a reputation for being hyperactive and disruptive. Which of the following would NOT be an ethical violation?

a. Telling the students that their former teacher has AIDS
b. Inviting your relative to come and speak to the class about his experience fighting for the Nazis during WWII
c. Being a little more lenient about Julie's behavior than you are with the other students, to make sure that the principal will not be upset with you
d. Giving Julie some of your prescription allergy medicine since it tends to have a sedative effect

19. Mrs. Emal often feels intimidated by computers in the classroom. Though she often tries to use computer applications in class, somehow the students always know more about them than she does. She feels self-conscious and embarrassed. She has tried to read up on new classroom technologies in education journals, but nevertheless, she always feels two steps behind the times. What should she do?

a. Clearly, Mrs. Emal's ignorance is undermining her authority. She should be stricter with the students, so that they do not laugh at her.
b. Technology changes quickly, and the articles she is reading may already be outdated. She would be better off discussing the problem with other teachers, or even taking a class at the local community college.
c. Since the students seem to understand the technology better, Mrs. Emal should get the students to teach her what she needs to know.
d. Mrs. Emal is obviously incompetent with computers. She would be better off relying on more traditional teaching methods and leave the electronics to the experts.

20. Which approach to assessment offers the strongest chance of quantifying what a student has learned?

a. Multiple choice tests
b. Essay questions
c. Combining several methods
d. Tests using a simple question-and-answer format

21. During in-class assignments and small group activities, how can a teacher best ensure that all of the students are on-task and not getting behind?

a. Watch the class quietly from the teacher's desk.
b. Respond to students promptly when they raise their hands.
c. Collect all student work several times during the class, check it, and then hand it back so that they can continue working.
d. Circulate among the students regularly to observe the students' work up close.

22. Which strategy works better for keeping students from losing focus during longer talks or explanations?

a. Break your lecture up with jokes or personal anecdotes.
b. Put a general outline of what you will discuss on the board.
c. Stop every minute or two and quiz a student at random on whether he or she understood the concept you are discussing.
d. Start off your lesson by asking the students what they already know about the subject.

23. Whose responsibility is it to ensure that a teacher remains current with new teaching techniques?

a. The county school system is required to set the standards and provide opportunities for teachers to learn new skills.
b. The principal is responsible for ensuring that the teachers in his or her school do not fall behind.
c. The senior teachers for each grade are responsible for taking the less experienced teachers under their wing.
d. Every teacher is responsible for taking the initiative for learning and applying new teaching methods as appropriate for the classes they teach.

24. It is your first week of class teaching a 12th grade history class. Because of the subject matter, and because most of these students will be going on to college, a significant portion of the course will be presented in the form of college-style lectures. How can you ensure that all of the students have the necessary note-taking skills they will need, both for this class and beyond?

a. This is not your responsibility. Since they are college-bound seniors, they should already have these skills.
b. Give a pop quiz at the end of every class.
c. Give a lecture on note-taking on the first day of class.
d. Inform the students that for the first couple of weeks, you will collect their notes at the end of class and give them back the next day with corrections.

25. When teaching Shakespeare's *Romeo and Juliet*, which technique might help students maintain interest despite the difficult language?

a. Give the students a glossary of archaic English words commonly found in the play.
b. Include a discussion of some modern interpretations of the story (movies such as *Romeo+Juliet*, or even *West Side Story*) and have students identify differences between the modern versions and the original.
c. Have the students read the parts out loud.
d. Hold a detailed discussion of English syntax and grammar of the period.

26. How can including cooperative learning strategies in the classroom teach practical life skills to students?

a. Students learn to work independently, even when others are around.
b. Students learn interpersonal problem-solving skills that they will need later in life.
c. Students learn ways to score better on standardized tests.
d. Students learn the importance of physical exercise in their daily lives.

27. All of the options below are important, but which is the single most important element of creating a productive classroom environment?

a. A well decorated classroom
b. A clean classroom
c. Planning
d. A good seating arrangement

28. Which method of lesson planning will help a teacher ensure that his lesson will take advantage of the multiple intelligences of different students?

a. Use a lesson-planning matrix to help devise learning activities that are organized according to different abilities.
b. Survey the students about what helps them to learn the most.
c. Design a seating plan so that the students who need the most help sit in the front.
d. Try to use more images and graphs in presentations.

29. What is the best way to handle current events that are relevant to your class?

a. Keep your lesson plans flexible, and integrate extended discussions of current events as they occur.
b. Don't allow current events to distract the class. Keeping to your schedule is more important.
c. Have students research current events on their own for extra credit.
d. Set strict parameters on the discussion of current events, such as holding such discussion during the last ten minutes of class on Fridays.

30. What is the most efficient way to apply a formula for determining final grades?

a. Paper, pencil, and a calculator
b. Database manager software
c. Spreadsheet software
d. Online resources

31. A student has exposed himself to a female student in the back of the classroom. What should be the immediate response of the teacher?

a. Assign the offending student to detention.
b. Physically restrain and remove the offending student from the classroom.
c. Send the offending student to the principal's office.
d. Attempt to shield the offended student and the rest of the class from the offending student.

32. How does the theory of multiple intelligences address the learning needs of students?

a. It suggests quite simply that some students are smarter than others, and that teachers must accept that while a *C* is a bad grade for some students, that it is a very good grade for others.
b. It suggests that different people learn in different ways, and that teachers can give more students a better chance by using a variety of teaching methods in the classroom.
c. It suggests that every student has only two areas of talent in which he or she can excel, and that once these talents are identified, students should not be pushed in other areas.
d. It suggests that all students are equally intelligent and that they will learn if they are motivated enough.

33. Which strategy is key for managing in-class group work sessions?

a. Avoid spending too much time with any one group and neglecting others.
b. Make sure that none of the students in any group are good friends.
c. Avoid the temptation to walk around the room and interact with the groups.
d. Grade only the final result of the assignment, and not the students' individual participation.

34. Mr. Holt is a new teacher, and has been teaching for three months. He is painfully aware that he is having trouble controlling his class. He knows that it is not simply a matter of one or two students being "bad apples." He is unable to effectively control his students and he feels intimidated. What should he do?

a. Be patient and give it a few more months. It takes time for a new teacher to find his stride and establish himself.
b. He must get control of the class immediately. Dole out harsh punishments to the whole class every time someone misbehaves. The students will be back in line in no time.
c. Inform the principal that he is a new teacher and request that the principal let him swap classes with another teacher who has students that are easier to get along with.
d. Consult with other teachers and administrators at your school and ask for advice and assistance.

35. What is the best starting point for deciding on the floor plan of your classroom?

a. Make sure that all student desks are oriented with their backs to the windows so as to ensure that no students will become distracted by events going on outside.
b. Consider the size and shape of the room, and decide where the optimal position would be for you to carry out most of your instruction.
c. Arrange student desks so that they all face the chalkboard.
d. Use whatever arrangement is already there. School administrators spend a lot of time before the beginning of the school year optimizing the floor plans of every classroom in the building.

36. Many of the students in your ninth-grade algebra class seem bored, and even though they are smart, they are having trouble following your class. What actions could you take that might get the students more involved?

a. Devote one entire class period as a question-and-answer session. Encourage the students to ask you about any aspect of the subject which they are having difficulty learning.
b. Set aside two class periods and meet with each student individually to address the problems they are having.
c. Revisit topics you have already covered so that you can make sure that everyone understands.
d. Periodically ask the students to meet in small groups and to come up with scenarios in which the kinds of problems you are covering can be applied.

37. Suppose that you are transitioning from one activity to another during class, but you notice that two of your students are still struggling to finish the current task. What is the best recourse?

a. Single the students out in front of the rest of the class so that they will feel more motivated to work more efficiently.
b. Do not go forward with the new activity, and have the rest of the class wait for the two students to finish their work.
c. Continue with the new activity, but allow the two students to continue and finish the activity they are on. Let them know quietly that they can meet with you after class to learn whatever they missed.
d. Give the two students a failing grade for the assignments because they did not finish their work on time.

38. After a month of class, Mr. Gupta notices that his 12th grade physics class has fallen well behind his planned curriculum. In-class experiments and other activities have taken significantly longer to complete than the teacher expected. What should he do?

a. Cease holding in-class experiments and stick rigidly with following the units in the textbook.
b. Ignore the planned curriculum; the students will learn more from doing the experiments than from lectures and written assignments.
c. Increase the amount of homework in order to catch up.
d. Evaluate the way students are carrying out experiments and develop more organized procedures to keep the students on track.

39. What is the most accurate indicator of overall student performance?

a. Final exams and other tests that cover course material on a comprehensive basis.
b. The combined results of frequent evaluations given throughout the term.
c. Studies show that in the end, a teacher's gut instinct about at student is usually right.
d. Homework and papers are usually the best indicator, since they show how a student thinks when not under direct teacher supervision.

40. What is the best tactic to use for displaying information in class if you must float from classroom to classroom?

a. Whatever classroom you are assigned to teach in is "yours" for that class period. Simply erase whatever is on the chalkboard and write your own information there.
b. Explain to the students that they need to take very thorough notes and give your lecture orally, without using any visual aids.
c. Email your notes and diagrams to all the students in advance and have them access them on school-supplied laptops. If no laptops are available, display information onto the whiteboard through the classroom's projector.
d. Prepare your notes on transparencies and display them using an overhead projector.

41. Suppose a particularly promising student in your 11th-grade physics class has become increasingly arrogant to the point that it is disrupting your lessons. The student constantly complains out loud in class that the problems are too easy, and he often blurts the answer to a problem out before you have even finished explaining it. The student is, in fact, one of your best students, and the class is probably not advanced enough for him. However, he must complete this class before moving on to more advanced science classes. How might a teacher best go about resolving the problem?

a. Discipline the student by lowering his grades until his behavior improves.
b. Try to come up with two or three options that could resolve the problem and work with the student to commit to one of them.
c. Recommend to the student's parents that they might want to consider enrolling him in a physics class at the local community college.
d. Send the student to the vice principal's office.

42. Suppose you are teaching a 10th grade US government unit on the role and structure of Congress, and many of your students are slow to understand the workings of the US Senate vs. the House of Representatives. Which of the following methods would be the most likely way to ensure that your students become more interested in the subject matter and take away a practical understanding of the material?

a. Have the students take turns reading the textbook aloud in class.
b. Assign each student to make a presentation on the biography of a current US senator or congress person.
c. Ask the students to follow the news closely at home and to identify ongoing activities in Congress that you can discuss in class.
d. Supplement the textbook material with charts and graphs to help the students better visualize the percentages of votes needed to pass a bill or override a veto.

Refer to the following for question 43:

Mr. Krick recently read an article about a new interactive computer game that is very effective at getting children interested in history. Although he has never seen the game himself, he is interested in the possibility of using it with his class.

43. What is the best course of action for Mr. Krick?

a. He should go to the local computer store, buy the game, and try it out with his class the next day.
b. He should forget about it. Computer games are bad for children.
c. He should make a copy of the article, note the website of the game, and consult with the school's technology coordinator to see if the coordinator knows anything about the product.
d. He should ask the class if they have heard of the game and if they think the game would be helpful to them in class.

44. In what areas do computers have the LEAST benefit for student learning?

a. Simple drills, such as teaching multiplication tables, because this frees up the teacher to work with the students on developing higher-level skills
b. Role-playing games that develop greater social awareness and that allow the students to participate more directly in the events they are learning about
c. Simulations of mechanical activities that help the students develop motor skills and reflexes
d. Exercises that teach higher-order thinking and professional skills

45. How can you best ensure that your students quickly settle down at the beginning of class so that you can get on with your lesson?

a. Establish a firm routine for the beginning of every class, so that all the students know what to expect
b. Use the time while the students are settling in to catch up on paper work
c. Threaten to send the whole class to detention
d. Tell the students that they can leave early if the class gets started on time

46. Suppose you are holding a class discussion of current events in your 8th grade social studies class. What is the most effective way to get the quieter students to participate in the discussion?

a. Ask the more active students to stop raising their hands.
b. Penalize students who do not participate in the discussion.
c. Periodically ask questions directly to the quiet students.
d. Offer extra credit to the students who participate the most.

47. Which of the following is consistent with constructive assertiveness on the part of a teacher?

a. Telling students in a literature class that there is only one acceptable point of view in regard to the novel you are teaching
b. A teacher who asks permission from her students to begin class
c. A teacher who halts his presentation and sternly insists that the students in the back of the room stop talking
d. A teacher who yells at students who answer questions incorrectly

48. Mike, a student in your 10th grade geometry class, is rapidly falling behind in class because he is having a harder time grasping concepts than are most of the other students. You have set up a meeting with Mike's parents and want to discuss options such as encouraging them to hire a private tutor, or possibly even transferring him to a remedial math class. What might be the best way to begin the discussion?

a. "Mike is working very hard in my class, but he is having a very tough time. I wanted to discuss a few ideas with you, and also to hear your input about what we can do to help him."
b. "Mike currently has one of the lowest averages in my class. I want to be frank with you. If something does not change, I'm afraid he will fail the class."
c. "Have you been working much with Mike at home to help him with his geometry? He just does not seem to be cutting it."
d. "Mike is having a little trouble with his geometry. I'm sure he will do fine, but I just wanted to let you know."

49. Which is an example of the how technology can be used to take advantage of the theory of multiple intelligences?

a. Students using the computer for math drills
b. Teaching students to use a word processor for writing papers
c. Offer students the option of doing class projects in the form of a blog or a video presentation
d. Instead of a lecture, give lessons using slide show presentations

50. How can a teacher end a lesson so that the students begin to process the material and keep it in their minds?

a. Take a moment to talk about how the day's lesson connects and fits in with previous lessons and/or the next day's lesson
b. Give a pop quiz
c. Call on a student at random to stand up before the class and explain what the most important thing he or she learned was
d. Be sure that the students have a homework assignment every single day

51. What is the most effective way to get through to a student who says to hate the subject you are teaching?

a. Don't give an inch. The student must see that the only option is submission to the curriculum.
b. Offer the student rewards for trying
c. Show empathy by asking the student to tell you his side of the problem
d. Threaten to call the student's parents

52. Which of the following is not an ethical violation?

a. A teacher becomes romantically involved with a student.
b. A teacher becomes romantically involved with the parent of a student in her class.
c. A teacher becomes romantically involved with another teacher in the same school.
d. All of the above are ethical violations.

53. After you send a student to the principal's office for repeatedly disrupting your class, the principal suspends the student for three days. Following the suspension, the principal informs you that he would like to put the student back in your class. You are concerned that the student will continue to disrupt the class. Which of the following best represents your obligations regarding welcoming the student back?

a. You should follow the leadership's decision and welcome the student back.
b. You are not obligated to allow the student back into your class if you feel uncomfortable.
c. You must file a petition with the board of education if you do not want the student back in your class.
d. You have to let the student back in your class only if you cannot find another teacher willing to take the student.

54. In your second-year French class, many of your students expressed surprise at how poor their grades were on the mid-term progress report. The grades in your class are calculated according to a very simple formula, a large part of which comes from the grades given on daily work. Which strategy would best ensure that your students remain aware of their grades?

a. Require the students to keep a running average of their daily grades in the front of their notebooks
b. Post a list of student grades every week on the bulletin board organized by student ID number
c. Send home a mini-report card every two weeks that the parents must sign
d. Explain your grading system to the students one more time, and then leave it up to them

55. What is the most productive order to structure a class period?

a. Seatwork, class discussion, content development
b. Class discussion, seatwork, content development
c. Seatwork, content development, class discussion
d. Content development, class discussion, seatwork

56. A school administrator recently sat in and observed Mr. Naylor's algebra class. Mr. Naylor received several criticisms. Which one should he take the most seriously?

a. The bulletin boards in his classroom could be better organized.
b. About a quarter of the students did not appear to be actively participating in class discussions.
c. Two students in the back of the class were passing notes back and forth, and the teacher did not notice.
d. The class was about a week behind where it should be according to the county guidelines.

57. Should students be allowed to use word processors to prepare written class assignments?

a. No. Word processors discourage students from learning grammar and spelling. It is better for teachers to require students to hand write or type their assignments.
b. The use of word processors should be mandatory on all written assignments and at all levels.
c. No. Word processors are commercial products, and it is inappropriate for a teacher to encourage or require students to use one piece of software instead of another.
d. Generally yes, but this depends on the nature of the assignment and the grade level of the class.

58. What is the best method for improving students' memorization skills?

a. Repetition
b. Break the item to be memorized into small sections and then learn the sections one at a time
c. Students should read the item once as rapidly as possible and then immediately try to repeat as much as they can recall
d. Play a distinctive piece of music in the background

59. Which strategy would best help a history teacher get students more involved in the subject?

a. Supplement the standard textbook with less academic materials, including narratives, biographies, and news articles from the time
b. Have students read from the textbook out loud in class
c. Make all of the class test questions essay questions
d. Have students act out battles in the classroom

60. Which subject area generally requires the most involved lesson planning?

a. English/language arts
b. Math
c. History
d. Computer science

Refer to the following for question 61:

A first-year science teacher has assigned her first group project of the year. She has divided the classroom into groups of four to conduct an experiment on the greenhouse effect by measuring the temperatures of two containers, with one having plastic wrap to simulate the greenhouse effect. The students must set up the project, conduct the experiment, and record their data. She wants all of the students to experience each part of the project and not divide into specialized roles.

61. How can the teacher ensure that all students are contributing equally during this cooperative learning exercise?

a. The teacher should circulate among the groups and observe how they are working together.
b. The teacher should assign one student in each group to monitor student participation.
c. The teacher should assign each student in each group a specific task to accomplish.
d. The teacher should avoid such exercises, since they inevitably end up with one or two students doing most of the work.

62. What is the best way to ensure overall good behavior from your students?

a. Establish a set of rules for your classroom, give the students a written copy, and go over the rules at the beginning of the year or semester
b. A good teacher is a strict teacher. From the very beginning, be gruff with the students, and show them that you have no tolerance for "nonsense."
c. Wait a few days before setting ground rules. Students will respect you more if you give them more leeway in the beginning as they are settling in.
d. Change your rules frequently to keep the students on their toes.

63. You are covering the American Revolution and the formation of the United States in your 10th grade US history class. Which task would NOT help your students process what they are learning?

a. Have the students write an essay on how the ideas of the founding fathers continue to influence us today
b. Have each of the students memorize a different part of the Constitution or the Declaration of Independence and recite it before the class
c. Ask the students to keep a learning log in which each day they write a short paragraph about the meaning of what they learned in class that day
d. Assign each student to research and prepare an oral presentation on one of the founding fathers or another important figure of the time

64. Suppose you have gone back to teaching after taking a few years off to spend with your young children. During the first couple of weeks in your new job, you notice that your classroom setup seems a little outdated compared with those of some of the other teachers. What should you do?

a. It is your classroom, and you have a right to run it as you see fit.
b. Do your best to make your classroom mimic the other classrooms for your grade.
c. Speak to some of your fellow teachers and ask them where they got their ideas, and what they can tell you about the latest trends.
d. Ask the students how they think you should set up the room.

65. What is the most accurate predictor of a student's achievement in school?

a. Socio-economic background of a student's peers
b. Family involvement in student's life
c. Education level of parents
d. Marital status of parents

66. Which of the following is an ethical or legal violation?

a. Physically restraining a student who is acting violently or endangering others
b. Informing a student's parents of the student's current grades
c. Approaching a student and asking if the student has a learning disability
d. Refusing to provide extra credit

67. Which of the following is the most appropriate point at which a teacher should first contact a student's parents?

a. Sarah gets a *D* in the class after consistently failing to turn in her work on time.
b. During the first week of class, you twice had to ask Brad to stop whispering to the girl sitting next to him.
c. Since the beginning of class a few weeks ago, Kristen often comes to class dressed inappropriately, wearing bikini bottoms and tee shirts with messages that border on being offensive.
d. During the first few weeks of the quarter, Rick made excellent grades on his weekly German vocabulary test; however, for the last two weeks his scores have steadily dropped. He also seems to be gloomier than usual.

68. Which equipment should be arranged first when deciding upon a classroom floor plan?

a. The teacher's desk
b. Computer workstations
c. Filing cabinets
d. Overhead projector

69. Which of the following teacher statements to a student represents the most constructive initial approach to talking in the classroom?

a. "Shut up!"
b. "Do you realize that when you whisper to your neighbor, it distracts the whole class?"
c. "Because of your behavior, I am now requiring the entire class to write 'I will not whisper in class' 500 times."
d. "Go outside and stand in the hall until class is over."

70. Which of the following is a commonly recognized benefit of computers in the classroom?

a. They allow the teacher more free time to spend as he or she pleases while students are working on computers.
b. Students can use them to communicate with each other during instruction.
c. They are more effective at facilitating discussion than in-person conversations.
d. They offer multiple methods of differentiation.

71. Suppose the students in your computer science class vary greatly in the amount of experience and knowledge they have about computers. What can you do as a teacher to make student evaluations fair to everyone?

a. Evaluate how much each student learns in addition to whether or not the student gets the correct answers on tests.
b. Grade class tests on a curve.
c. Put more weight on class research projects than on tests.
d. Grade students only according to test results.

72. What is the best time to establish direct contact with a student's parents regarding concerns with the student's work or behavior?

a. On the first day of school
b. Whenever a student makes a mistake
c. As soon as you notice a negative pattern developing in the student's work or behavior
d. Only when a problem becomes extreme

73. What can a teacher do to prevent students from falling into a pattern of incomplete assignments?

a. Ask the students to keep an eye on each other and report to you if someone else is having a problem.
b. Increase the penalty for not finishing assignments.
c. Approach a student privately the first time the student fails to turn in an assignment, and let the student know you are available to help.
d. Assign extra credit work to students who fail to turn in assignments.

74. What is the most productive teacher response to an uncooperative student who says: "I hate grammar. It's a waste of time, and I don't want to take it anymore!"

a. "You do seem to be having a tough time with it lately. Why don't you tell me about what is causing you the most trouble?"
b. "Don't you want to be able get a good job?"
c. "Hang in there, sport. You'll get it. It just takes a little more work."
d. "Grammar is not an elective. You have to take it."

75. Which method is the most helpful in making sure that students fully understand their progress throughout the term?

a. In addition to your own records, require that each student keep a grade book for him or herself.
b. Once a week, read each student's current average out loud to the class.
c. Have students check their own work.
d. Issue an informal written progress report every month.

76. Which of the following is a good example of a learning goal that a teacher should set for a poetry unit in an English literature class?

a. Students will learn to identify the most common meters used in English literature, with a focus being placed upon iambic pentameter.
b. Students will learn to appreciate and enjoy poetry as an art form.
c. Students will learn how to identify the elements of good poetry.
d. Students will learn the cultural importance of poetry to English speakers around the world.

77. Which of the following is a good way for a new teacher to build useful connections and knowledge of the school resources available to her?

a. Volunteer to participate on school committees and other events
b. Take the time to get to know school administrators and other teachers
c. Attend local education conferences and workshops
d. All of the above

Refer to the following for questions 78–81:

Eric, one of the students in Mr. Nielsen's 2nd year French class, has gotten *C*'s on his last three weekly vocabulary quizzes. Mr. Nielsen is surprised, because Eric has always seemed like a good student in French until now. Additionally, Eric also seems less energetic than before. In fact, Eric often appears on the verge of falling asleep. Mr. Nielsen goes over Eric's records and verifies that Eric was a consistent *A-* student during first year French. Granted, since beginning second year French, Eric's French had grades dropped to a steady *B+* until this latest situation. It is true that the second year class is significantly more difficult and intense than first year, but even so, the latest drop in Eric's grades goes beyond what Mr. Nielsen would normally expect. Although Eric does not "fit the profile," Mr. Nielsen wonders if Eric could have become involved in drugs because he seems so lethargic in class.

78. What would be the best initial step for Mr. Nielsen to take?

a. Contact Eric's parents and notify them that Eric's French grades have dropped, and that he might be taking drugs
b. Approach Eric directly and ask him about his grades
c. Approach some of Eric's friends and ask them if Eric is taking drugs
d. Assign extra credit work to Eric so that he can bring his grades back up

79. After speaking to Eric, Mr. Nielsen is perplexed. When Mr. Nielsen asked why his French grades were dropping, Eric responded that he was taking some harder classes this year, and was having trouble balancing everything. During the conversation, Eric seemed conflicted. On the one hand, he said he still loved French as much as ever, but at the same time, he kept repeated that it was not as important as his computer science and trigonometry classes.

What would the next logical step be for Mr. Nielsen?

a. Contact Eric's parents
b. Ask Eric's computer science and trigonometry teachers if they could cut back on Eric's work
c. Speak with Eric's guidance counselor
d. Suggest to Eric that he should drop the second-year French class

80. Mr. Nielsen speaks with Eric's father, Jim, who is an accountant. Jim tells Mr. Nielsen that he accepts full responsibility for the drop in Eric's French grade. Jim says that he has been pushing Eric to work harder in his math classes, so that he can get into a better college. Jim said that he knows Eric likes French, but that as a parent he feels that math and computer science are more important for Eric's future than French. Jim says that he told Eric to put less time into French, and that he is not worried about the drop in his grades.

How should Mr. Nielsen respond to Jim?

a. Try to convince Jim that French is just as important as math
b. Recommend that Eric drop the French class
c. Tell Jim that getting a *C* or worse in French will not help Eric's GPA.
d. Thank Jim for his candor, and suggest that a conference with Eric's guidance counselor might be useful in sorting out Eric's priorities

81. How should Mr. Nielsen handle it, if Eric comes to him and says that he disagrees with his father and wants to focus all his energy on French class so that he can study abroad?

a. Recommend another conference with the guidance counselor
b. Encourage Eric to follow his heart, regardless of what his father wants
c. Tell Eric that his father knows what is best for him
d. Call Eric's father and try to convince him that Eric should focus on what he is best at

Refer to the following for questions 82–85:

Mrs. Marx teaches a 9th grade composition class. She is not very comfortable with computers, and has always been wary of allowing students to write essays on their home computers because she has heard that using a computer makes it easier to plagiarize. However, her students and even some of their parents ask her over and over again every year to allow them to write their assignments using a word processor. Recently, one parent made a point that really stuck with her. He explained that he was a businessperson, and that without good computer writing skills, he simply could not survive in the modern work place. He said that students needed extensive exposure and training in the use of computers for writing in order to get jobs later on. After the conversation, Mrs. Marx began to feel very much behind the times, and realized that she might actually be doing her students a disservice by forbidding the use of computers in her class.

82. Considering that Mrs. Marx's own experience with computers is limited, what should she do in order to teach writing with computers effectively?

a. Enroll in a computer science class at the local community college
b. Form a study group with other teachers to discuss and share new teaching techniques using computers
c. Tell the parents that "writing is writing," with or without computers, and that the students can pick up computer skills in other classes
d. Ask the students to teach her about using word processors

83. After careful thought, Mrs. Marx decided to allow her students to begin using computers for completing class writing assignments, and even told her class that she would permit them to bring laptops to class to take notes. After some time, however, she realized that some students were using the wireless connections on their laptops to chat with each other during class, which is against school policy. How should she respond?

a. She should firmly warn students that this is not allowed, and that continuing to do so will jeopardize their privilege to use laptops in class.
b. She should allow the students to chat, since this helps them learn technology.
c. She should go back to the old policy of not allowing any use of computers at all.
d. Since she is unable to identify which students are guilty, she should assign detention to the entire class.

84. As her class goes on, Mrs. Marx continues to worry about students using the Internet to plagiarize their papers. However, Mrs. Marx does not know if this is really happening, nor does she understand how to detect or fight it. What should she do?

a. Approach one of her better students privately and ask him to show her how students usually go about downloading papers
b. Start visiting the social networking websites popular with teens and run a search on her student's names
c. Email all of the students' parents and ask them to monitor their children's Internet activities more closely
d. Visit the school's technology coordinator and ask for more information about resources available to teachers for fighting plagiarism

85. Phillip, a student in Mrs. Marx's class, is the only student who did not take up Mrs. Marx's offer to do assignments on a computer. However, his grades have also dropped a little since she began encouraging the class to use a computer. Curious, Mrs. Marx approaches Phillip privately and asks why he does not want to use a computer and what is going on with his grades. He tells her that his parents cannot afford a computer and that he feels self-conscious about it since all the other students have computers. What should Mrs. Marx do?

a. Tell the rest of the class to stop using computers on their assignment, since it is unfair that Phillip does not have one
b. Go to a discount store and buy Phillip the cheapest laptop she can find
c. Tell Phillip that she can arrange for him to use the school computer lab either before or after school to work on his assignments, and also suggest that he consider using the computers at his local public library
d. Tell Phillip that he can do his assignments however he wants, but that he needs to keep his grades up

Refer to the following for questions 86–90:

This quarter there are several non-native English speakers in Mr. Michael's literature class. One student, Vlad, is from Russia. He seems to understand English very well, but he has a heavy accent, that can sometimes be hard to understand. Some of the other students make fun of his accent in class. This makes Vlad angry, and he often responds by using profanity. Another student, Maria, is Mexican and is having a lot of trouble keeping up with the reading assignments. A third student, Akiko, is from Japan.

86. How should Mr. Michaels deal with the students who are making fun of Vlad's accent?

a. Hold them after class and firmly explain to them that this is not acceptable, and that they will be punished if it continues. Explain to them that if they moved to Russia, they would have accents too.
b. Join in with the students and make fun of Vlad. This will quickly teach him that he should stop speaking with an accent.
c. Ask Vlad to teach the class some Russian folk dances. This will make everyone more comfortable.
d. Give the whole class extra assignments. This way they will be too busy to make fun of Vlad.

87. How should Mr. Michaels deal with the problem of Vlad's use of profanity?

a. Send Vlad to the principal's office and recommended that he be suspended
b. Calmly explain to Vlad in private that he understands that Vlad is upset about being made fun of, but that the words Vlad is using are extremely offensive and cannot be used at school
c. Ignore the profanity. Since he is a foreigner, he probably does not know better.
d. Give Vlad detention

88. How should Mr. Michaels handle Maria's situation?

a. Give the class shorter assignments so that Maria does not fall behind
b. Ask her to transfer to another class because her English is not good enough
c. Arrange for her to have a textbook with larger print to make it easier for her to read
d. Spend some time with her after class to evaluate her reading skills. If necessary, consult with her guidance counselor or her parents, and suggest either a private tutor or a class more appropriate to her level.

89. Vlad approaches Mr. Michaels and says that he is ashamed of his accent and asks what he can do to get rid of it. How should Mr. Michaels respond?

a. Make inquires with the school administration about the availability of a speech therapist for Vlad
b. Tell Vlad that it is natural to have an accent, and that he should not be ashamed of it
c. Offer to provide accent coaching to Vlad, but tell him that it will cost $30 per hour
d. Tell Vlad that this is not the school's responsibility

90. Akiko is a fast reader and speaks well, but her writing is filled with mistakes and is way below her reading level. Akiko approaches Mr. Michaels and asks if she could write her assignments in Japanese and submit them to Mrs. Suzuki, the school's music teacher, who is also Japanese. She is very concerned about getting bad grades since she always got excellent grades in Japan. How should Mr. Michaels respond?

a. If Mrs. Suzuki is in agreement, Akiko should be allowed to submit her work in Japanese until her English improves.
b. Mr. Michaels should tell Akiko that she must write in English, but that he will "go easy on her grades" since she needs time to learn to write better.
c. Mr. Michaels should consult with Akiko's guidance counselor and parents to discuss whether she is in the right class, or perhaps needs a tutor.
d. Mr. Michaels should simply tell her that this is not Japan, and that she must produce work by American standards if she wants a good grade.

Answer Key and Explanations

1. C: Learning these skills early will help students to mature and become responsible adults. Answer A is hardly necessary. Most students find themselves under stress anyway. Answer B should not be an issue as long as the teacher is attentive and properly checks the students' work. Answer D is a very cynical viewpoint. While this may happen on occasion, such projects are still very much worthwhile.

2. B: This creates a temptation for some of the students to dishonestly change their grades. Answer A works well but does require more time from the teacher. Answer C is a very efficient method for recording grades in this situation, although it does require sacrificing a little bit of class time. Answer D is ideal, although not all teachers have a teacher's aide to rely on.

3. A: At the very least, parents should have a list of the basic requirements of the class, including any term papers or long-term projects that the students will have to complete. Answer B is great if you have the time to put it together, but it is not essential. Answer C might be too much information for some parents and is not the most essential information most parents need to help their children succeed. Answer D is simply unrealistic. Unfortunately, not all parents are willing or able to become experts in all of the subjects their children are studying.

4. C: Having each student write out his own step-by-step instructions will help them visualize the process in their minds and make them feel more confident about what they are doing. During the actual lab session, the students will also find it helpful to have the procedure spelled out in their own words. Answer A will do little if anything to calm their nerves, and nothing to help them learn about the process. Answer B will likely only make the students more nervous and more likely to make mistakes, since they will feel rushed. Answer D is not a bad idea except that with so many people talking in one classroom, it may be a bit chaotic.

5. B: At this level, it can often be difficult to sustain a productive discussion for longer than 15 minutes or so. After that, students will tend to lose interest or veer the discussion off topic.

6. B: When a teacher is consistent in how he or she runs her classroom, the students will more quickly understand the rules and will also recognize that the rules apply equally to everyone. Answer A can work in some classrooms, but some students will find this to be too intense. Answer C will lead to the students taking advantage of the teacher and misbehaving even more. Answer D will likely lead to chaos. While it is wise not to let the students "get a rise out of you," the teacher should always react so that it will be clear that misbehavior is not tolerated.

7. D: When Jethro is reprimanded in class, his behavior becomes worse. Speaking to him in private may prove more beneficial, and he may open up about his problems. Jethro, having grown up in a rough neighborhood, likely learned to be defensive and project a strong image. He may let his guard down when not around the other students.

8. C: Introducing new material using several different strategies will help make it more accessible to a larger group of students, regardless of their specific backgrounds. While surveys and general knowledge about cultures may be useful, relying too much on generalized beliefs about cultures and what they value and find useful in instruction can be problematic.

9. C: Though many people would look the other way, Mr. Calhoun would be committing an ethical violation by selling products such as Girl Scout cookies on school property. It may not seem like much of an offense, but it does not benefit the school in any way, and some parents might complain about a teacher who is selling sweets to their children. Moreover, Mr. Calhoun's students might even get the idea that if they do not buy Mr. Calhoun's cookies, that they will not get good grades.

10. C: In a highly diversified class, teachers often fall into the trap of allocating too much time to the higher performing students while neglecting the lower performing students. As a result, the lower performing students can become resentful and feel little incentive to work harder. The other options are generally recommended practices in classes with diverse levels of skill.

11. B: Using additional visual aids and hand gestures will help get your points across more clearly. Answer A is inappropriate. The parents should not have to pay for a translator, and such a strategy would also not encourage the student to increase his or her English skills. Answer C would make it even harder for the student to understand. Answer D would be unfair to the other students, since it would greatly slow down the class and make it impossible for the teacher to cover the material on schedule.

12. A: Planning out the lesson yourself in writing is the only way to ensure that all of the parts of your lesson will fit together logically. The more time you put into your preparations, the better your lesson will go in the classroom. Answer B is unreliable for this purpose. The students do not know what your goals are for the lesson. Occasionally checking in with your students is useful, but not as a substitute for lesson planning. Answer C is equally ineffective and will bore even your best students to tears. Most classes need to go beyond the scope of the textbook, and many classes use more than one book. Answer D is a very poor way to teach. Each teacher needs to customize his or her own lesson. This will make it more interesting and will take into account aspects of your school's particular curriculum, as well as the needs of your specific students.

13. C: Large projects should receive several grades, and students tend to be more motivated if the teacher grades them as the project moves along. Answer A might be appropriate for seniors, but otherwise, students of this age are not organized enough to handle that level of responsibility. Answer B has little to do with the overall grading strategy. Answer D tends to punish students who make extra effort, since they get nothing for it in return. Instead it encourages students to only do what is absolutely necessary to meet the criteria.

14. C: Many new teachers make the mistake of getting so caught up in their lesson that they fail to notice problem behavior in the classroom before it gets out of hand. Teachers must learn to divide their attention between all aspects of the class environment and to periodically scan the room and take account of what is going on. Like juggling, this is a skill that takes time and practice to develop. All new teachers must work hard to become competent at it.

15. C: Giving the students an active task, such as taking notes, will force the students to focus on the content of the tour. Answer A will do little to change or inspire the students to pay more attention. Answer B also has little to do with what students get out of the experience. Answer D is backwards. Having a quiz after the field trip would make more sense.

16. B: Bulletin boards are a great way to make your classroom more appealing to students and can also be a useful way to communicate rules, schedules, and other information; however, it is not absolutely essential that the bulletin boards be perfect on the first day of school. Answer A is much more important since students must have a good view of the main teaching area and if you have to move them around, it will make it harder for you to learn their names. Answer C is essential so that all students have access to the materials necessary for the class. Of course, this is not as critical with materials that will not be used until later in the term. Answer D is equally important if you intend to rely on these items in your teaching.

17. B: Learning to constructively sort out differences is an important life skill that is worth pursuing in class. It is important, however, that other students are also allowed to share their perspectives. The two disagreeing students should not be allowed to take up the entire discussion. Answer A denies the students a chance to benefit from a true discussion. Answer C assumes that there is always a correct perspective that can be decided upon and incentivizes the type of heated exchange that is currently occurring. Answer D would have the same stifling effect as answer A.

18. B: There would be nothing wrong with inviting your relative to speak to the class about his experience in WWII as long as his talk is appropriate and respectful to all of the students. In fact, it could be a very interesting and educational experience. Answer A would violate the other teacher's right to privacy, unless she personally told you that it was okay to tell the students. Answer C would also be ethically wrong. Julie should receive the same treatment as any other student. If you genuinely feel that you are being pressured by the principal to do otherwise, then you should contact a school system administrator regarding the matter. Answer D is not only unethical, it is illegal.

19. B: Mrs. Emal will need to work harder to stay current. She does not have to become an expert, but she should not allow herself to fall so far behind that she feels intimidated. She should be more creative or proactive about the resources she uses to educate herself. Answer A is not a solution. Certainly the students should not be permitted to disrespect her, but that is only a symptom and not the real problem. Answer C is risky. While the students may know more than the teacher, they understand the technology from a very different perspective, and may not be the most reliable source of information. Answer D is a cop-out. Technology is too important to simply set it aside because the teacher is behind the times. Mrs. Emal will continue to feel inadequate until she makes the effort to get herself current.

20. C: Some students perform better on tests, while others do better with papers or other projects. Just as students learn in a variety of ways, their talents for expressing what they have learned also varies widely. A teacher that evaluates students based on a wide variety of tasks will come away with a much more complete picture of each student's strengths and weaknesses.

21. D: Circulating around the class allows the teacher to observe firsthand how things are going without interrupting the students' work. Answer A does not permit the teacher to see how the students are doing. Answer B is much too passive and does not allow the teacher a chance to solve problems before they happen. Answer C is not practical, since it requires too much time.

22. B: Putting up a general outline will make it easier for the students to follow your talk. Answer A would likely make it harder for the students to follow your lesson. Answer C would also be disruptive. An occasional question to a student who is not paying attention is fine, but doing this too much will cause your lesson to veer off schedule and may also interfere with other students' note taking. Answer D would not be very effective. While asking students what they already know about a subject is a good way to prepare a lesson and engage students, it does not help them focus during longer talks or explanations.

23. D: The individual teacher is ultimately responsible for keeping up with the latest ideas. The school system, the principal, and other teachers can often be excellent resources and may even set up programs or continuing education requirements to help teachers stay current, but this does not always occur, and in any case, it remains a teacher's responsibility to ensure that his or her skills are constantly improving.

24. D: Reviewing the students' notes will quickly identify anyone who lacks good note-taking skills. Depending upon how many students are having trouble, you can then either devote some class time to a discussion of note-taking or meet with students individually. Answer A is not a solution. As a teacher preparing children for college, it is your responsibility to ensure that they have skills such as these. Answer B would seriously interrupt the flow of your lesson plan and test general recollection ability more than note taking. Answer C wastes valuable class time and does not allow the teacher to verify that students actually develop their note-taking skills.

25. B: This will bring the story into a modern context, making it easier to understand. Having them search for differences will ensure that they actually read the original as well. Answer A would certainly be helpful, but it is not likely to prevent students from losing interest by itself. Answer C is also a useful practice, but without a real understanding of the context, much of the drama will be lost upon the students. Answer D will almost certainly put most of the students to sleep and is unnecessary for studying a single play.

26. B: Cooperative learning exercises (working in small groups) teach students how to solve problems in groups. These skills are essential to success in many jobs. Answer A is the opposite of cooperative learning. Answers C and D are unrelated to the topic of the question.

27. C: Planning, above all else, will help a teacher ensure that a class will proceed smoothly. All of the other items will follow if a teacher exercises good planning skills.

28. A: A lesson-planning matrix makes it easier for teachers to plan their lessons around a variety of useful strategies. Answer B does not take into account how one will incorporate the students' various skills into lesson. Moreover, students are not always fully aware of their learning abilities. Answer C fails to address lesson planning at all, and it also might make the slower students feel that they are being unfairly singled out. Answer D is in fact one way to improve the comprehension of some students, but it is only one method, and will not especially help students who are not visually oriented.

29. A: If you are teaching a class while relevant current events are taking place, it is beneficial to devote a significant amount of time to addressing them in class. There are few things that motivate students as much as seeing how what they are learning applies to "real life," especially in the present. Answer B is a mistake. The teacher should be flexible and make judgments on a case-by-case basis as to how much time is appropriate to devote. Answer C is a great idea but should not be a substitute for in-class discussion. The students need to hear the teacher's explanation of events before taking on extracurricular assignments independently. Answer D is also not very practical, as some events are more relevant than others.

30. C: Once you know the necessary formula, a spreadsheet is the best tool to use for applying it across the board. While answer A will certainly work, and some people still prefer it, using a spreadsheet is much more efficient and will also guard against careless arithmetic errors. If you are unfamiliar with spreadsheets, it is well worth taking the time to learn, as it will greatly improve your efficiency in calculating grades.

31. D: The first response is to protect the students from the immediate threat of exposure if at all possible. Following that, the next step is to send the offending student immediately to the principal's office. An offense involving sexual misconduct should be treated very seriously. Depending on the age of the students involved and state law, it may be necessary to involve the police. In case of investigation, it is best to follow the chain of authority of the school and ensure effective documentation of the incident. Answer A, detention, is not an effective and timely response to an incident that requires immediate action. Answer B, physically restraining and removing the student, is generally unlawful unless the student is an active physical threat to the safety of the other students. Generally, there is a better way to handle the situation than to use physical force. For offenses this serious, the teacher should do what is necessary to end the situation and then refer the problem to the principal or vice principal. In such cases, punishment is not usually the teacher's responsibility.

32. B: The theory suggests that some students learn better through verbal interaction, while others are more visual, physical, or artistic. By using a variety of teaching methods, rather than just lecturing or working problems on a chalkboard, a teacher will help ensure that more students will grasp a given topic. Any of these methods may be applied in the teaching of any subject.

33. A: The teacher should circulate around the room but should avoid spending too much time with any one group since this tends to distract the teacher's attention from what is going on in other groups. Answer B is not important, although the teacher should be sure that all students cooperate effectively on the project. Answer C is the opposite of what the teacher should be doing. By circulating among the groups and taking notes, the teacher can help with problems and verify that all students are actively participating. Answer D is incorrect, as it could lead to situations in which those who do not meaningfully participate receive good grades because other students work hard to finish the group work.

34. D: If you are overwhelmed and losing control of your class, it is very important that you step forward and ask for help promptly, rather than allowing things to keep getting worse. Most of your colleagues will have had similar experiences and can help you find a workable solution. This is a challenge faced by nearly all new teachers, and they need to be able to ask for help when they need it. Answer A is too risky. While any teacher needs time to adjust and adapt to new challenges, this should not be done at the expense of the students. They are not guinea pigs. Answer B is unfair. You have already established that the problem is not with the students.

It is with you. Answer C is absurd. There is no such thing as an "easy class." Each one has its challenges. You will not impress your principal and colleagues by giving up.

35. B: Classrooms come in a variety of shapes and sizes. Moreover, the arrangement that works for one class will not necessarily work for another. Answer C, with the desks facing the chalkboard, seems logical and might work in many cases, but you need to consider the needs of your class first. For example, some teachers prefer to use an overhead projector instead of a chalkboard. Also, some classrooms have more than one chalkboard. Answer A is not a good idea unless there really is a major source of distraction outside the window. Answer D is incorrect because school administrators do not typically spend much time optimizing the floor plans of classrooms.

36. D: Having the students consider real life applications of math problems is a great way to help make the subject seem less abstract and more interesting. Answer A is an invitation to chaos, and it also uses up a lot of class time. Answer B wastes even more class time. It is unfair to have the whole class wait while the teacher speaks individually with each student. Such a meeting should be held after class. Answer C may sometimes be useful, but it is probably not in this case. You have already determined that your students are bored, and repeating material will likely be even more boring for them.

37. C: Do not interrupt the flow of your class when only a couple of students need more time; however, do make sure the two slower students do not get lost in the shuffle. Set aside a few minutes after class, or while the other students are doing seatwork, to catch them up. Answer A could needlessly traumatize the two slower students. Answer B would not be fair to the other students and would interfere with the flow of your lesson plan. Ia majority of your students are having trouble, however, it might be worth spending more time on the subject. Answer D would discourage the two students from learning unless the activity is a timed test.

38. D: If Mr. Gupta knows that the experiments are where the time is being lost, then he needs to closely evaluate why they are taking so long. Are the students spending more time talking than working? Are they getting stuck and waiting a long time for Mr. Gupta to get around to them? Are some of the experiments simply too ambitious for this class? In any case, he must determine where the problem is and then reorganize the way experiments are conducted to make the process more efficient. Answer A is too drastic and deprives students of an important opportunity to gain a hands-on understanding of the principles being covered. Answer B is also not the way to go. This will eventually result in a class that fails to cover a lot of important material. Answer C is unfair to the students. Mr. Gupta should not overburden the students because he failed to properly organize the class in the first place.

39. B: Frequent evaluations show how students perform on a weekly or daily basis. Moreover, they often reveal problems earlier enough that they can be effectively address without ruining the student's grades. Answer A is not always reliable since a student may be nervous or not functioning at his/her best on the particular day of the test. Answer C is nonsense. A teacher's evaluation should always be based on objective indicators. Answer D can certainly be useful, but these assignments do not indicate how a student performs under controlled conditions and without access to references such as calculators, encyclopedias, or help from family members.

40. C: Modern technological advancements have given many school districts the ability to provide classroom laptops for individual student use. Emailing students your material will provide each student with their own copy of the materials while limiting the use of paper. If no student laptops are available, using the classroom's projector to display information is also an efficient option. Answer A is a sure way to annoy your fellow teachers. Just because you are floating does not mean that the other teacher using the room is floating too. Answer B might be okay for college teaching, but it is unacceptable in a secondary school environment. Answer D is an outdated way of displaying information within a classroom. Many schools don't keep overhead projectors on hand anymore.

41. B: In this case, the teacher should work with the student to come up with several acceptable options for solving the problems and ask the student to commit to one of them. It may also be helpful to involve the student's parents or guidance counselor. The student is much more likely to cooperate if he has more than one option. Answer A will likely lead to more problems. Answer C might be a practical option depending on the school, but once more, the student will be more likely to respond constructively if there are multiple options. Answer D, like answer A, does not get at the root of the problem. Since this attitude is not typical of the student, it indicates a bigger problem.

42. C: Following current events is a great way to show the students how the work of Congress affects their everyday lives. Holding in-class discussions will reveal areas where the students' knowledge is weak and will make your explanations more interesting. Answer D illustrates a useful tool, but charts and graphs alone will not motivate your students. Answer B does represent a way to get the students more actively involved in the subject, but learning the biographies of senators will not help the students to understand the overall structure and function of Congress. Answer A is quite simply an ineffective way to make students learn.

43. C: It might be a good idea to purchase the game, but it is best to do a little research first and talk to the technology coordinator. It is important to make sure that the game is truly educational, practical for class use, and also appropriate for use with the age group of the students in his class. Answer A is risky. At the very least, the teacher should spend some time with the game and verify that it looks promising. Answer B is closed minded. After all, there are indeed some useful educational games that can successfully be used in class. Answer D is unreliable, as most students would be happy to play a game instead of listening to a lecture.

44. A: While useful in some contexts, computer-monitored drills do not represent the greatest use of computers. These drills can be accomplished without computers. Even if using computers for drilling exercises, the teacher should remain active with the students and would not be more "freed up" than if the drills were administered on paper. Role-playing games, simulations, and exercises that teach higher-order thinking represent uses of computers that provide benefits that are difficult to obtain without computers.

45. A: Establish a firm routine, such as leading a roll call or reviewing the previous day's homework. When everyone knows exactly what to expect, and when to expect it, they will fall in with the routine as well. Answer B will result in the students taking even longer to settle down. Answer C is impractical and, unless you actually enforce it, will result in the students not taking you seriously. Answer D sets a very bad example and implies that good discipline is negotiable.

46. C: Asking questions directly to the quieter student will encourage them to participate. It will also encourage them to participate more on their own if they do not want to be called on directly. Answer A will have little effect, other than to stifle students who are participating. Answer B will create a tense and distasteful atmosphere that will not foster very productive class discussion. Answer D will only serve to encourage the more active students to participate even more than before.

47. C: Constructive assertiveness means that a teacher is confidently in control of the class and communicates clearly without losing control of his or her emotions. Such a teacher also easily adapts to different situations and different points of view. Answer A is an example of a teacher who is extremely inflexible. This is not constructive assertiveness. Answer B is an example of a teacher who is unable to control the class. Answer D illustrates a teacher who fails to control his or her emotions. This is a sign of weakness and insecurity.

48. A: This approach clearly communicates the problem, while at the same time showing respect for the student. Additionally, it invites input from the parents. This is a very good way to lay the groundwork for a cooperative discussion. Answer B needlessly compares Mike's performance to the other students in the class, and worse yet, it offers no solution. Answer C would likely put the parents on the defensive since it questions whether they are helping Mike. Answer D does not effectively communicate the seriousness of the problem. The parents will leave the meeting thinking that it's no big deal.

49. C: Offering students an option of formats for class projects is a great way to take advantage of both new technologies and of multiple intelligence theory. Some students are much more likely to succeed by doing a video project or a blog than a traditional written report. Moreover, students will need to know how to use these technologies after graduation anyway. However, it is very important that the teacher verifies that the content is substantive and of high quality, regardless of the format in which the project is completed. Teachers should also be competent enough with the available technologies that they know how to guard against plagiarism.

50. A: It greatly helps the learning process when the teacher illustrates how the new material fits together with what the class has already learned. This also serves to remind students of past lessons and to keep the information fresh. Answer B can be useful occasionally, but is not practical as a daily option. Answer C would substantially raise tension in the classroom, and would do little to assist the students in processing information. Answer D is certainly helpful, but once more it does not substitute for a teacher tying things together at the end of a lesson.

51. C: If the student sees that you are genuinely interested in why he feels the way he does, he is much more likely to listen to your side. Moreover, you may even discover a larger problem that you were not even aware of. Answer A will generally result in more of the same behavior, or even worse. It is rarely helpful to back a student into a corner. Answer B might work in the short term, but will fail in the long term since it does not address the underlying problem. Answer D is very counterproductive, as this will tend to predispose the parents to be enemies. If you feel that you need to contact the student's parents, just do so. Do not try to use it as leverage.

52. C: As long as neither teacher is subordinate to another teacher, then there should be no problem with two teachers becoming romantically involved, unless the school, or school district, has a specific policy against this. Answer A is most certainly a violation. Answer B is also an ethical violation, since this could create grounds upon which the teacher's grading practices could be questioned.

53. A: Laws regarding removal from class vary some from state to state, but generally, permanent removal from class is seen as a last-resort measure. When a student is disruptive, the teacher can remove and recommend suspension. Upon return, the student should generally be given a second chance, as the consequences have already been established. The teacher may follow the same removal procedure if the student continues to be disruptive, at which point, the teacher should recommend a permanent removal by the principal or administration if the student seems likely to participate. Permanent removal should not take place after one or few events but should be the result of a pervasive and persistent disruption to the class. When a teacher is physically threatened or harmed, no administration can oblige that teacher to take the student back.

54. A: Requiring students to keep a running tally of their average in the front of their notebook will force them to think about their grade every day. It will also directly involve them in the process and teach them to be independently responsible about keeping up with their grades. Answer B is too passive, since some of the students would forget to check it. Answer C will be seen by some as overly invasive. It also lacks the advantages of teaching the students to keep track of their grades themselves. Answer D will be insufficient for many students.

55. D: The teacher should first instruct the class on the subject matter, then the class should discuss it, and then the students should engage in independent activity. This order ensures that the students have the most opportunity to absorb the new material before attempting to complete a related assignment on their own.

56. B: It is extremely important that the class meet the needs of all students in the class. If a quarter of the students are disengaged, they are probably not learning as much as they should be, and the teacher should try a different approach. Answer A is a low priority, as long as the class itself is proceeding well. Answer C needs to be addressed, but it is not necessarily a serious problem, as long as the teacher pays attention. Answer D, falling a little behind schedule, is okay as long as the students are learning. Sometimes it is appropriate for a teacher to take a little more time on a particular lesson if the whole class is having trouble with it.

57. D: Teachers should apply common sense in this decision, and consider the needs of their class as appropriate. Answers A and B both represent closed-minded approaches to the question. Word processors are a part of modern life and employment, and it is completely appropriate for students to learn the use of these programs since they will likely need to know how to use them later in life. Obviously, it does not make sense for students to have access to a word processor during a spelling test. Answer C is illogical. After all, students are asked to use commercial products in their schoolwork all the time, including their own textbooks.

58. B: Breaking the item in to smaller sections makes memorization much easier. Answer A is an important part of memorization, but without breaking a topic up into smaller sections, many students will have a hard time. Answer C is ineffective unless the student has a photographic memory. Playing music in the background is helpful to some, but later the student may have difficulty if the same music is not playing when the student tries to recall the subject matter.

59. A: Textbooks are often dry and abstract in the way that they present material. Having the students read some first-person accounts of events, or other less formal materials, can bring the subject to life, and may even encourage students to read more on their own. Answer B will be of little use if the material is dry. Answer C is irrelevant, since the question regards helping students to learn rather than how to evaluate their progress. Answer D is a bit overly ambitious to pull off in a classroom; however, it is rooted in a very good idea. Having students act out certain events can be a very effective way to get students more involved emotionally. However, this would be time consuming and could cause safety issues.

60. A: English and language arts classes tend to cover very wide areas in a single term (such as spelling, grammar, literature, and writing) and therefore they often require the use of several textbooks. Since the teacher must shift gears more often, he/she must carefully plan the logical approach, and must also make sure to keep the students cued in so that they bring the appropriate books on the appropriate days.

61. A: It is the teacher's responsibility to observe and verify that students are following the instructions and participating equally. Answer B is likely to produce biased results. Answer C defeats the purpose of the exercise. The point is for the students to learn how to effectively work together on the group task. Answer D simply denies students the experience of learning this valuable lesson.

62. A: Establishing a clear set of rules for your classroom from the very beginning is the best way to let your students know what is expected of them. Giving the students the rules in writing ensures that they have no excuse to not know what the rules are. Answer B works for some teachers but not for all. Moreover, it is not necessarily to your advantage to establish yourself in a negative light before your students. Answer C is a very bad idea. Waiting to establish the rules will likely result in chaos, and students will get the idea that they can get away with anything. Answer D is also unhelpful. Your rules should be consistent. Changing them often will confuse your students and might cause them to take your rules less seriously.

63. B: Simply memorizing words from the Constitution or the Declaration of Independence does nothing to ensure that students actually understand the meaning behind the words. *Processing* means the activity requires students to interpret new material and to express it in an original way. Answer A requires the students to consider the Revolution from a modern perspective. Answer C requires the students to spend some time every day thinking about what they learned, which helps keep the new material active in their brains. Answer D requires the students to do their own research and ask and answer their own questions about important figures in the history of our country.

64. C: Talking to your colleagues is the best way to catch up with the current trends. Of course you are under no obligation to copy them, but you may come away with some ideas to make your classroom more functional. Answer A is like sticking your head in the sand. You should always be open to new ideas. Answer B may cause you to miss out on understanding the reasons behind some of the new trends, and also if you copy other rooms too closely, your students may get the wrong idea about you. Answer D will not result in a classroom that serves your purposes. However, there is nothing wrong with asking a couple of your more artistic students to help you decorate, once you have decided what you want to do.

65. B: Studies have shown that no other factor affects a student's performance in school as much as the degree to which the student's family is involved in his or her life. All of the other factors listed also have their influence too, but if a student's family takes an active interest in the student's performance in school, the other factors are more likely to be overcome, and the student's grades, attitude, and likelihood of graduation are all likely to be higher.

66. C: It is inappropriate for a teacher to directly approach a student and ask him or her about any disability he or she may have. This could be interpreted as harassment. A student may volunteer this information if he or she likes, or a teacher may approach the student's guidance counselor or the principal with such concerns, who may then contact the parents and recommend a medical consultation, but it is not a teacher's job to attempt to diagnose any such condition.

67. D: This is a classic situation in which a teacher observes a dangerous pattern in a student's performance. The parents should be consulted as soon as possible. Answer A represents a situation that is already out of control. The parents should have been contacted long before, since the grade is final. Answer B represents a situation that should continue to be monitored but which does not yet necessitate contacting a parent. Answer C represents a situation which might be better referred to the assistant principal's office, since the student is probably in violation of the school dress code and not just of a class rule.

68. B: The placement of computer workstations or other student technology stations is dictated by the location of electrical outlets and Internet connections. Therefore it is highly desirable to arrange their location before bringing in other equipment. Answer A, the teacher's desk, is less critical, but should be positioned so that it affords the teacher a good view of the classroom when the teacher is working. Answer C, filing cabinets, are the least critical item, and may usually be left until last, since the only issues concerning their placement are that they should be out of the way of student traffic and should be easily accessible from the teacher's desk. Answer D, the overhead projector, needs to be positioned within a direct line of sight to the projection screen.

69. B: This statement clearly lets the student know that you are unhappy with his behavior and why. It also calls the attention of the whole class that the student for misbehaving, adding additional incentive. Option A is rude and unprofessional. It shows that the teacher is losing control, which actually empowers the misbehaving student. Option C is disruptive and punishes everyone for the actions of one individual. It could also result in retaliatory behavior on the part of other students. Answer D would at least remove the problem student from the class, but it also prevent student from learning. This might be reasonable if the misbehavior continues, but the teacher should begin with the more constructive option, especially if this is not a "problem student."

70. D: Computers provide teachers with many options for differentiation due to the various tools and programs available. Teachers should remain active in the classroom even when computers are being used. While especially useful in remote settings, computers are not generally believed to be better for facilitating discussions within the class.

71. A: Evaluating individual student progress will make evaluation much fairer in such a situation. Answer B is more about making the teacher look good than about fairness to the students. Answer C, shifting the grading priority to research projects, will not necessarily make the evaluations fairer if student progress is not considered. Answer D is the opposite of what a teacher should do in this situation.

72. C: The moment when you first observe a detrimental pattern forming in the student's behavior or schoolwork is the time to bring the parents into the picture. Answer A is incorrect because communicating on the first day of school does not prevent concerns from showing up later. Answer B is incorrect because it may be impractical to contact parents after every mistake. One-off mistakes, depending on severity, are common and don't always necessitate communication with the parents. Answer D is waiting too late. Once a problem becomes extreme, it becomes much more difficult to solve.

73. C: Teachers should not procrastinate about getting involved if a student is in danger of falling behind. Instead, they should talk to the student kindly to find out what the problem is. It may not be what was expected. Answer A is quite simply not an effective way to keep tabs on students. Moreover, it will likely create dissension among the class. Answer B does nothing to help a student who may be having trouble understanding the work. Answer D is only occasionally appropriate. Otherwise, the student will simply begin to assume that he or she can always get extra credit if he or she does not finish an assignment.

74. A: This response shows empathy to the student and is more likely to get him to open up a little and tell you where the main problem is. Answer B is a taunting answer that will likely only make the student angrier. Answer C is at least encouraging, but if the student really is having trouble, this approach will not reveal where the problem is. Answer D may be a statement of fact, but it will probably cause the student to clam up and continue to do badly on his assignments.

75. A: When students keep their own grade books, it causes them to be more involved in their grade and to understand exactly where it is coming from. This way, they will know exactly how they is doing on any given day. Answer B is inappropriate. Reading students' grades to the class violates their right to privacy. Answer C is not a bad idea for some classes, but it does not necessarily keep the student informed of his or her own progress. Answer D is a good idea, but it also would generate a lot of extra work for the teacher and does not involve the student as directly.

76. A: This is a specific, practical goal that can be taught, tested, and evaluated. Answer B is ambiguous, and it cannot be effectively evaluated. Answer C sounds specific but in fact deals in opinion. What makes a poem good is a subjective matter about which people disagree. Answer D is also ambiguous. The learning goals for each unit should be specific and measurable.

77. D: Answer A is a great way to learn how decisions are made at your school and to get your voice heard. Answer B is very helpful. Your fellow colleagues are the people you will need to turn to when you need help. Answer C is a great source of new ideas and teaching techniques.

78. B: The first step is for Mr. Nielsen to approach Eric directly and ask him what is wrong. This offers the best opportunity to gain the student's trust, which is an important part of solving whatever the problem. Answer A, contacting the parents, is not a bad idea, but suggesting that Eric is taking drugs with so little evidence would be reckless. Answer C is inappropriate. A teacher should not violate a student's right to privacy by discussing his performance or habits with fellow students. Answer D would be premature. Before finding a solution, the problem must first be identified.

79. A: Mr. Nielsen should contact Eric's parents. It may be necessary to make some tough decision in the near future, and Eric's parents should be involved before the process goes any further. Answer B is inappropriate. It is not Mr. Nielsen's place to interfere in the way another teacher teaches a class. Answer C is actually a good idea, but Eric's parents need to be notified of the problem first. Answer D is rather drastic, especially since Mr. Nielsen knows that Eric has a talent in this area and enjoys the subject.

80. D: This type of situation is tricky, and it would probably be very helpful for Eric, his parents, and his guidance counselor to sit down together and search for a solution. Answer A will not work. Jim has already made up his mind. It is tempting for a teacher to get proprietary about his or her subject, especially if the teacher knows that the student has a talent in that area. However, this is not a fight a teacher wants to take on. Answer B would be a rash recommendation. First all options should be considered. This is why bringing in the guidance counselor could be helpful. Answer C is a hostile stance, and will not help gain the parents' trust and respect.

81. A: This is not a good place for a teacher to take sides. The guidance counselor is in a good position to help bring about a diplomatic solution. Answer B could result in a major conflict with Eric's father. Answer C will make Eric feel boxed in. Clearly he needs assistance in dealing with the situation. Answer D is risky. Unless Mr. Nielsen feels that he has a very strong report with Eric's Dad, intervening in this way could create a much more hostile situation.

82. B: Forming a study group with other teachers is a terrific way to share techniques and learn in a comfortable low-pressure environment focused specifically on the needs of teaching. Answer A is great, but this may be overkill, and might not even address her specific needs. After all, she is not teaching programming. Answer C would indicate that the teacher is in serious denial and refuses to accept changes in the modern world. Answer D is backwards. The goal is for the teacher to teach the students what they do not already know.

83. A: In fact many schools do not permit students to even have laptops in class. You should consult the school rules, or ask your school's technology coordinator how to handle the use of laptops in class. Answer B would be a direct violation of school policy and could even get the teacher in trouble. Answer C is overkill. Answer D is wrong. There is no reason to punish the whole class for something only a couple of students are doing.

84. D: In most cases, the technology coordinator will have useful information and suggestions in regard to this, possibly including software or websites that teachers can use to search for copied papers. Answer A is unlikely to be of very much use, since few cheaters will willingly give up their secrets. Answer B would be a very inefficient method, since few students would use their own names online while cheating. Answer C is unlikely to help, as few parents have absolute control over their children's access to the Internet. Moreover, some would take offense to an unsubstantiated suggestion that their child is a cheater.

85. C: Mrs. Marx should be proactive in helping Phillip to find access to a computer if he wants to learn. Suggesting resources like the school computer lab or the local library is a great way to start. Answer A is ridiculous and does not help anyone. Answer B would be very generous, but supplying students with computers is not Mrs. Marx's responsibility. Answer D is a bit insensitive and lazy. There is more Mrs. Marx can to do help her student get the most from the class.

86. A: Speak to the students who are mistreating Vlad and punish them if the problem continues. Answer B would be unethical and cruel. Answer C has nothing to do with the problem. Answer D is unfair to the rest of the class.

87. B: Foreigners often underestimate the offensiveness of such words, because the language is foreign to them. They should however be taught which words are acceptable and which are not. Answer C will result in the problem continuing, which is unacceptable regardless of whether Vlad understands the meaning of what he is saying. The teacher must correct the behavior. Answer D would only be appropriate if the student continues using inappropriate language after you confront him.

88. D: Before taking action, Mr. Michaels must first evaluate the situation. Answer A is unfair to the other students in the class. They should not be slowed down because of another student. Answer B is unlikely to solve Maria's language difficulties. Answer C is irrelevant. She is not visually impaired. She needs help with her English reading skills.

89. A: Many schools have a speech therapist on staff, or at the very least there may be such a therapist who floats between schools. Such a specialist may be able to help Vlad. Answer B is simply a cop-out. Answer C is unethical. Teachers cannot charge students for tutoring. However, if there is no other option, the teacher could recommend that the student find a professional language coach. Answer D is once again a cop-out, and Vlad will quickly get the message that Mr. Michaels does not care if he falls through the cracks.

90. C: This is a sensitive situation, and Akiko should be given every chance to improve her skills. Answer A would not help her to improve her English writing skills. Answer B would be unfair to the other students. Answer D is unfair to Akiko, who is openly asking her teacher for help.

Online Resources

Due to our efforts to try to keep this book to a manageable length, we've created a link that will give you access to all of your online resources:

mometrix.com/resources719/texespprte370

It's Your Moment, Let's Celebrate It!

Share your story @mometrixtestpreparation